D0989850

FRANK **CHO**

SKYBOURNE™

BOOM!
STUDIOS

BOOM! STUDIOS

SKYBOURNE, September 2018. Published by BOOM! Studios, a division of Boom Entertainment, Inc. Skybourne is ™ & © 2018 Frank Cho. Originally published in single magazine form as SKYBOURNE No. 1-5. ™ & © 2016-2018 Frank Cho. All rights reserved. BOOM! Studios™ and the BOOM! Studios logo are trademarks of Boom Entertainment, Inc., registered in various countries and categories. All characters, events, and institutions depicted herein are fictional. Any similarity between any of the names, characters, persons, events, and/or institutions in this publication to actual names, characters, persons, and events, whether living or dead, events, and/or institutions is unintended and purely coincidental. BOOM! Studios does not read or accept unsolicited submissions of ideas, stories, or artwork.

BOOM! Studios, 5670 Wilshire Boulevard, Suite 400, Los Angeles, CA 90036-5679. Printed in China. First Printing.

ISBN: 978-1-60886-986-2, eISBN: 978-1-61398-657-8

Cards, Comics & Collectibles Baltimore Comic-Con Limited Edition
ISBN: 978-1-68415-286-5

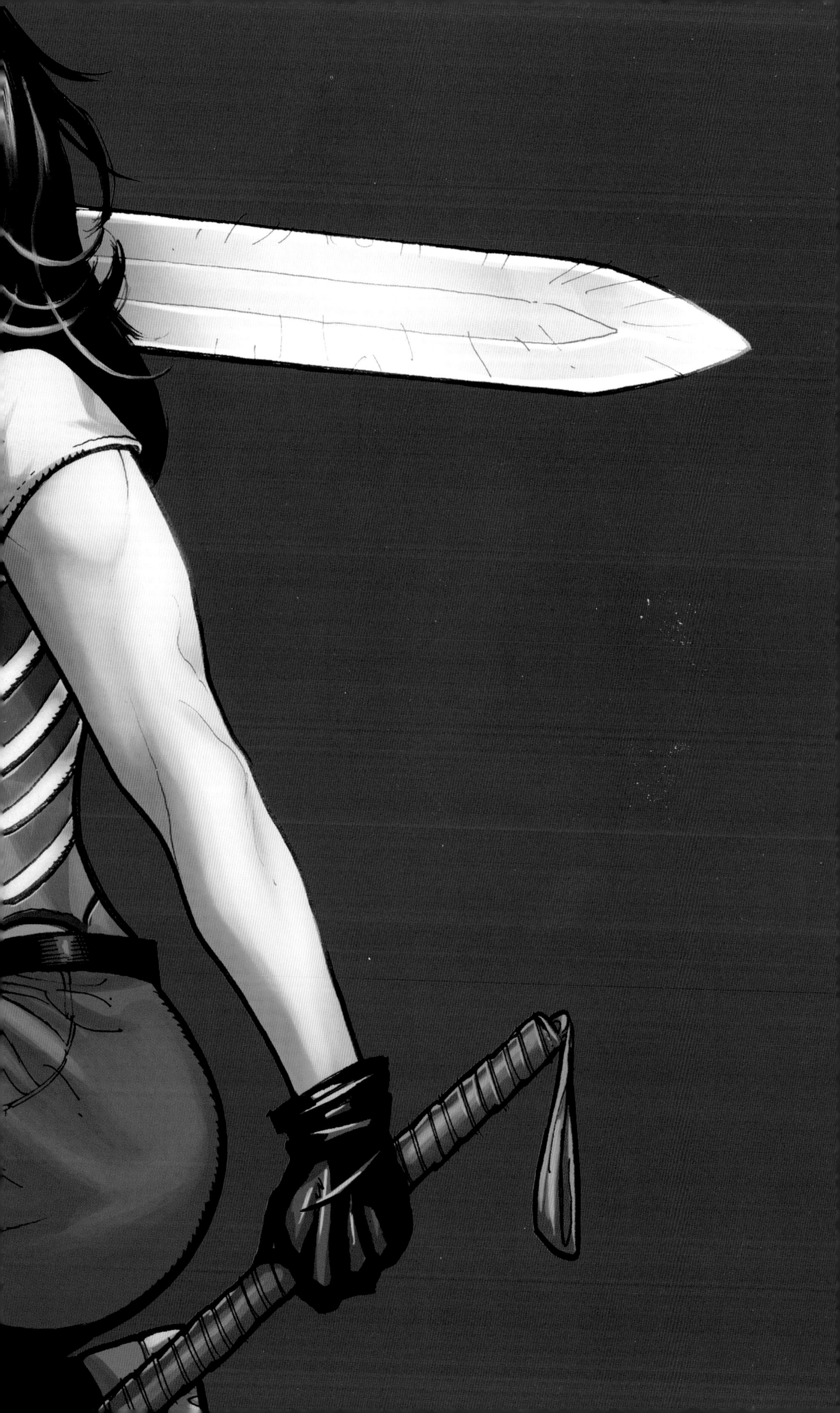

SKYB

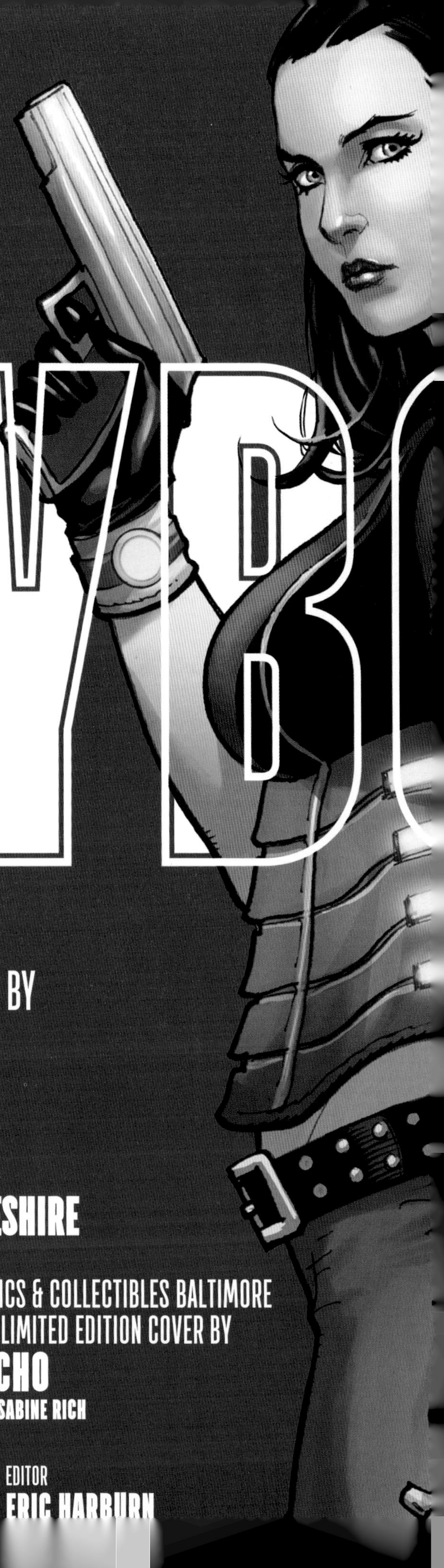

CREATED, WRITTEN & ILLUSTRATED BY

FRANK CHO

COLORED BY
MARCIO MENYZ

LETTERED BY
ED DUKESHIRE

COVER BY
FRANK CHO
WITH COLORS BY **SABINE RICH**

CARDS, COMICS & COLLECTIBLES BALTIMORE COMIC-CON LIMITED EDITION COVER BY
FRANK CHO
WITH COLORS BY **SABINE RICH**

DESIGNER
SCOTT NEWMAN

ASSOCIATE EDITOR
CHRIS ROSA

EDITOR
ERIC HARBURN

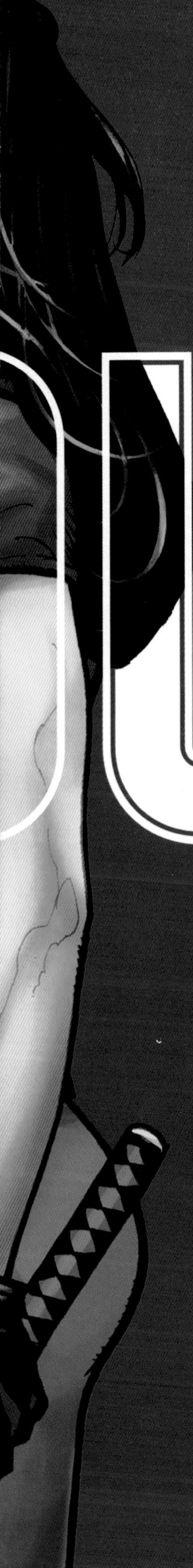

URNE

Lazarus, after his miraculous resurrection, fathered three children: **Abraham Skybourne**, **Thomas Skybourne**, and **Grace Skybourne**.

All three children were blessed with superhuman strength, impenetrable skin, and immortality.

This is their story.

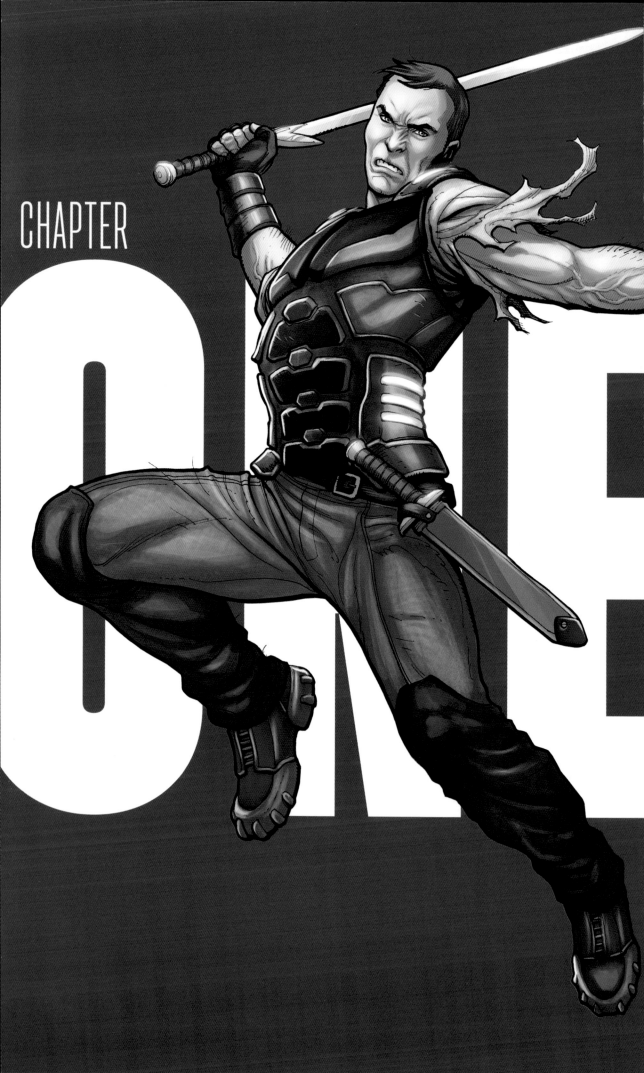

CHAPTER

ONE

29 YEARS AGO.
SOMEWHERE OVER CHINA.

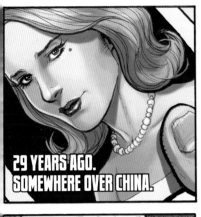

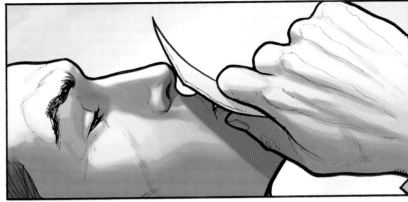

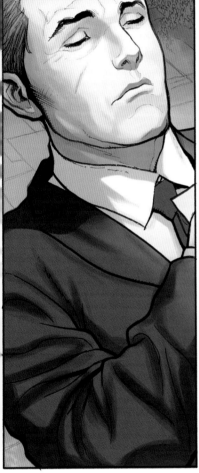

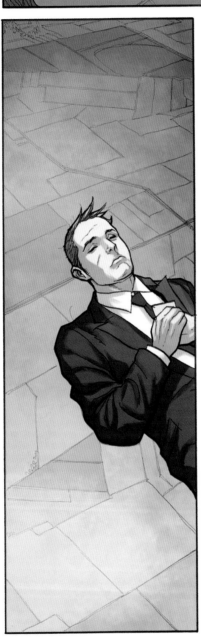

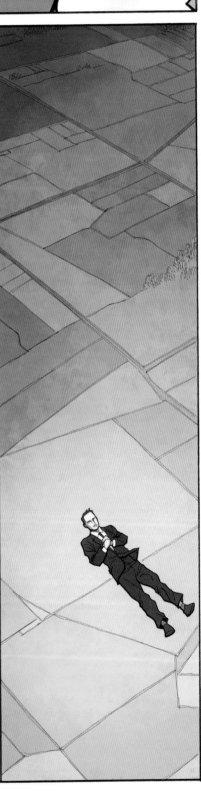

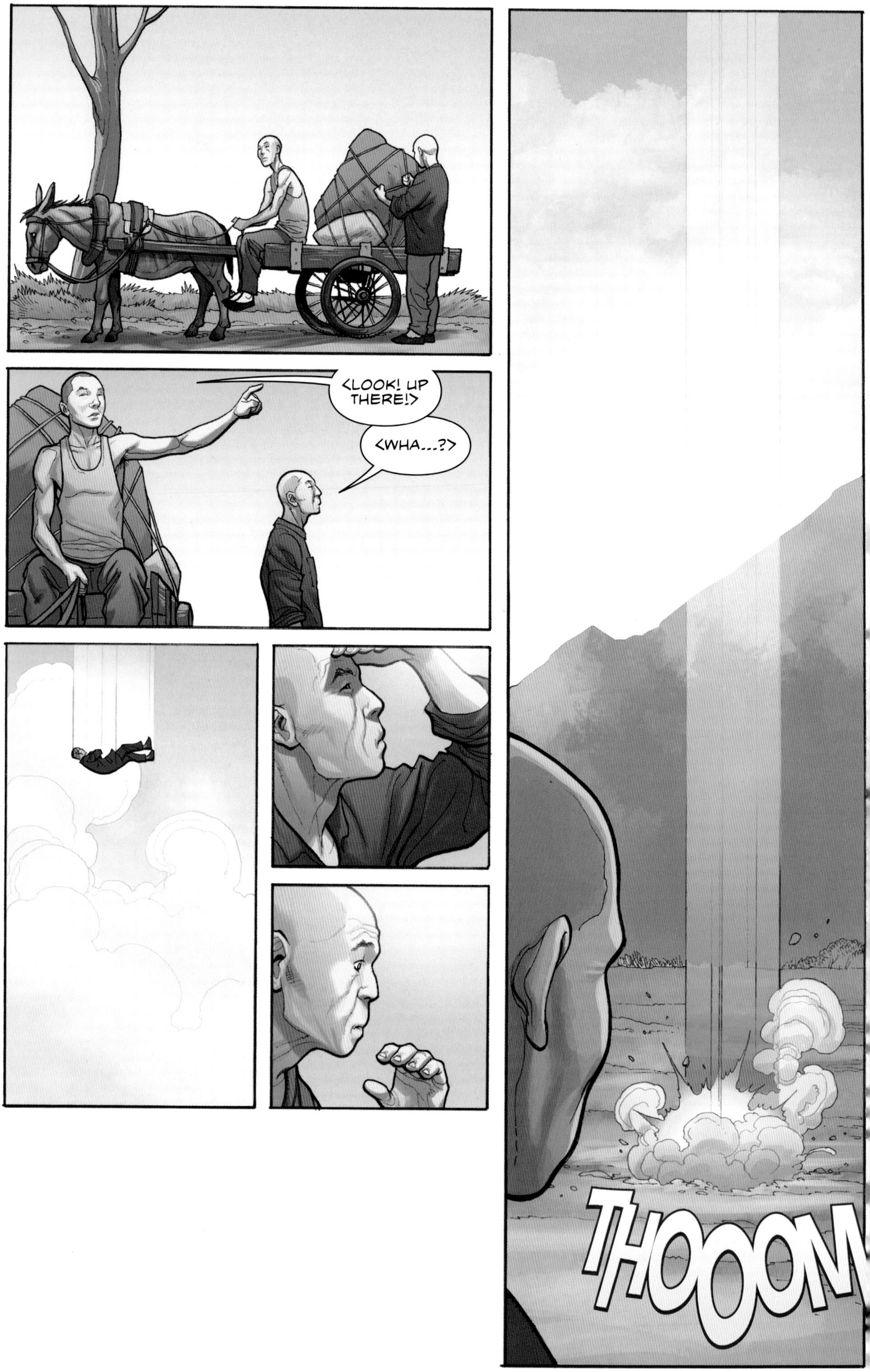
<LOOK! UP THERE!>
<WHA...?>
THOOOM

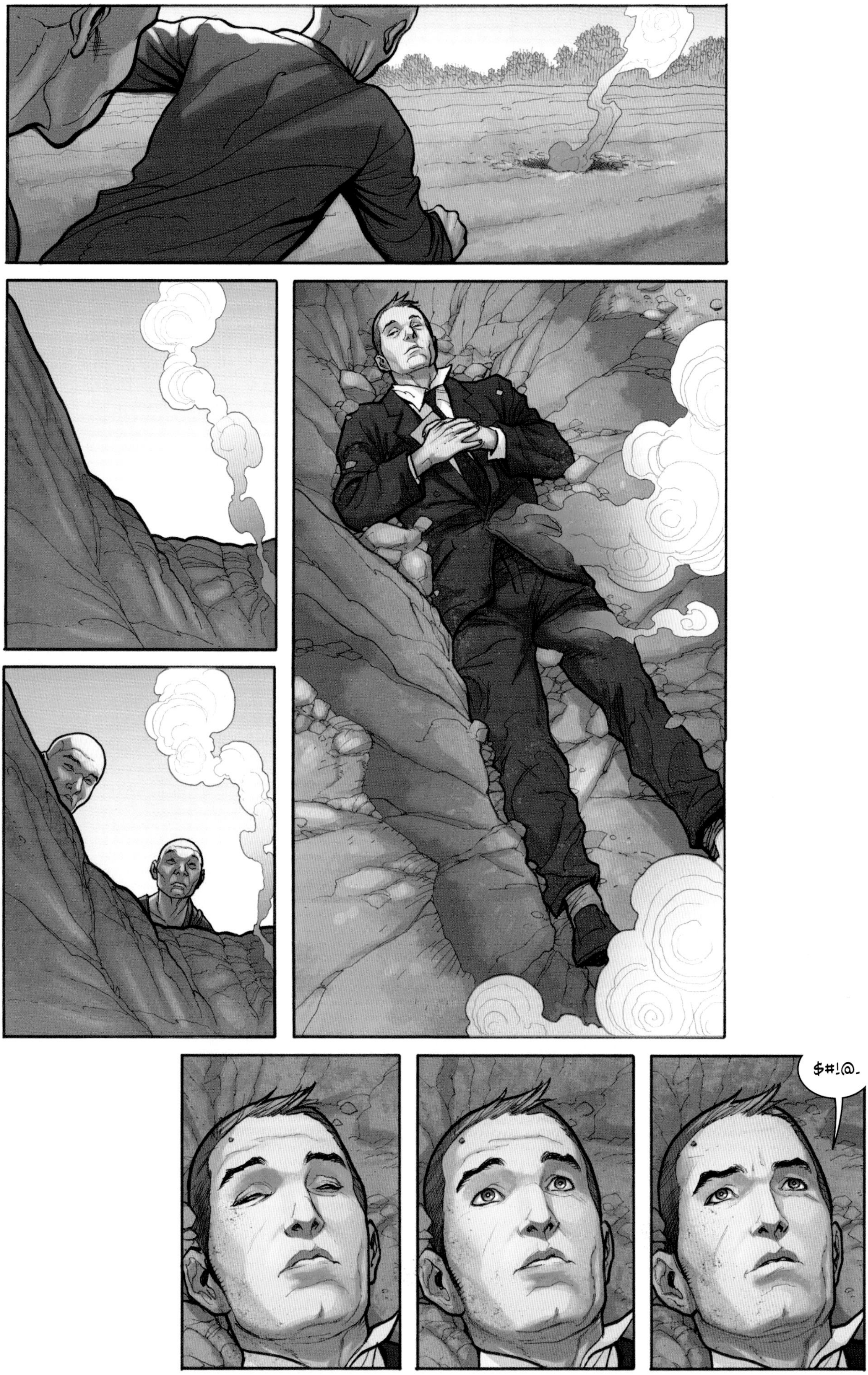
$#!@-

BOOM! STUDIOS
PRESENTS

SKYBOURNE™

CREATED, WRITTEN & ILLUSTRATED BY
FRANK CHO

WITH COLORS BY
MARCIO MENYZ

AND LETTERS BY
ED DUKESHIRE

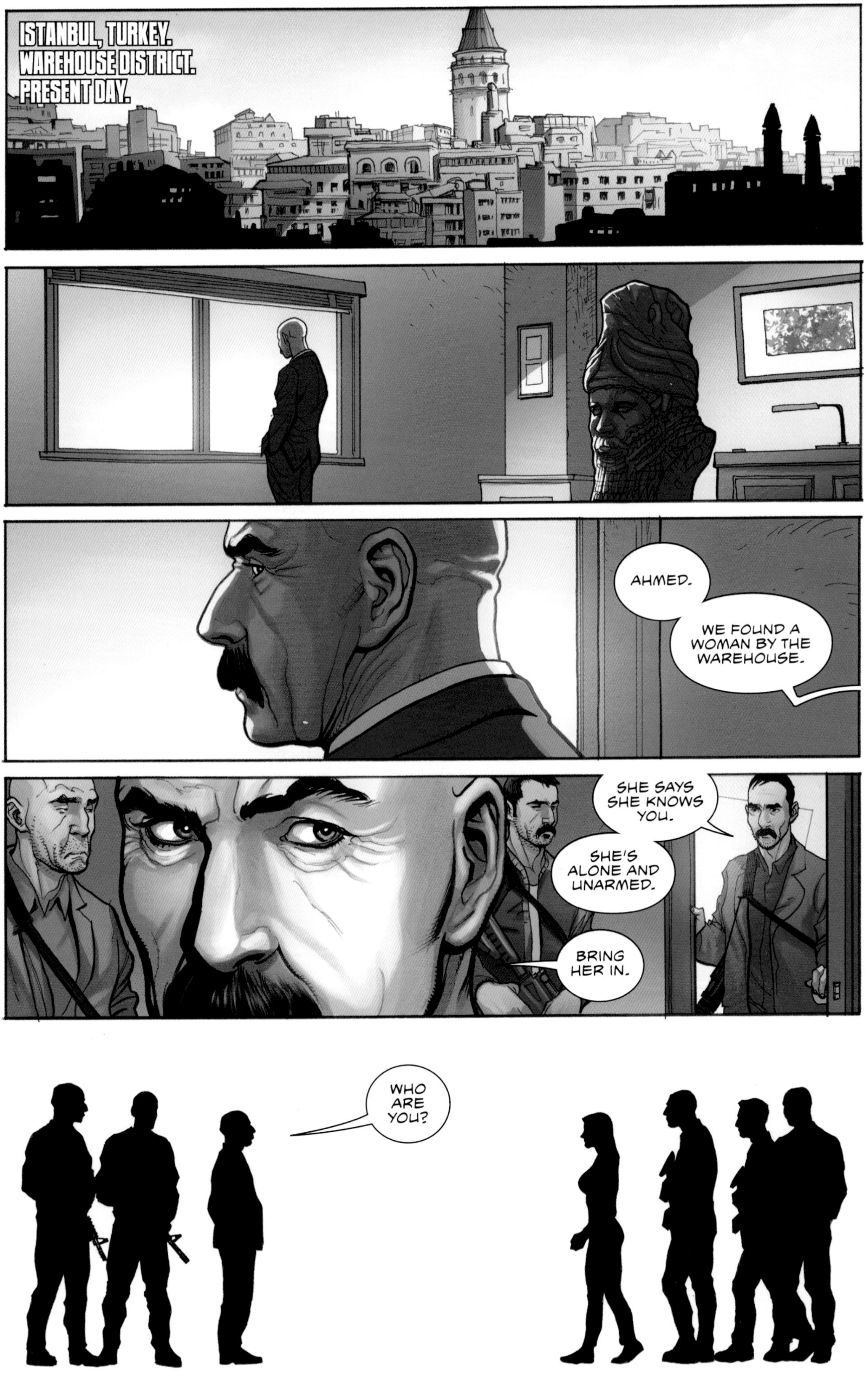
ISTANBUL, TURKEY.
WAREHOUSE DISTRICT.
PRESENT DAY.
AHMED.
WE FOUND A WOMAN BY THE WAREHOUSE.
SHE SAYS SHE KNOWS YOU.
SHE'S ALONE AND UNARMED.
BRING HER IN.
WHO ARE YOU?

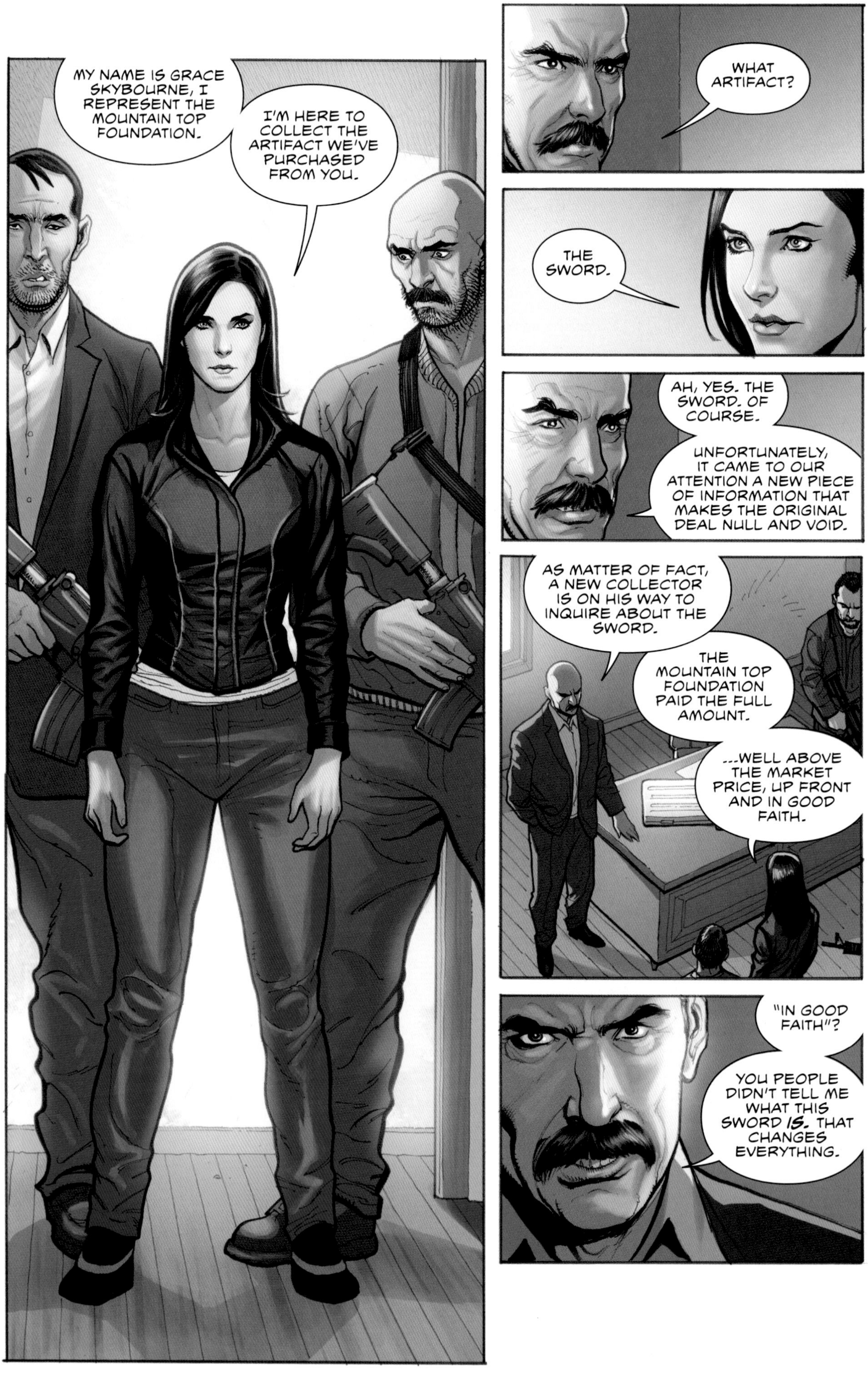
MY NAME IS GRACE SKYBOURNE, I REPRESENT THE MOUNTAIN TOP FOUNDATION.
I'M HERE TO COLLECT THE ARTIFACT WE'VE PURCHASED FROM YOU.
WHAT ARTIFACT?
THE SWORD.
AH, YES. THE SWORD. OF COURSE.
UNFORTUNATELY, IT CAME TO OUR ATTENTION A NEW PIECE OF INFORMATION THAT MAKES THE ORIGINAL DEAL NULL AND VOID.
AS MATTER OF FACT, A NEW COLLECTOR IS ON HIS WAY TO INQUIRE ABOUT THE SWORD.
THE MOUNTAIN TOP FOUNDATION PAID THE FULL AMOUNT.
...WELL ABOVE THE MARKET PRICE, UP FRONT AND IN GOOD FAITH.
"IN GOOD FAITH"?
YOU PEOPLE DIDN'T TELL ME WHAT THIS SWORD IS. THAT CHANGES EVERYTHING.

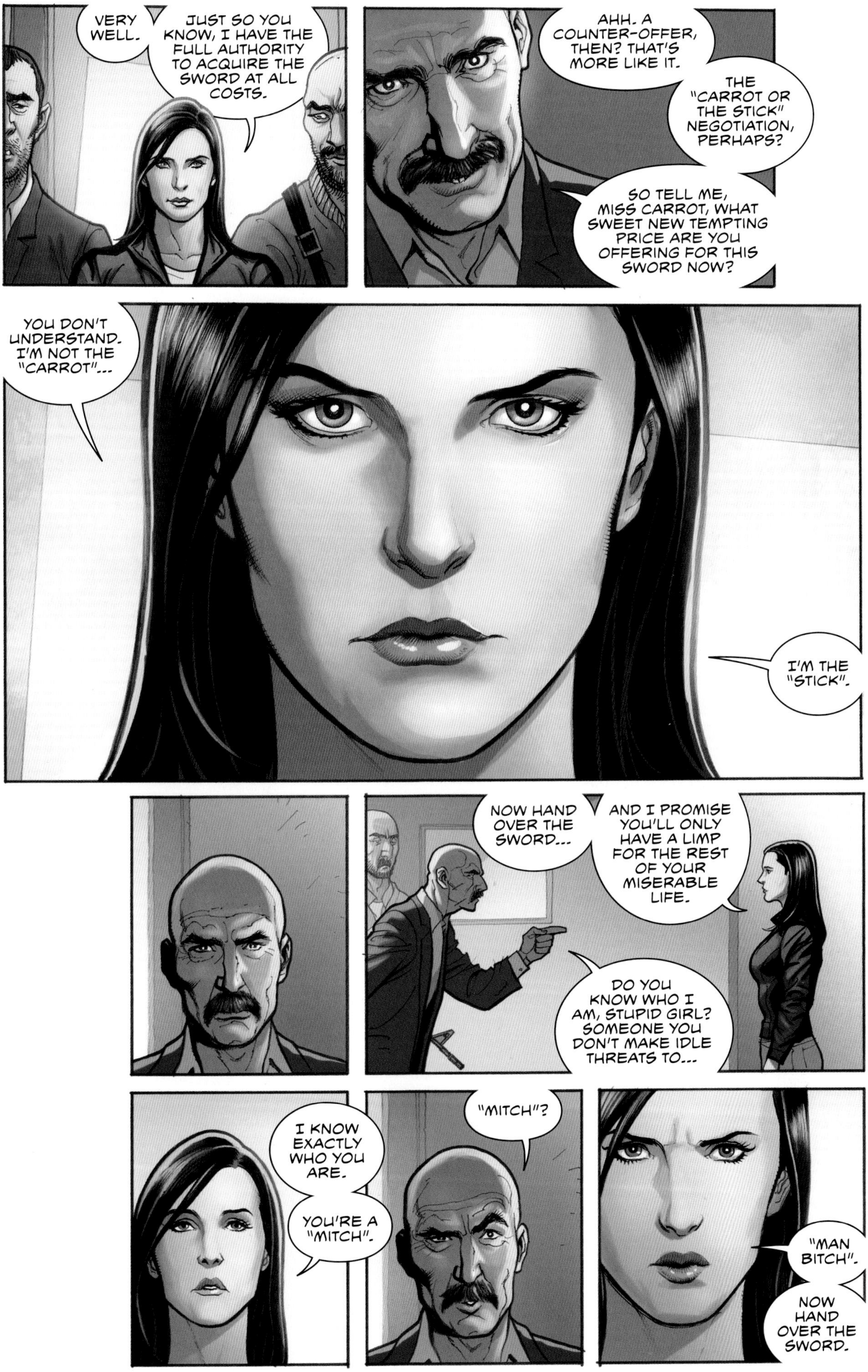
VERY WELL.
JUST SO YOU KNOW, I HAVE THE FULL AUTHORITY TO ACQUIRE THE SWORD AT ALL COSTS.
AHH. A COUNTER-OFFER, THEN? THAT'S MORE LIKE IT.
THE "CARROT OR THE STICK" NEGOTIATION, PERHAPS?
SO TELL ME, MISS CARROT, WHAT SWEET NEW TEMPTING PRICE ARE YOU OFFERING FOR THIS SWORD NOW?
YOU DON'T UNDERSTAND. I'M NOT THE "CARROT"...
I'M THE "STICK".
NOW HAND OVER THE SWORD...
AND I PROMISE YOU'LL ONLY HAVE A LIMP FOR THE REST OF YOUR MISERABLE LIFE.
DO YOU KNOW WHO I AM, STUPID GIRL? SOMEONE YOU DON'T MAKE IDLE THREATS TO...
I KNOW EXACTLY WHO YOU ARE.
YOU'RE A "MITCH".
"MITCH"?
"MAN BITCH".
NOW HAND OVER THE SWORD.

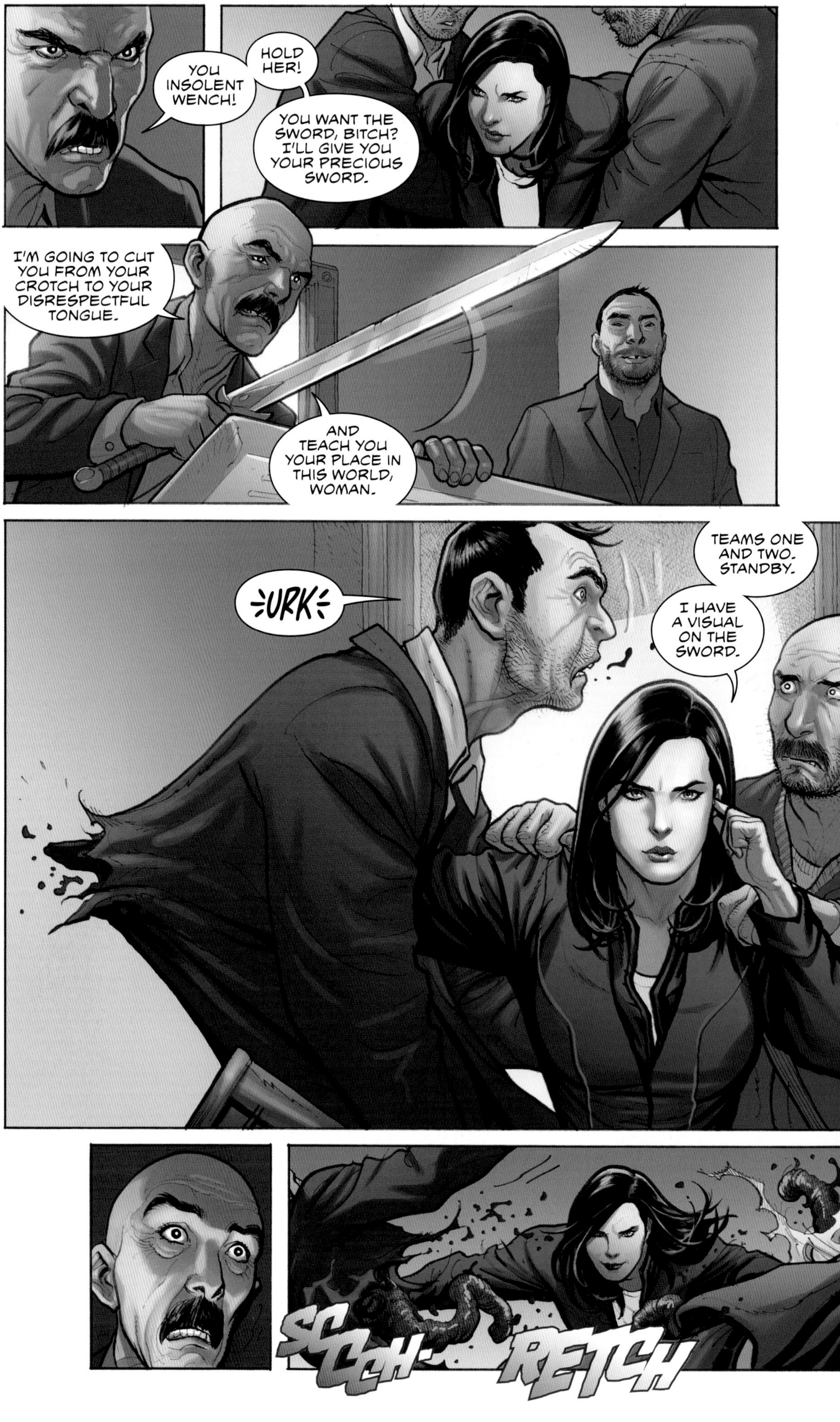
YOU INSOLENT WENCH!
HOLD HER!
YOU WANT THE SWORD, BITCH? I'LL GIVE YOU YOUR PRECIOUS SWORD.
I'M GOING TO CUT YOU FROM YOUR CROTCH TO YOUR DISRESPECTFUL TONGUE.
AND TEACH YOU YOUR PLACE IN THIS WORLD, WOMAN.
URK
TEAMS ONE AND TWO. STANDBY.
I HAVE A VISUAL ON THE SWORD.
SCCCH-RETCH

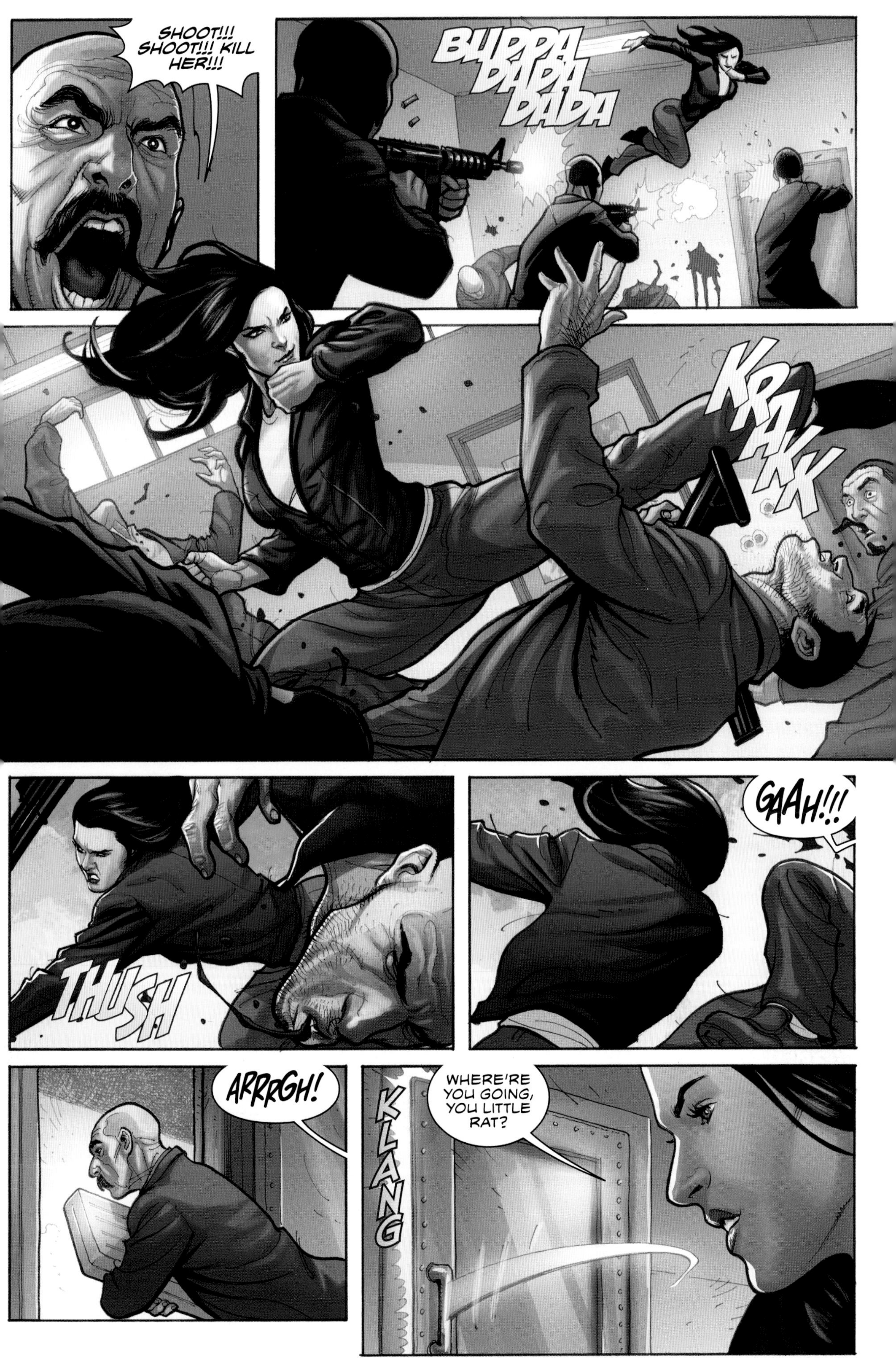
SHOOT!!! SHOOT!!! KILL HER!!!
BUDDA DADA DADA
KRAKK
THUSH
GAAH!!!
ARRRGH!
KLANG
WHERE'RE YOU GOING, YOU LITTLE RAT?

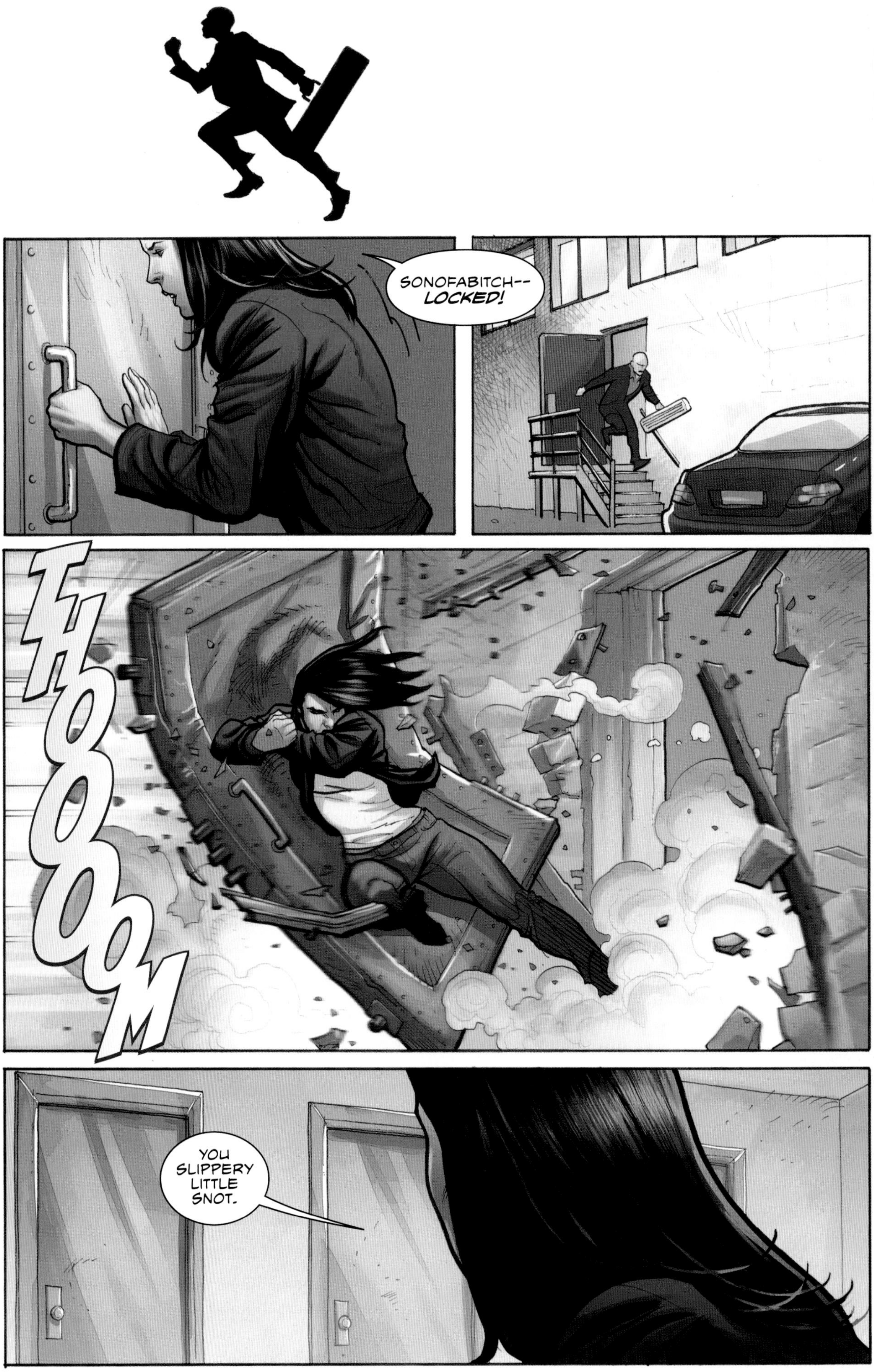
SONOFABITCH--
LOCKED!
THOOOOOM
YOU SLIPPERY LITTLE SNOT.

OW!

BLAM
BLAM
BLAM

PHOOM!

:URK:

HE'S EXITED THE BUILDING WITH THE SWORD. DO YOU HAVE A VISUAL?

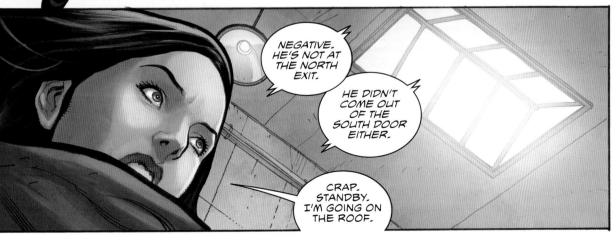

NEGATIVE. HE'S NOT AT THE NORTH EXIT.

HE DIDN'T COME OUT OF THE SOUTH DOOR EITHER.

CRAP. STANDBY. I'M GOING ON THE ROOF.

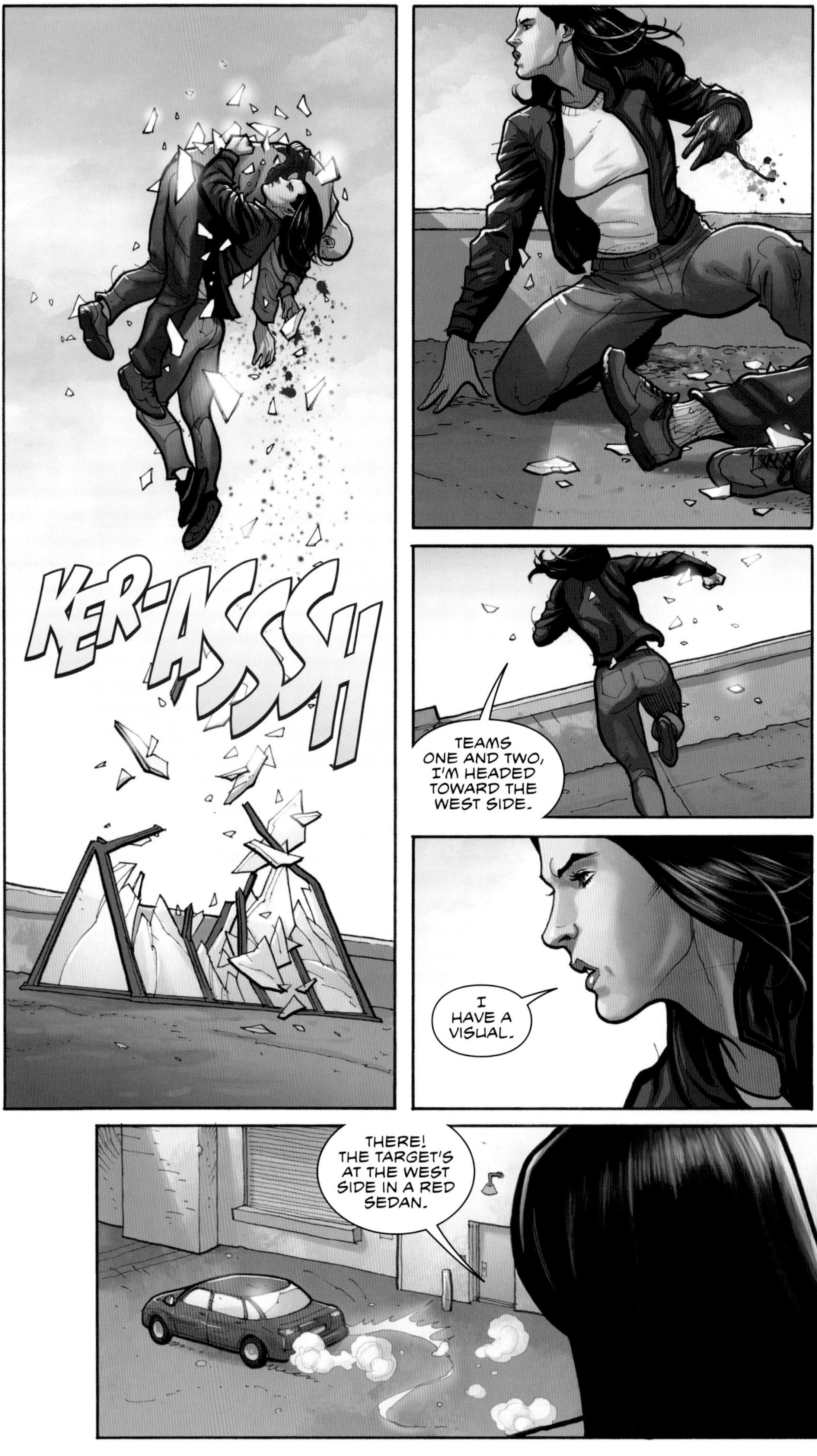
KER-ASSSH
TEAMS ONE AND TWO, I'M HEADED TOWARD THE WEST SIDE.
I HAVE A VISUAL.
THERE! THE TARGET'S AT THE WEST SIDE IN A RED SEDAN.

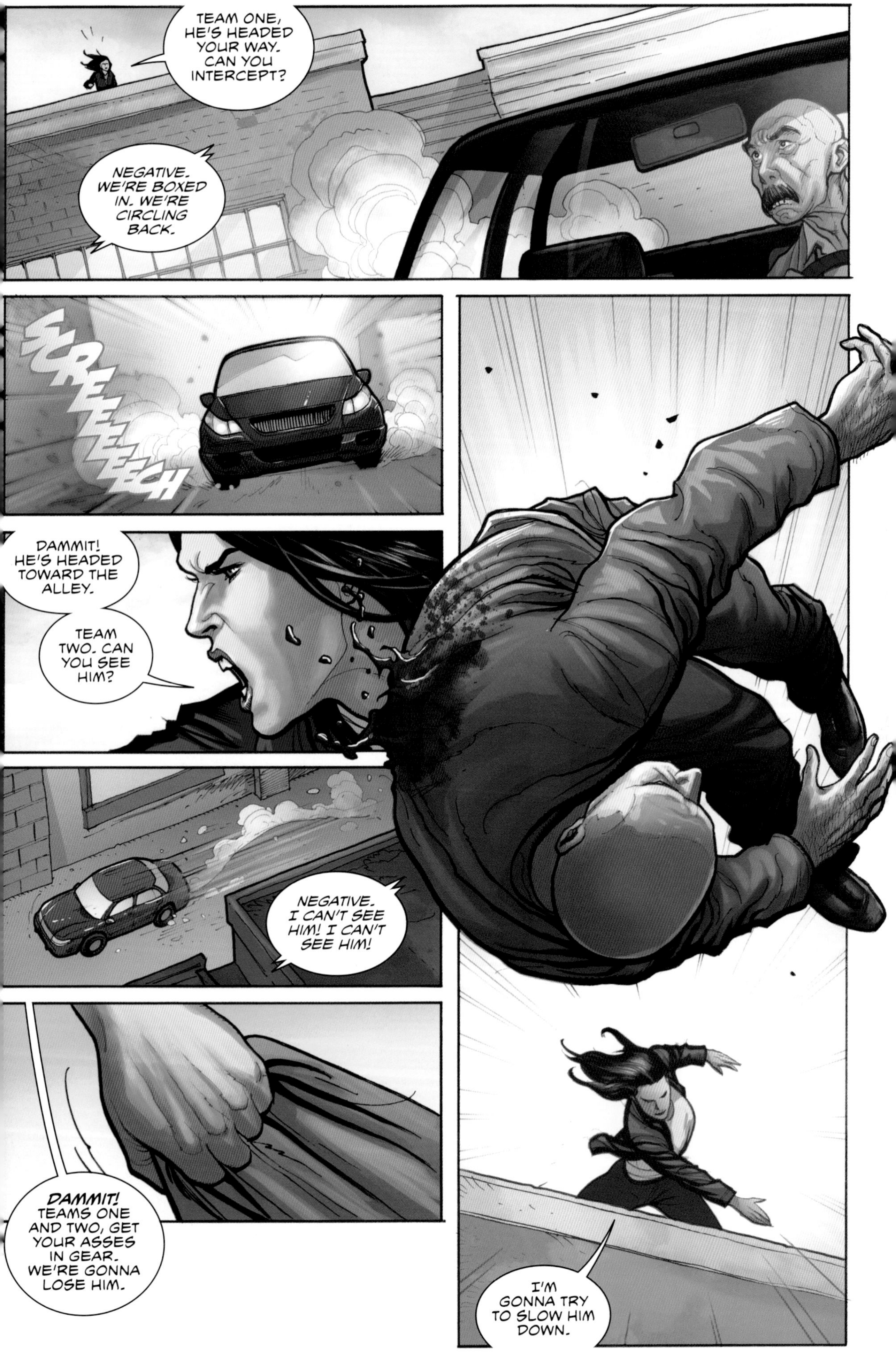
TEAM ONE, HE'S HEADED YOUR WAY. CAN YOU INTERCEPT?
NEGATIVE. WE'RE BOXED IN. WE'RE CIRCLING BACK.
SCREEEEEEECH
DAMMIT! HE'S HEADED TOWARD THE ALLEY.
TEAM TWO. CAN YOU SEE HIM?
NEGATIVE. I CAN'T SEE HIM! I CAN'T SEE HIM!
DAMMIT! TEAMS ONE AND TWO, GET YOUR ASSES IN GEAR. WE'RE GONNA LOSE HIM.
I'M GONNA TRY TO SLOW HIM DOWN.

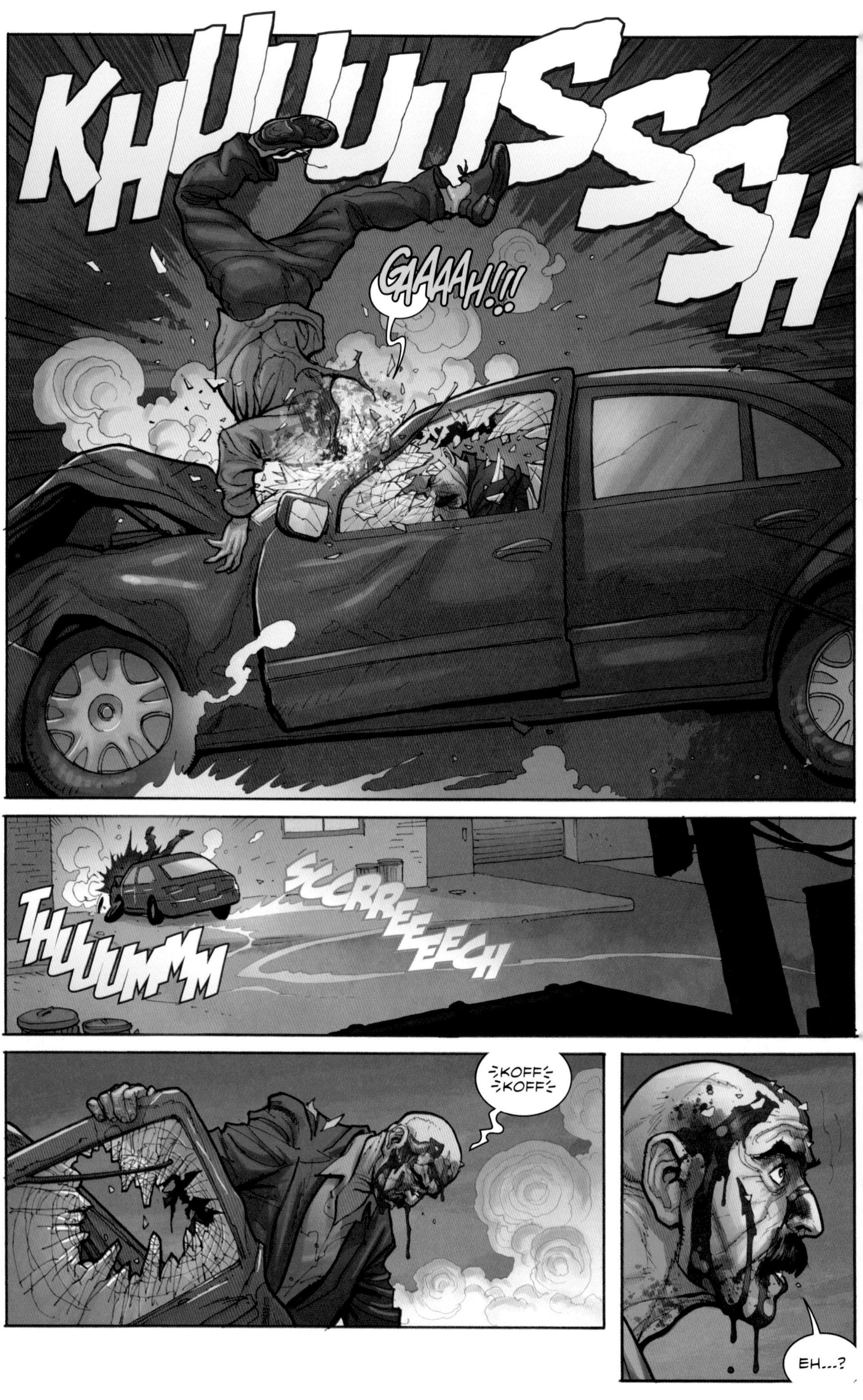
KHUUUTSSSH
GAAAAH!!!
THUUUMMM
SCCRREEEEECH
KOFF KOFF
EH...?

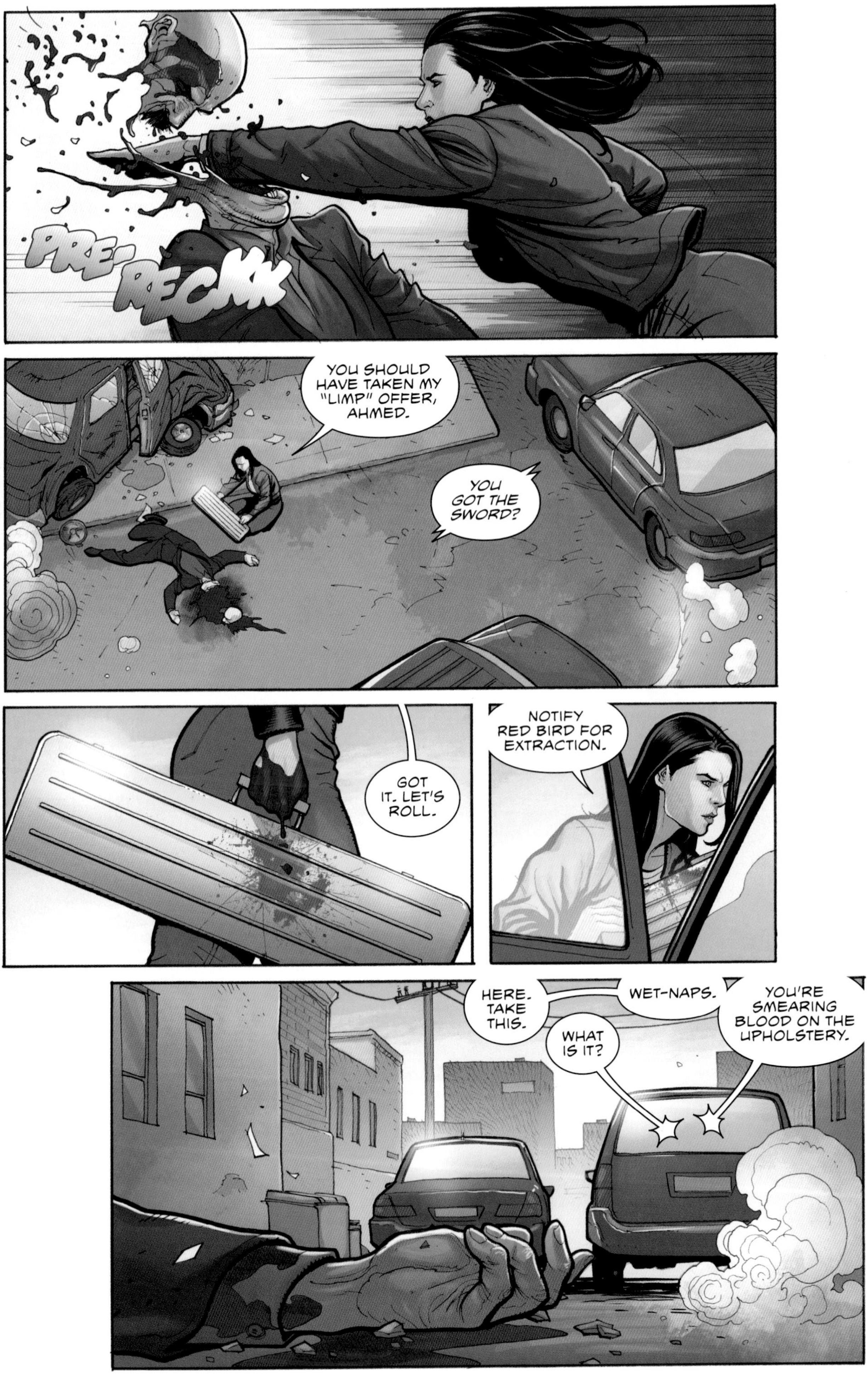
PRE-RECKK
YOU SHOULD HAVE TAKEN MY "LIMP" OFFER, AHMED.
YOU GOT THE SWORD?
GOT IT. LET'S ROLL.
NOTIFY RED BIRD FOR EXTRACTION.
HERE. TAKE THIS.
WHAT IS IT?
WET-NAPS.
YOU'RE SMEARING BLOOD ON THE UPHOLSTERY.

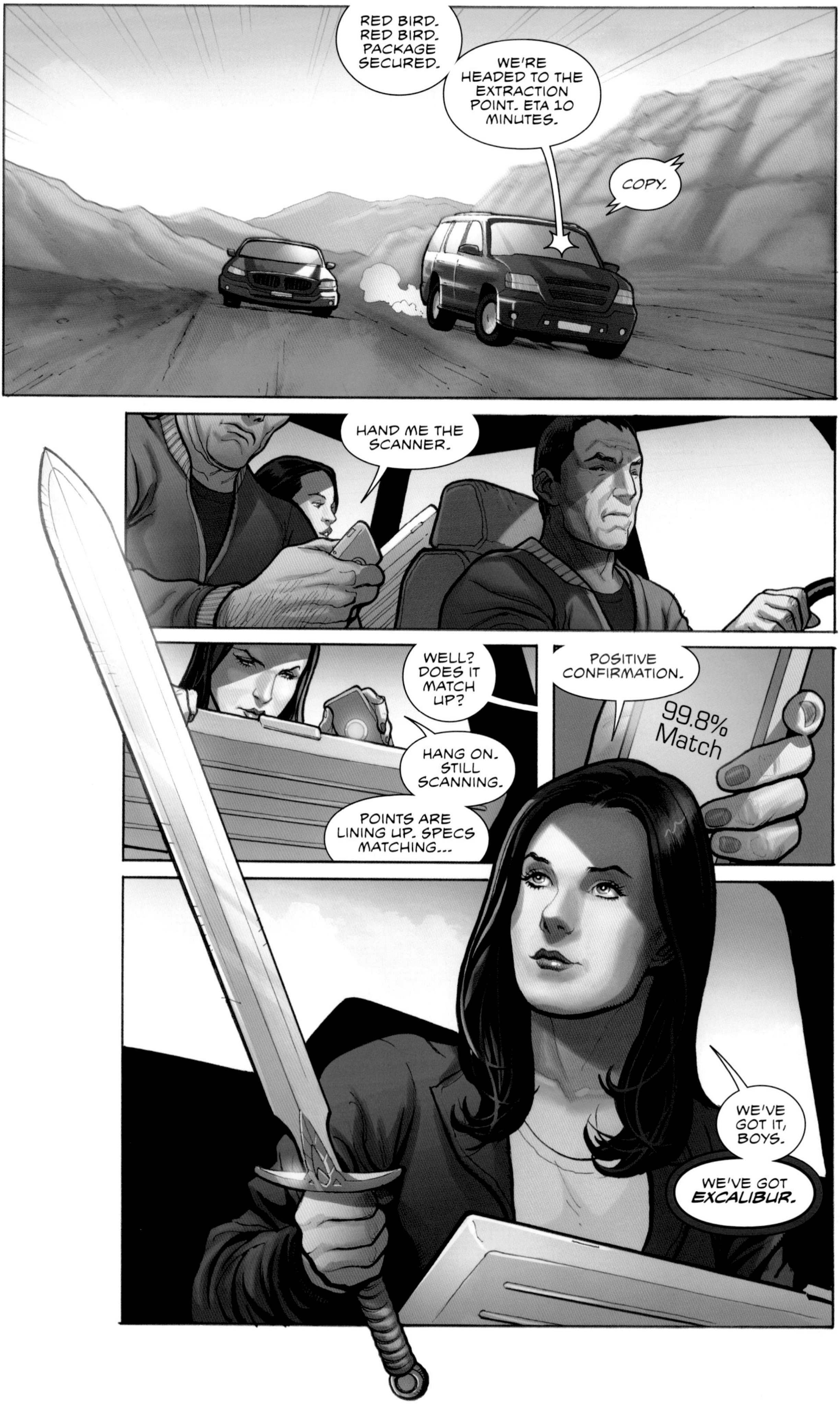

RED BIRD. RED BIRD. PACKAGE SECURED.
WE'RE HEADED TO THE EXTRACTION POINT. ETA 10 MINUTES.
COPY.
HAND ME THE SCANNER.
WELL? DOES IT MATCH UP?
HANG ON. STILL SCANNING.
POINTS ARE LINING UP. SPECS MATCHING...
POSITIVE CONFIRMATION.
99.8% Match
WE'VE GOT IT, BOYS.
WE'VE GOT *EXCALIBUR.*

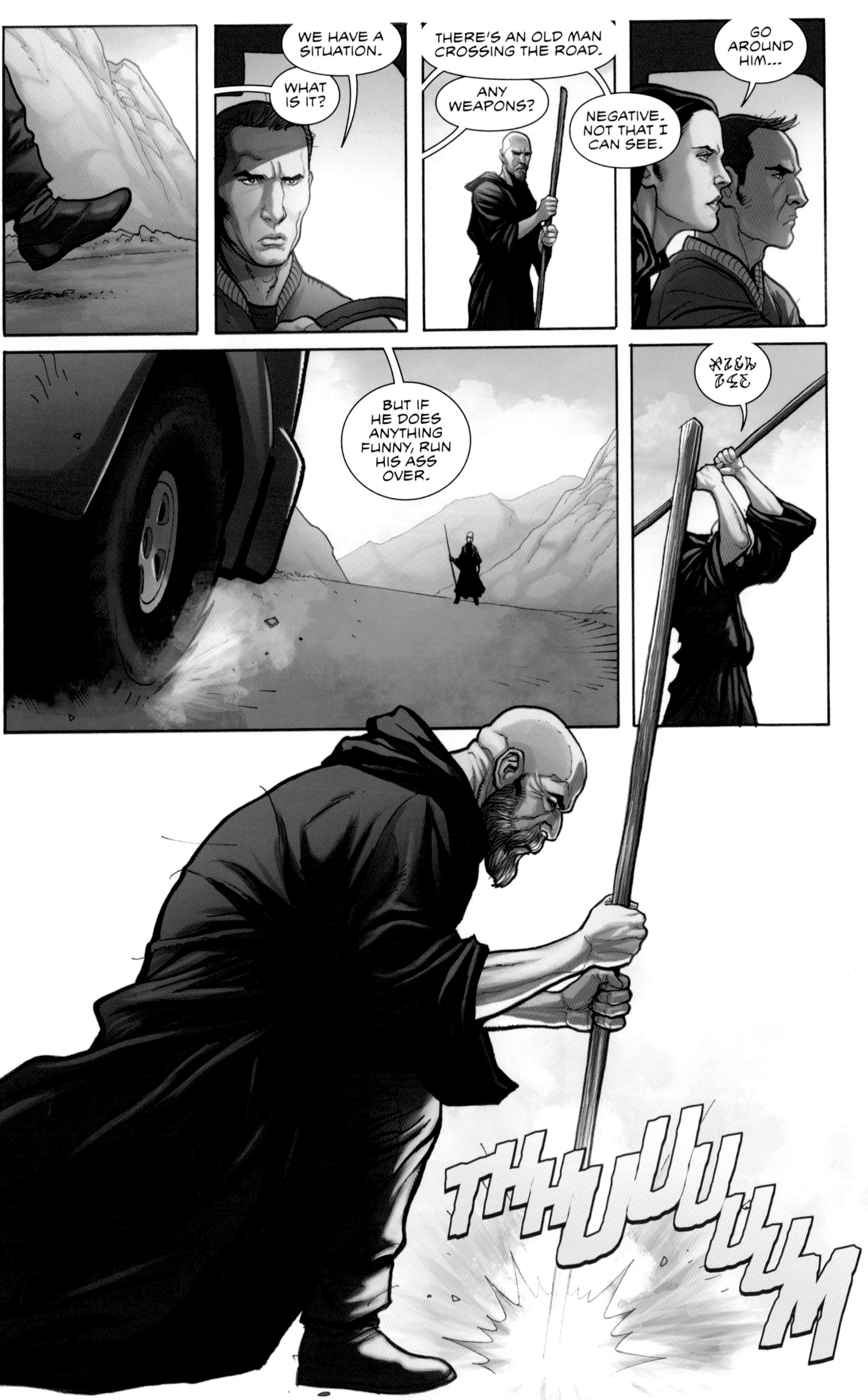
WE HAVE A SITUATION.
WHAT IS IT?
THERE'S AN OLD MAN CROSSING THE ROAD.
ANY WEAPONS?
NEGATIVE. NOT THAT I CAN SEE.
GO AROUND HIM...
BUT IF HE DOES ANYTHING FUNNY, RUN HIS ASS OVER.
THUUUUUM

KA-BOOOM

AARHHH!

ᒣGHARK!ᒧ

FOOMP

$#%@!

KLUK- THUP

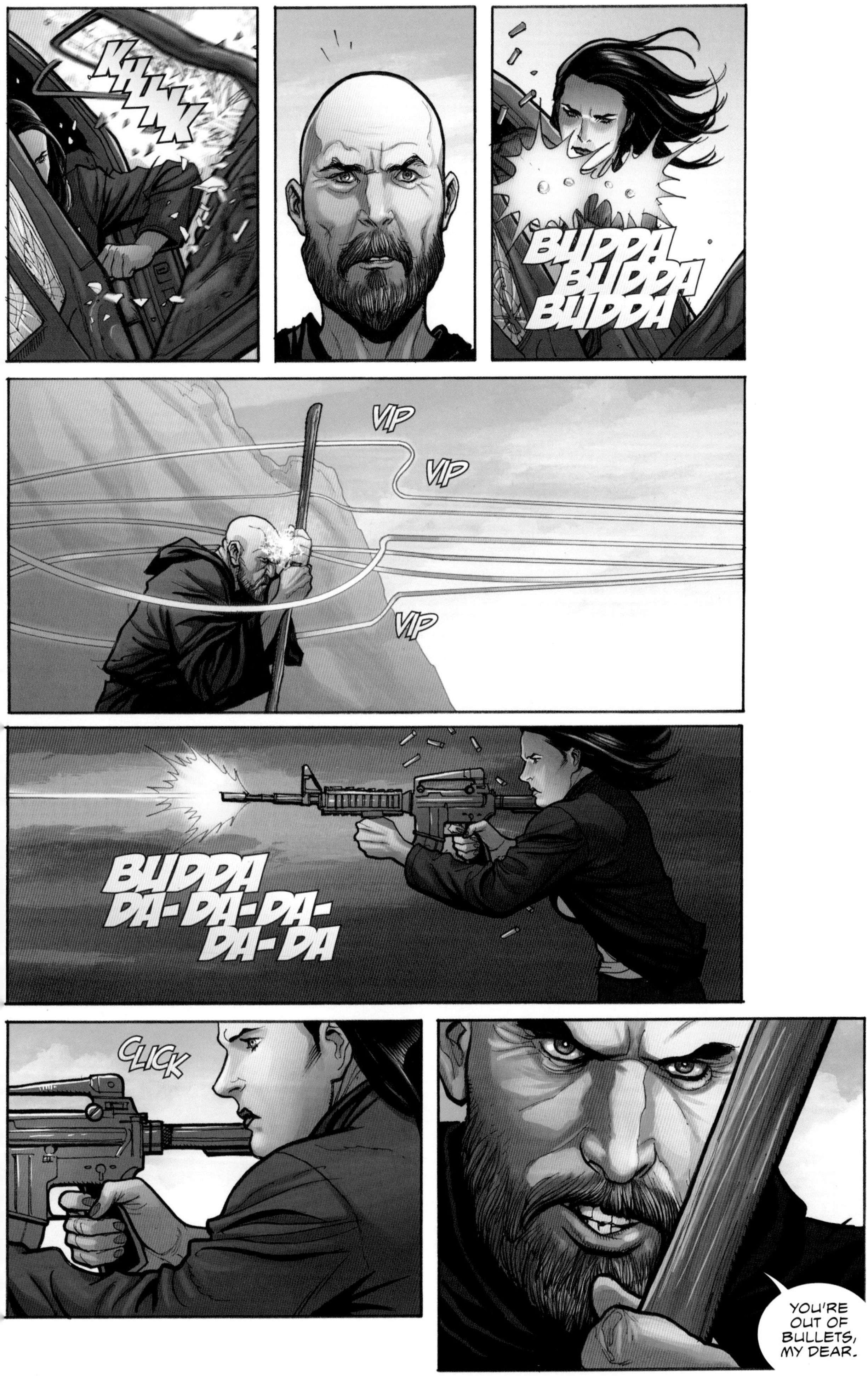
KHUNK
BUDDA BUDDA BUDDA
VIP
VIP
VIP
BUDDA DA-DA-DA-DA-DA
CLICK
YOU'RE OUT OF BULLETS, MY DEAR.

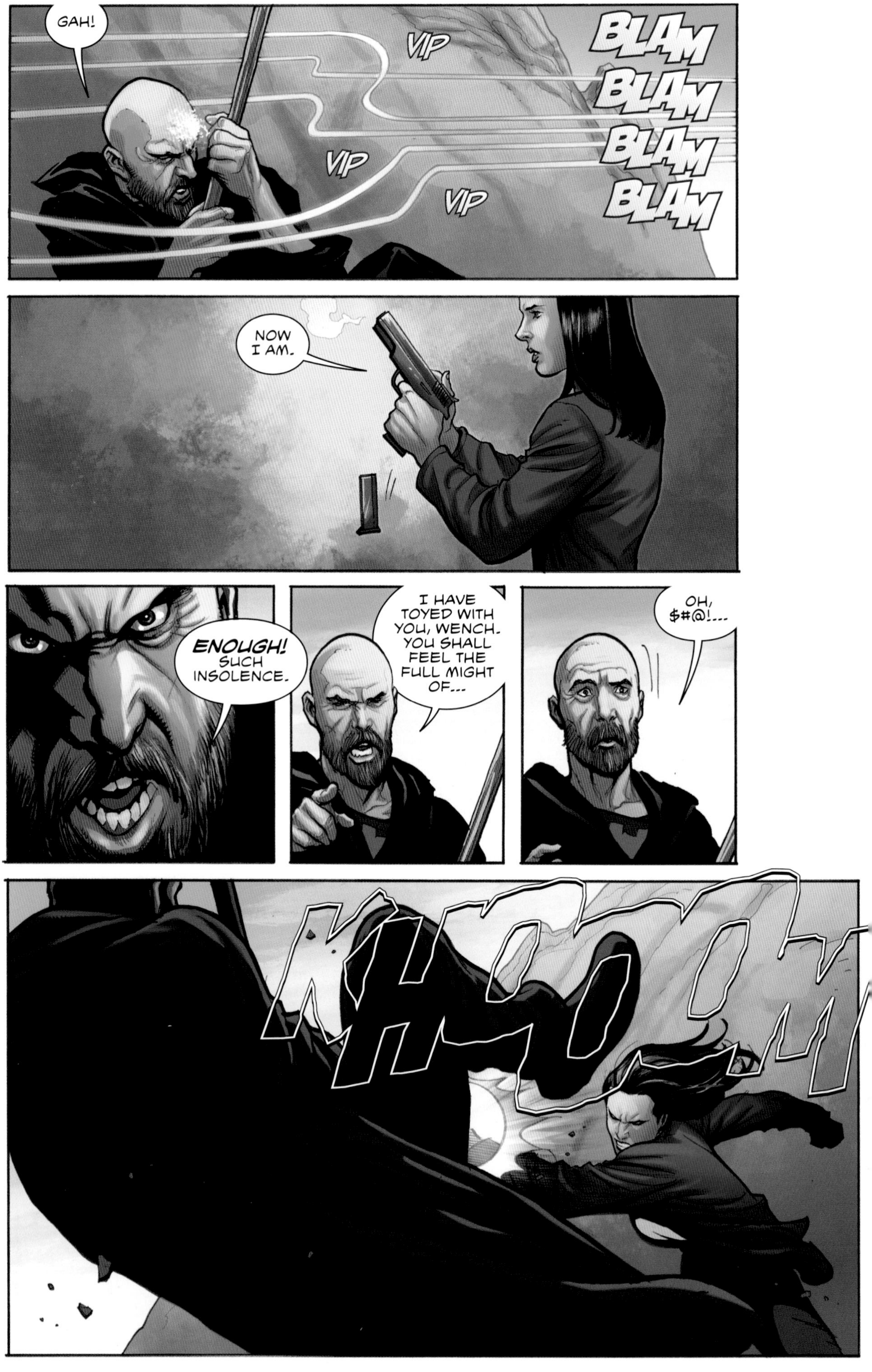
GAH!
VIP
BLAM
BLAM
BLAM
BLAM
VIP
VIP
NOW I AM.
ENOUGH! SUCH INSOLENCE.
I HAVE TOYED WITH YOU, WENCH. YOU SHALL FEEL THE FULL MIGHT OF...
OH, $#@!...
KH-O-OOM

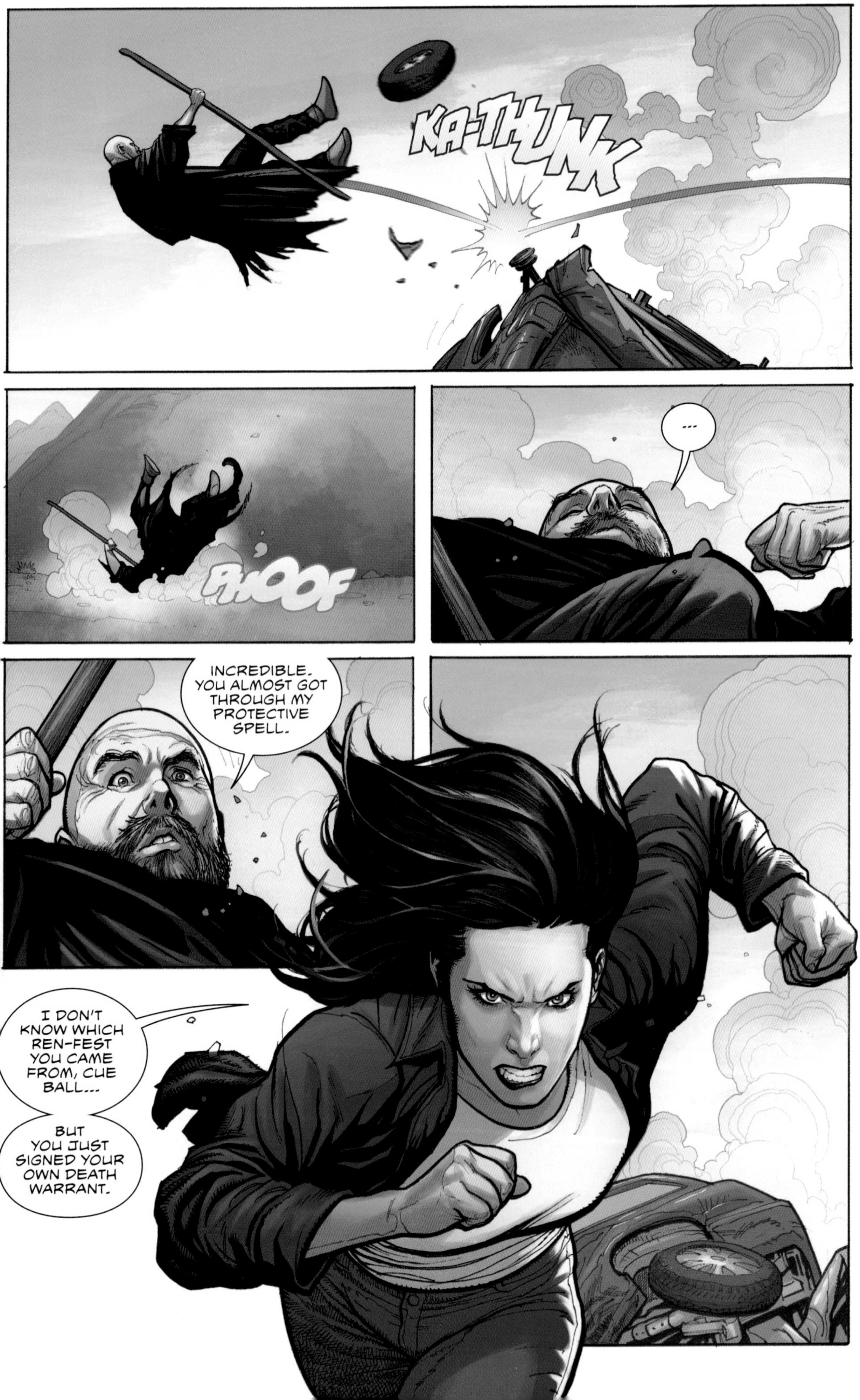
KA-THUNK
PHOOF
...
INCREDIBLE. YOU ALMOST GOT THROUGH MY PROTECTIVE SPELL.
I DON'T KNOW WHICH REN-FEST YOU CAME FROM, CUE BALL...
BUT YOU JUST SIGNED YOUR OWN DEATH WARRANT.

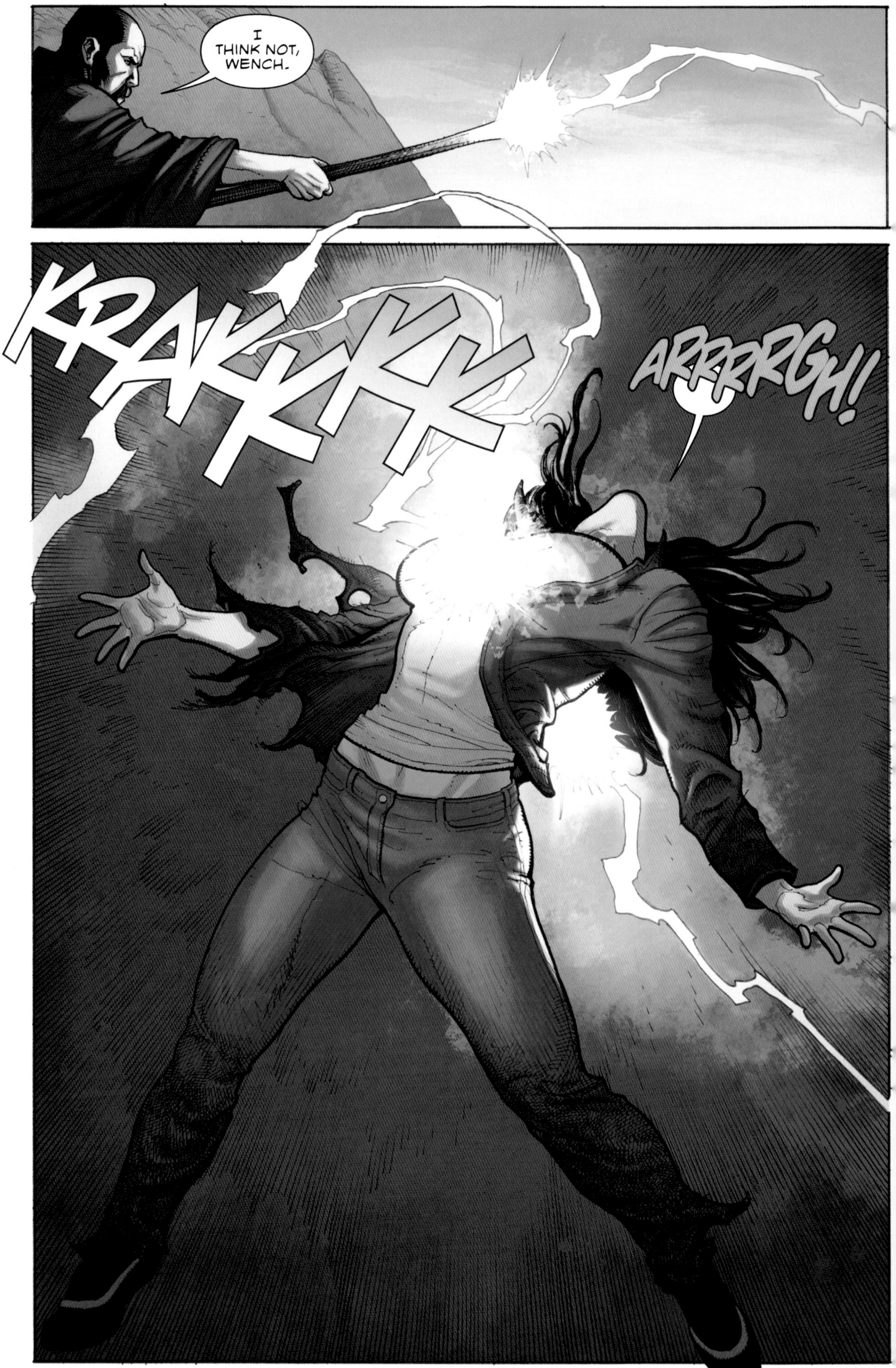
I THINK NOT, WENCH.
KRAKKKK
ARRRRGH!

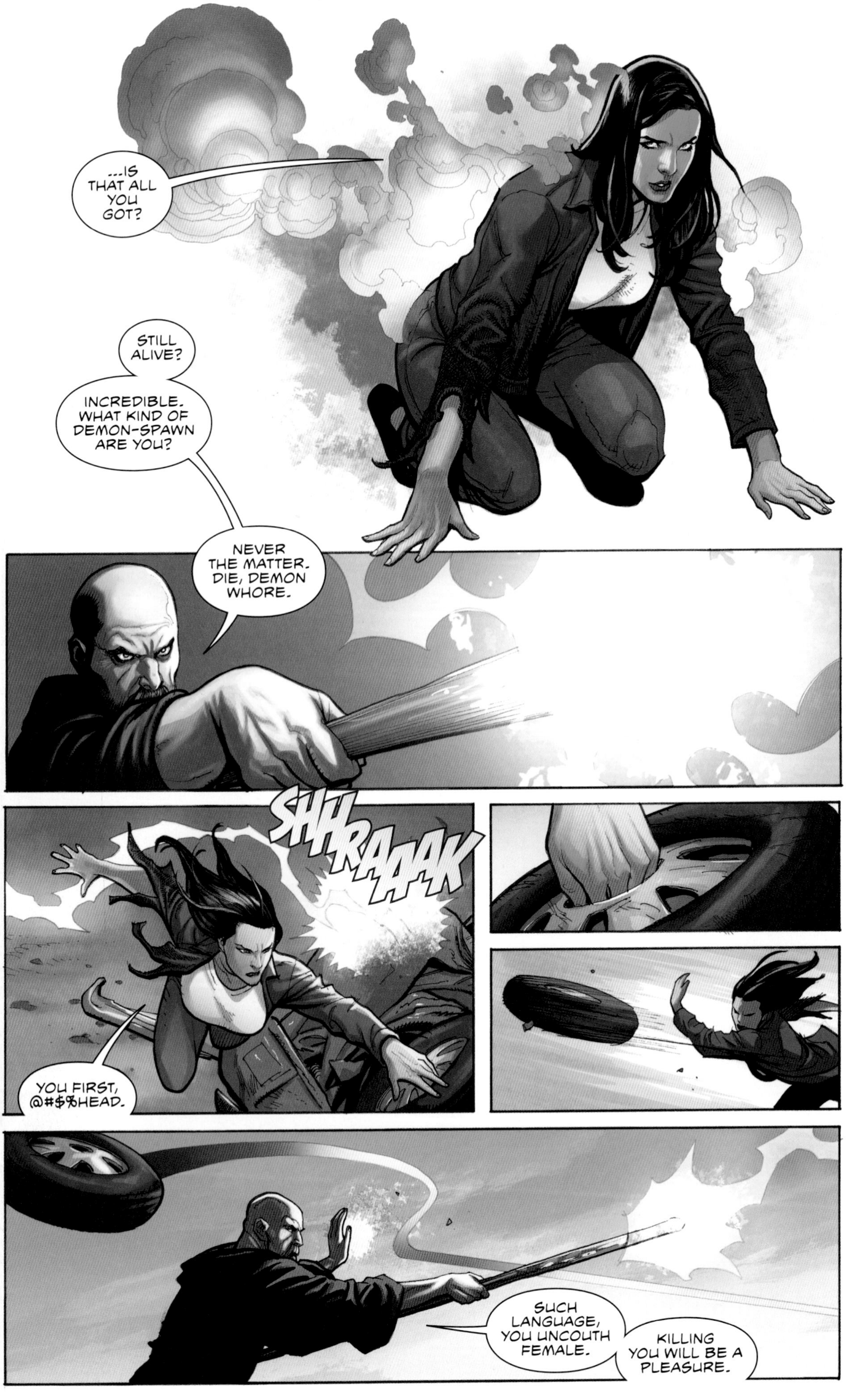
...IS THAT ALL YOU GOT?
STILL ALIVE?
INCREDIBLE. WHAT KIND OF DEMON-SPAWN ARE YOU?
NEVER THE MATTER. DIE, DEMON WHORE.
SHHRAAAK
YOU FIRST, @#$%HEAD.
SUCH LANGUAGE, YOU UNCOUTH FEMALE.
KILLING YOU WILL BE A PLEASURE.

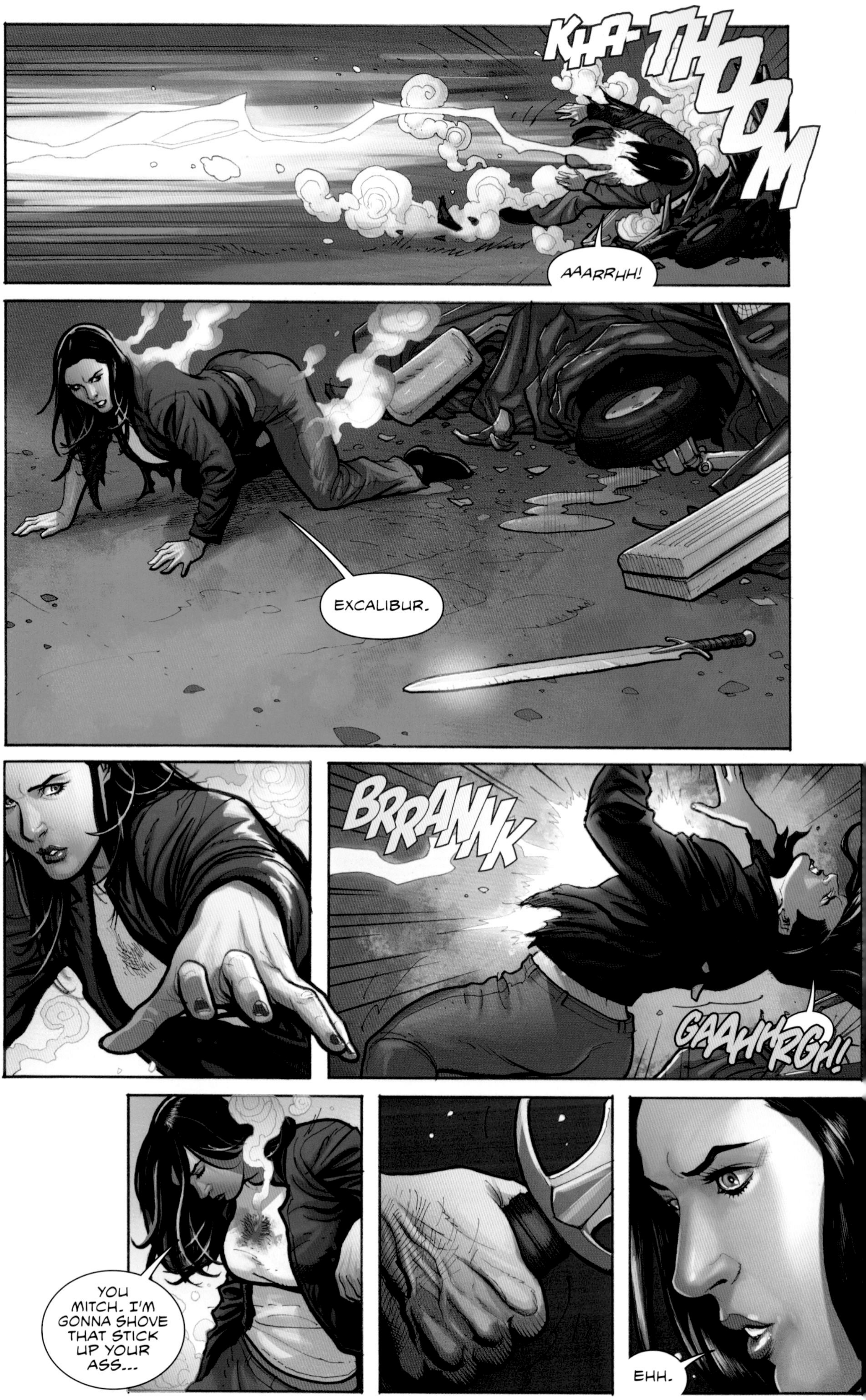
KHA-THOOOM
AAARRHH!
EXCALIBUR.
BRRANNK
GAAHHRGH!
YOU MITCH. I'M GONNA SHOVE THAT STICK UP YOUR ASS...
EHH.

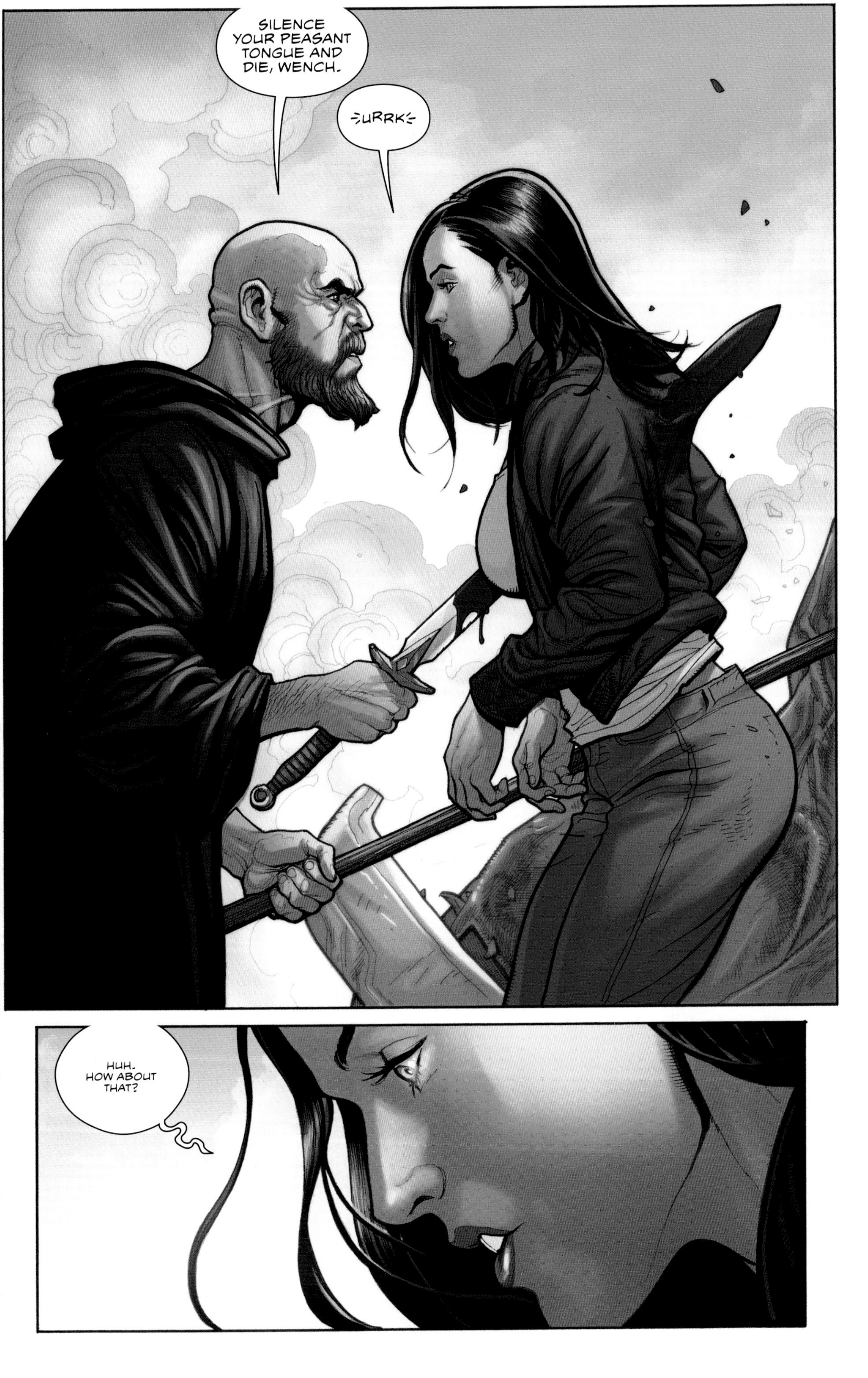
SILENCE YOUR PEASANT TONGUE AND DIE, WENCH.
URRK
HUH. HOW ABOUT THAT?

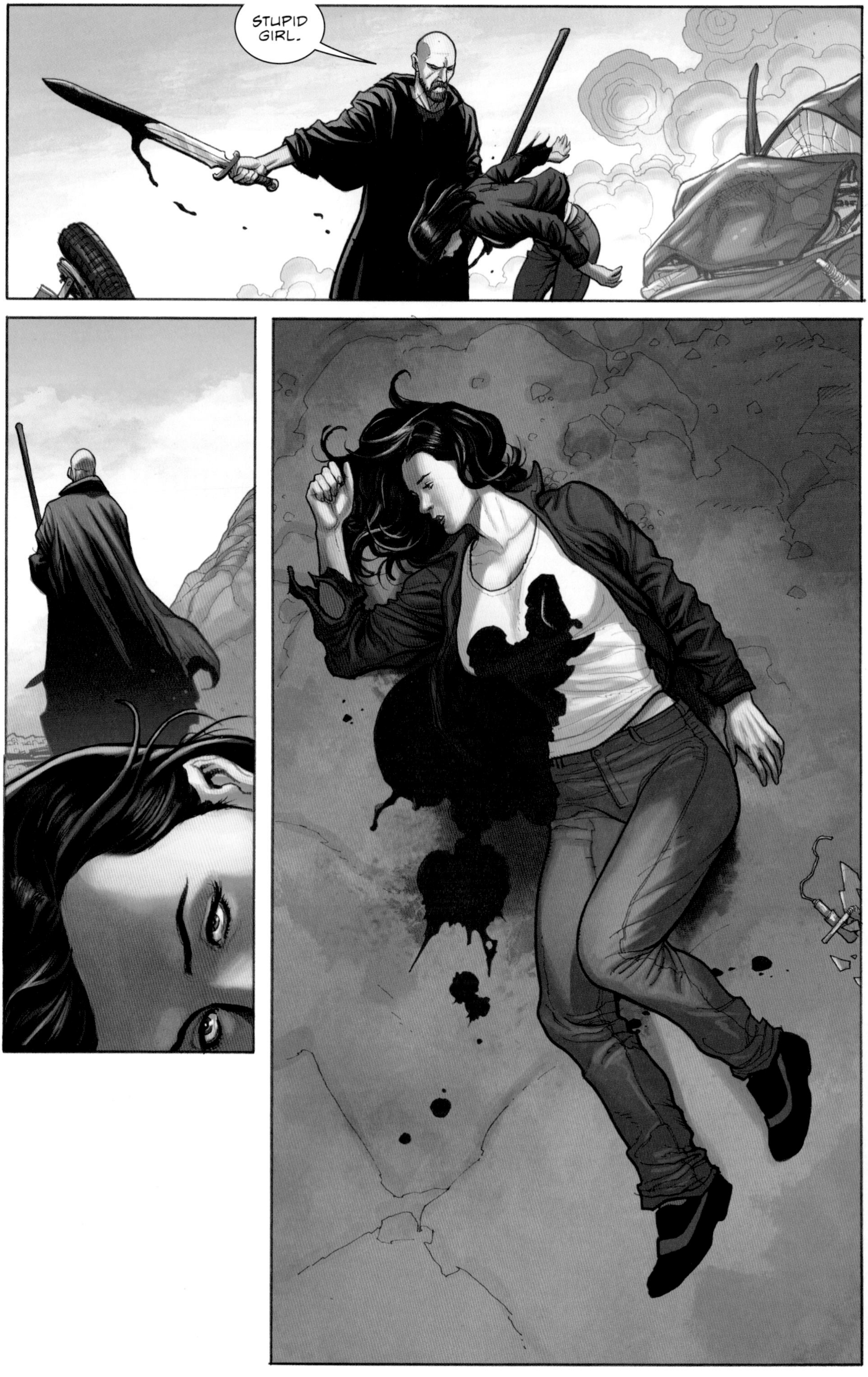
STUPID GIRL.

Issue One Cover by **FRANK CHO**
with colors by **MARCIO MENYZ**

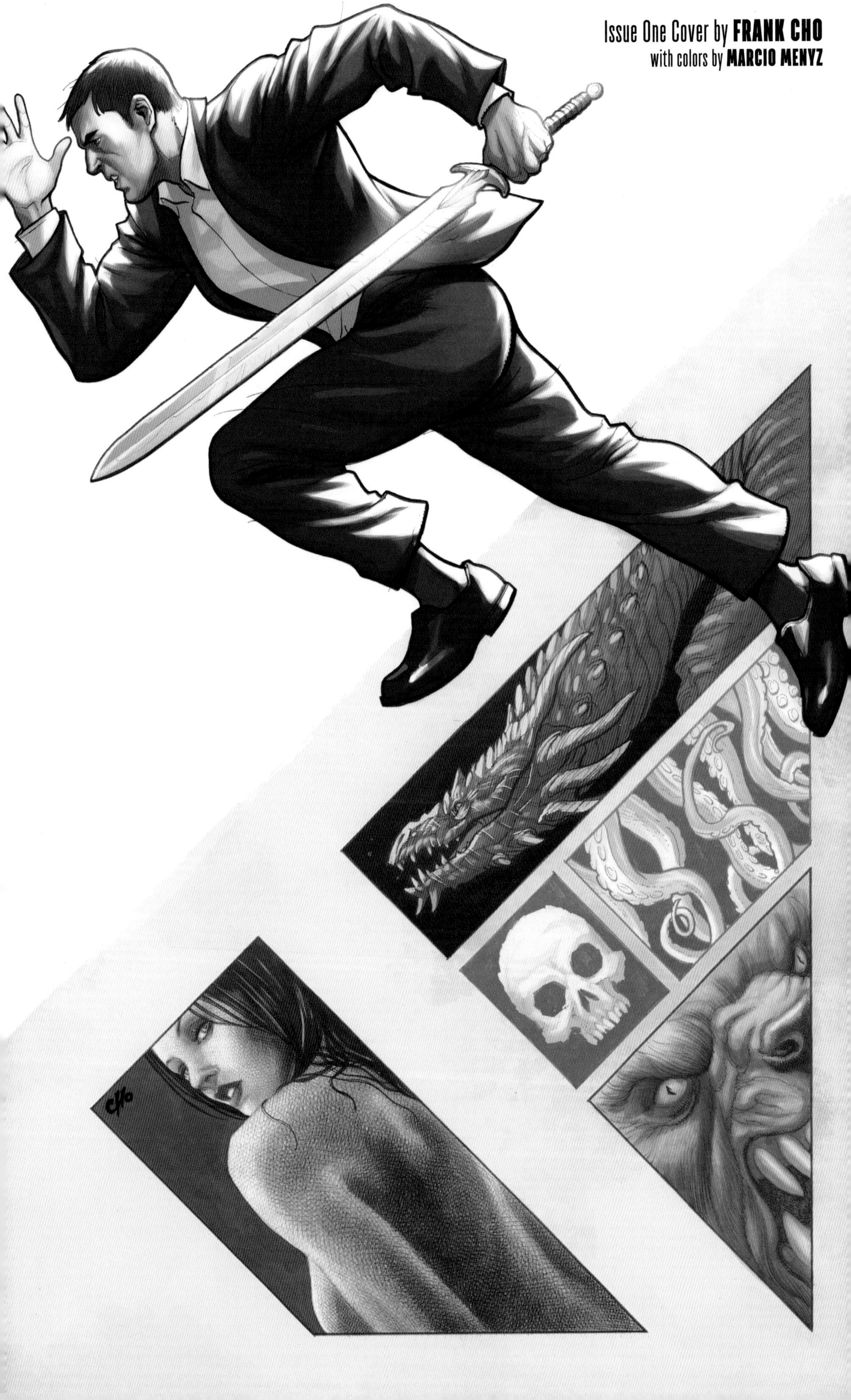

CHAPTER TWO

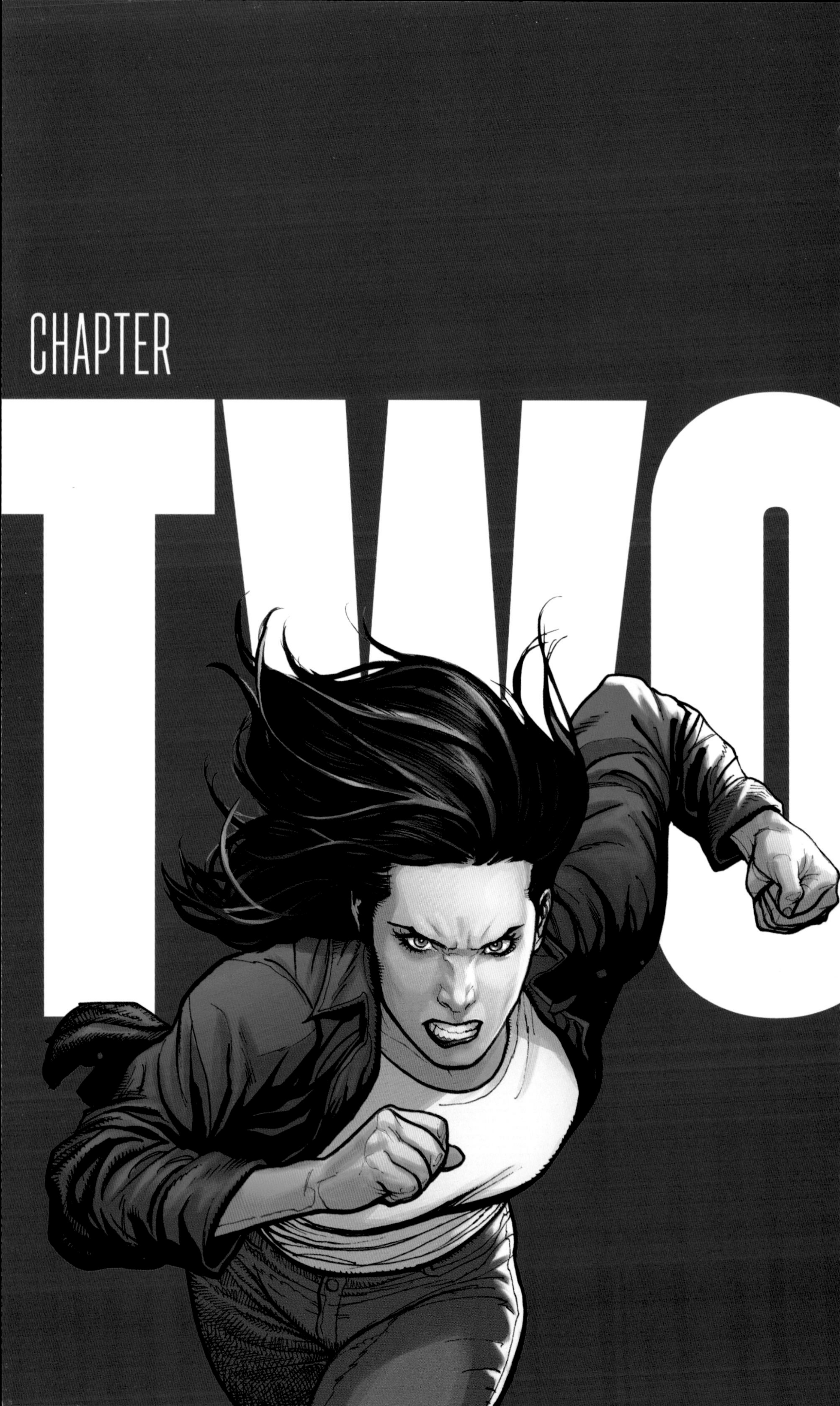

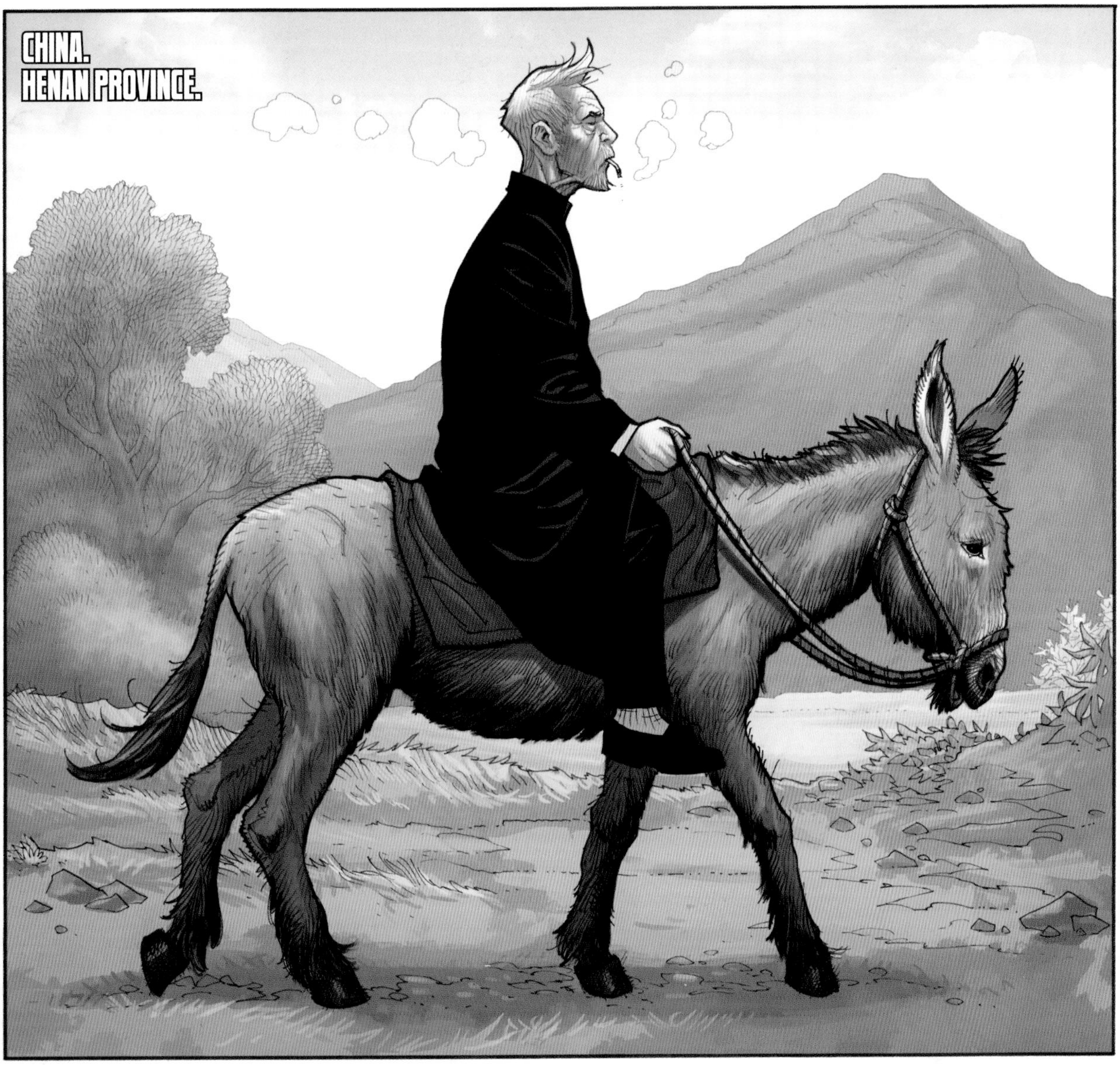
CHINA.
HENAN PROVINCE.

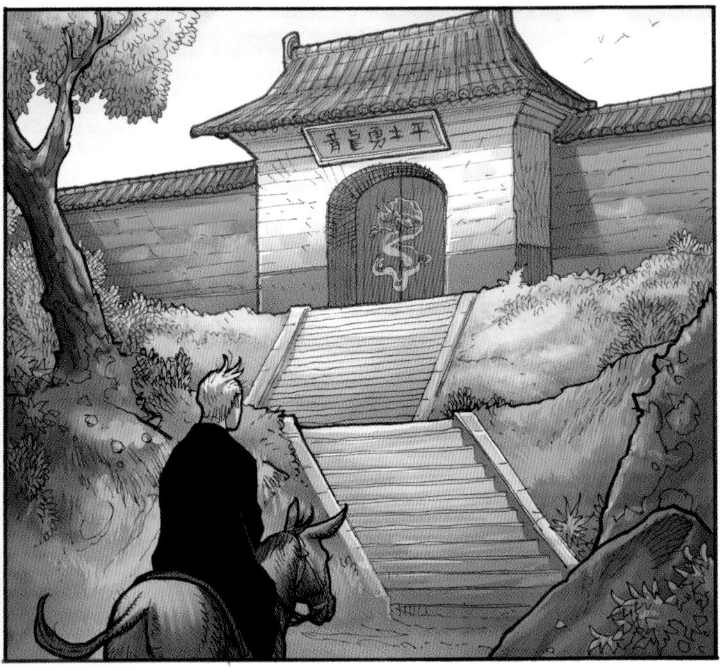

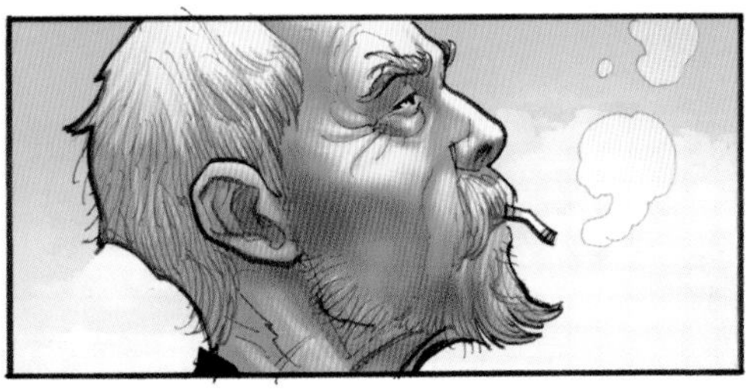

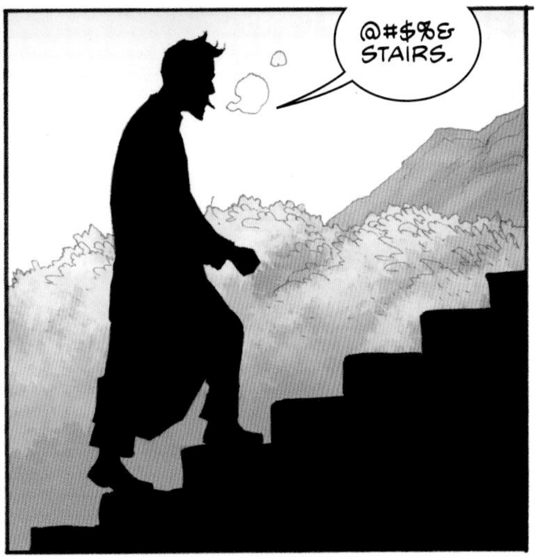
@#$%& STAIRS.

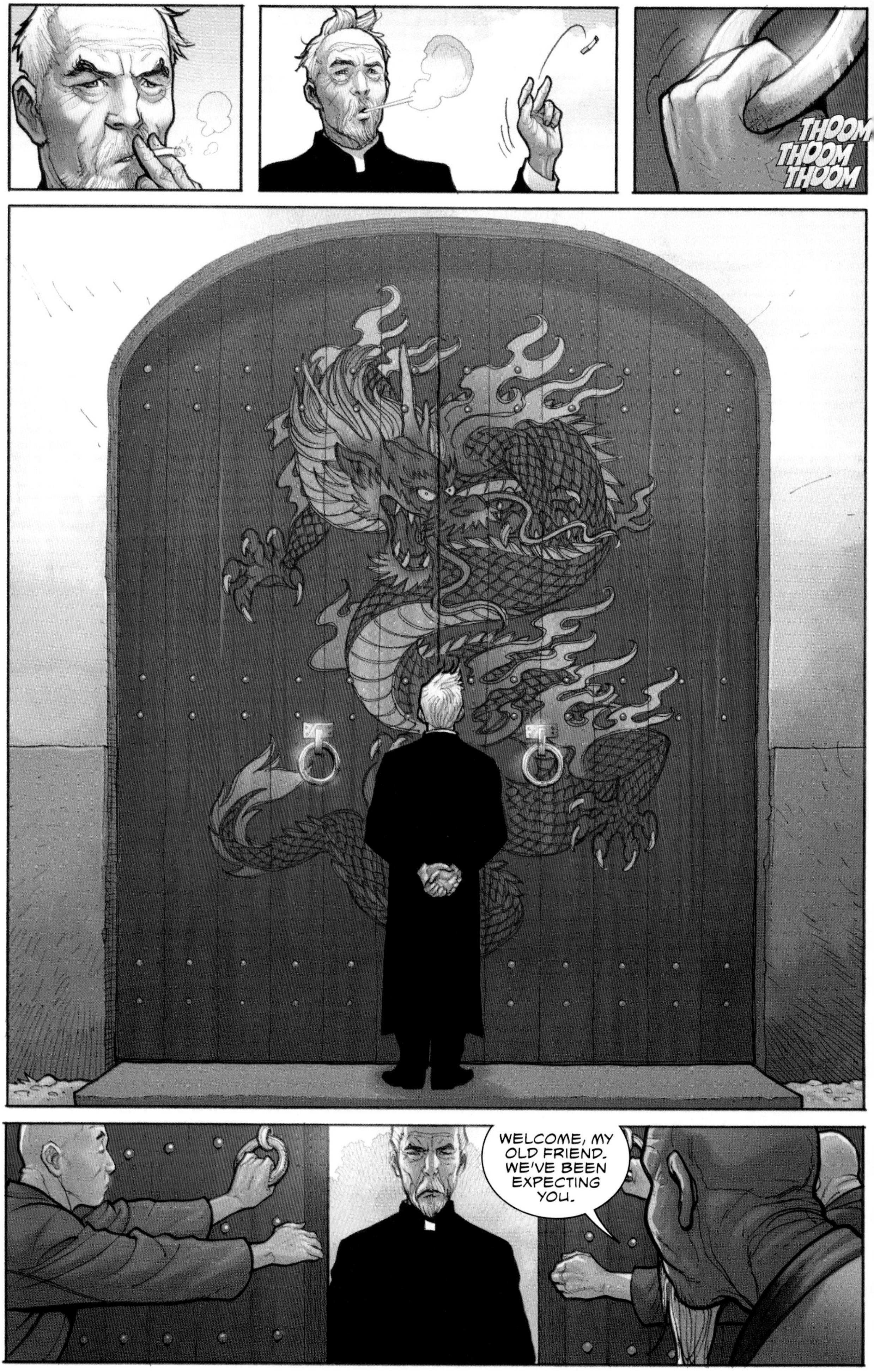
THOOM
THOOM
THOOM
WELCOME, MY OLD FRIEND. WE'VE BEEN EXPECTING YOU.

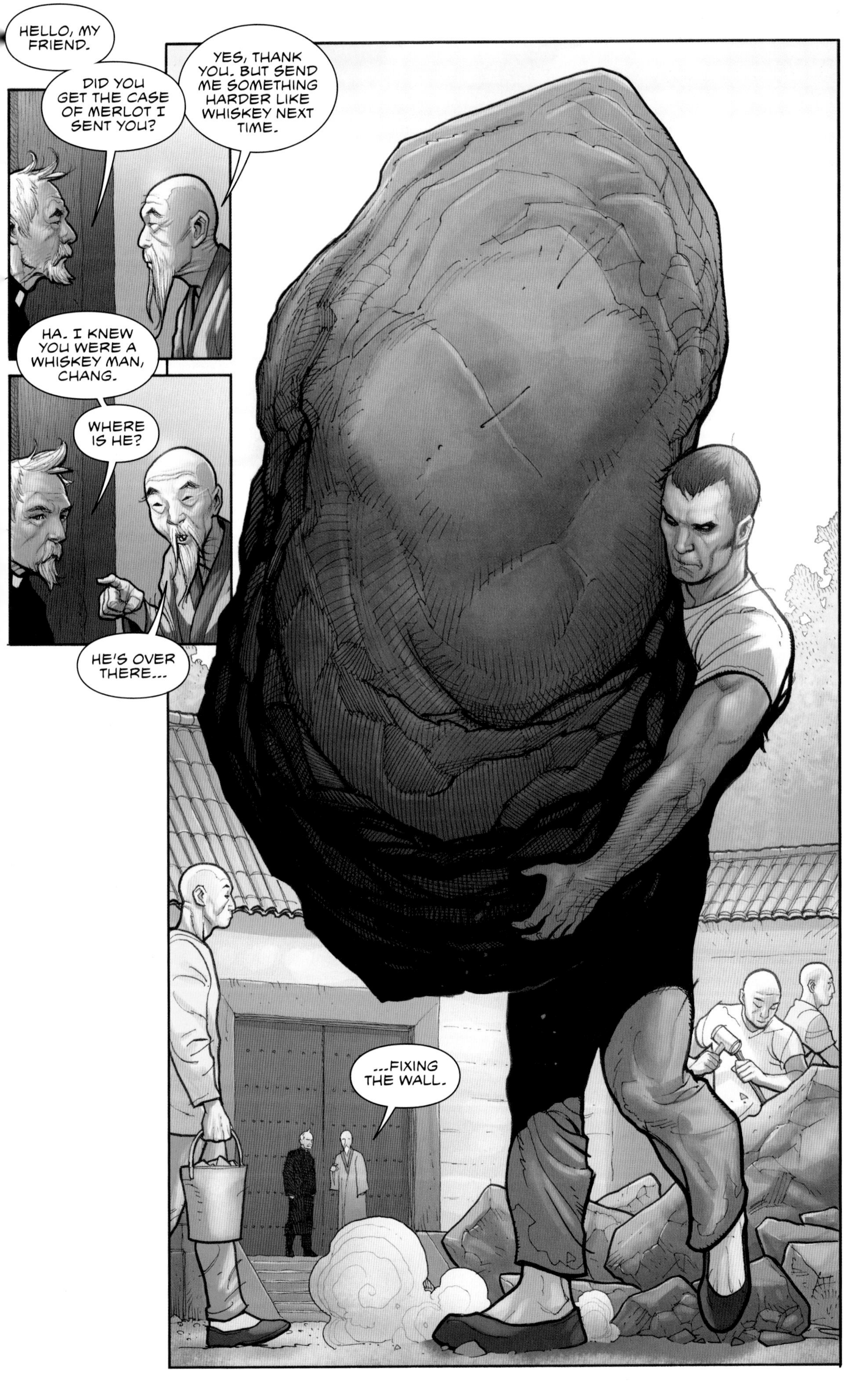
HELLO, MY FRIEND.
DID YOU GET THE CASE OF MERLOT I SENT YOU?
YES, THANK YOU. BUT SEND ME SOMETHING HARDER LIKE WHISKEY NEXT TIME.
HA. I KNEW YOU WERE A WHISKEY MAN, CHANG.
WHERE IS HE?
HE'S OVER THERE...
...FIXING THE WALL.

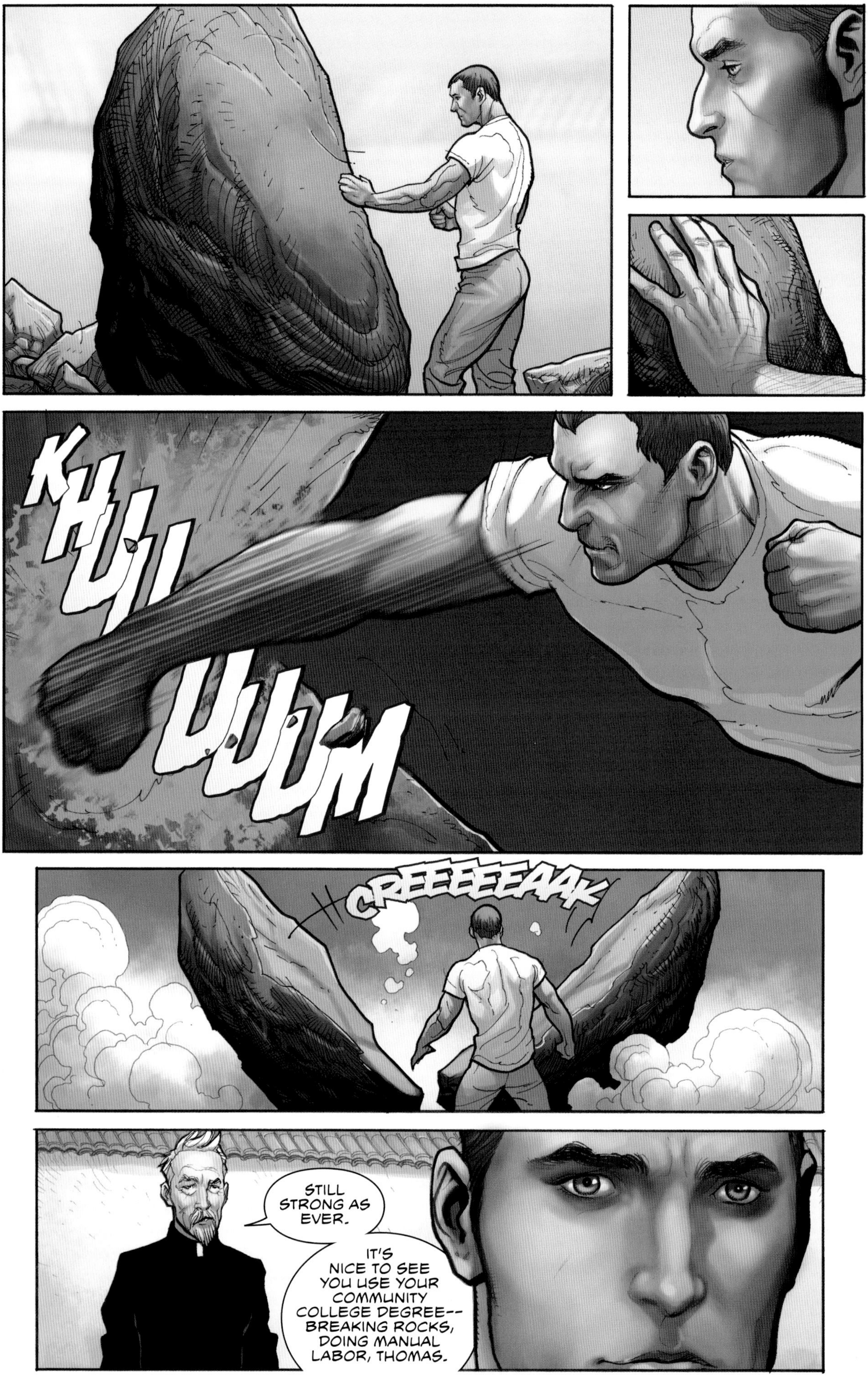
KHUUUUUM
CREEEEEEAAK
STILL STRONG AS EVER.
IT'S NICE TO SEE YOU USE YOUR COMMUNITY COLLEGE DEGREE-- BREAKING ROCKS, DOING MANUAL LABOR, THOMAS.

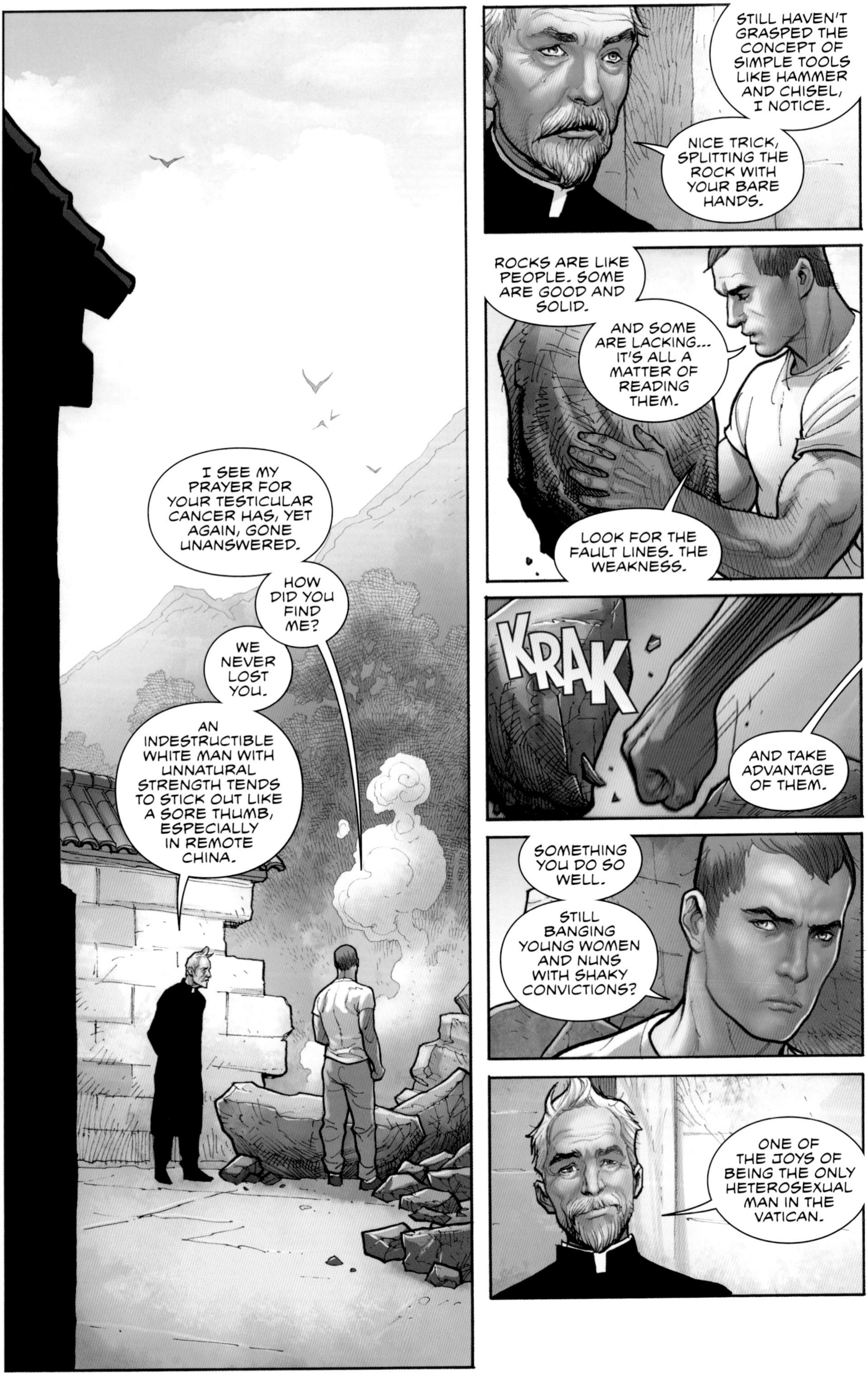

I SEE MY PRAYER FOR YOUR TESTICULAR CANCER HAS, YET AGAIN, GONE UNANSWERED.
HOW DID YOU FIND ME?
WE NEVER LOST YOU.
AN INDESTRUCTIBLE WHITE MAN WITH UNNATURAL STRENGTH TENDS TO STICK OUT LIKE A SORE THUMB, ESPECIALLY IN REMOTE CHINA.
STILL HAVEN'T GRASPED THE CONCEPT OF SIMPLE TOOLS LIKE HAMMER AND CHISEL, I NOTICE.
NICE TRICK, SPLITTING THE ROCK WITH YOUR BARE HANDS.
ROCKS ARE LIKE PEOPLE. SOME ARE GOOD AND SOLID.
AND SOME ARE LACKING... IT'S ALL A MATTER OF READING THEM.
LOOK FOR THE FAULT LINES. THE WEAKNESS.
KRAK
AND TAKE ADVANTAGE OF THEM.
SOMETHING YOU DO SO WELL.
STILL BANGING YOUNG WOMEN AND NUNS WITH SHAKY CONVICTIONS?
ONE OF THE JOYS OF BEING THE ONLY HETEROSEXUAL MAN IN THE VATICAN.

HEH...

HA! HA. HA. HA.

HEH. HEH. HEH. SNORT!

IT'S GREAT TO SEE YOU, SWIGGY.

LET ME LOOK AT YOU...

YOU LOOK EXACTLY THE SAME SINCE I LAST SAW YOU 29 YEARS AGO... YOU STILL LOOK LIKE $#!&.

ONE OF THE PERKS OF BEING AN IMMORTAL.

WHAT'S GOING ON HERE?

WE'RE BUILDING A DRIVE-THRU WINDOW.

SMARTASS.

STORM KNOCKED DOWN THE WALL. WE'RE JUST REPAIRING IT. HERE, HAVE A SEAT.

WHAT BRINGS YOU UP HERE, MAN?

I JUST WANTED TO SEE MY OLD FRIEND.

FOR A GUY WHO WORKS IN THE SECRETS BUSINESS, YOU HAVE THE WORST POKER FACE SOMETIMES.

WHAT'S TROUBLING YOU, SWIGGY?

ALRIGHT. ALRIGHT.

THOMAS, THE WORLD'S COMING APART AT THE SEAMS.

THE WORLD'S FULL OF STUPID PEOPLE. IT'S *ALWAYS* COMING APART AT THE SEAMS, SWIGGY.

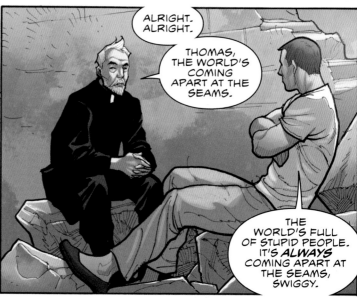

NOT LIKE THIS.

THE PSY DEPARTMENT CONFIRMED SOMETHING IS IN THE AIR. SOMETHING IS AGITATING THE WORLD'S COLLECTIVE PSYCHE, LIKE WIND BEFORE A STORM.

SOMETHING BIG. SOMETHING MAGICAL.

...SOMETHING YOU GUYS CAN EASILY HANDLE.

IF YOU NEED ANY ASSISTANCE, NOTIFY DULCE BASE IN NEW MEXICO.

THAT'S JUST IT. THOSE GRAY BASTARDS AT DULCE, NEW MEXICO ARE MORE TIGHT-LIPPED THAN EVER. I JUST GOT REPORT THAT THEY ARE MOVING KEY TECHNOLOGY TO THEIR MOON BASE.

IT'S AS IF THEY KNOW SOMETHING IS COMING. LIKE RATS LEAVING A SINKING SHIP.

HELL, THOMAS. HALF THE MAGICAL ITEMS IN THE VAULT ARE ACTIVE. THE DARK MIRRORS OF BURGUNDY ARE CONSTANTLY FLASHING RANDOM IMAGES OF DESTRUCTION.

THE PSYCHIC FEEDBACK HAS KNOCKED OUT HALF THE REMOTE VIEWERS AND THE SENSITIVES OUT OF THE ROTATION. WE'RE FLYING BLIND HERE. WE NEED...

WHOA. STOP RIGHT THERE, SWIGGY.

I KNOW WHAT YOU'RE DOING. I DIDN'T COME TO CHINA BECAUSE I LIKE CHINESE FOOD AND SLENDER, SUBMISSIVE WOMEN.

I DON'T WORK FOR MOUNTAIN TOP FOUNDATION ANYMORE. I'M OUT. I'M DONE. I'M *RETIRED.*

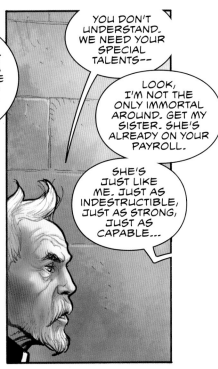

YOU DON'T UNDERSTAND. WE NEED YOUR SPECIAL TALENTS--

LOOK, I'M NOT THE ONLY IMMORTAL AROUND. GET MY SISTER. SHE'S ALREADY ON YOUR PAYROLL.

SHE'S JUST LIKE ME. JUST AS INDESTRUCTIBLE, JUST AS STRONG, JUST AS CAPABLE...

THOMAS, WE DID.

SHE'S DEAD.

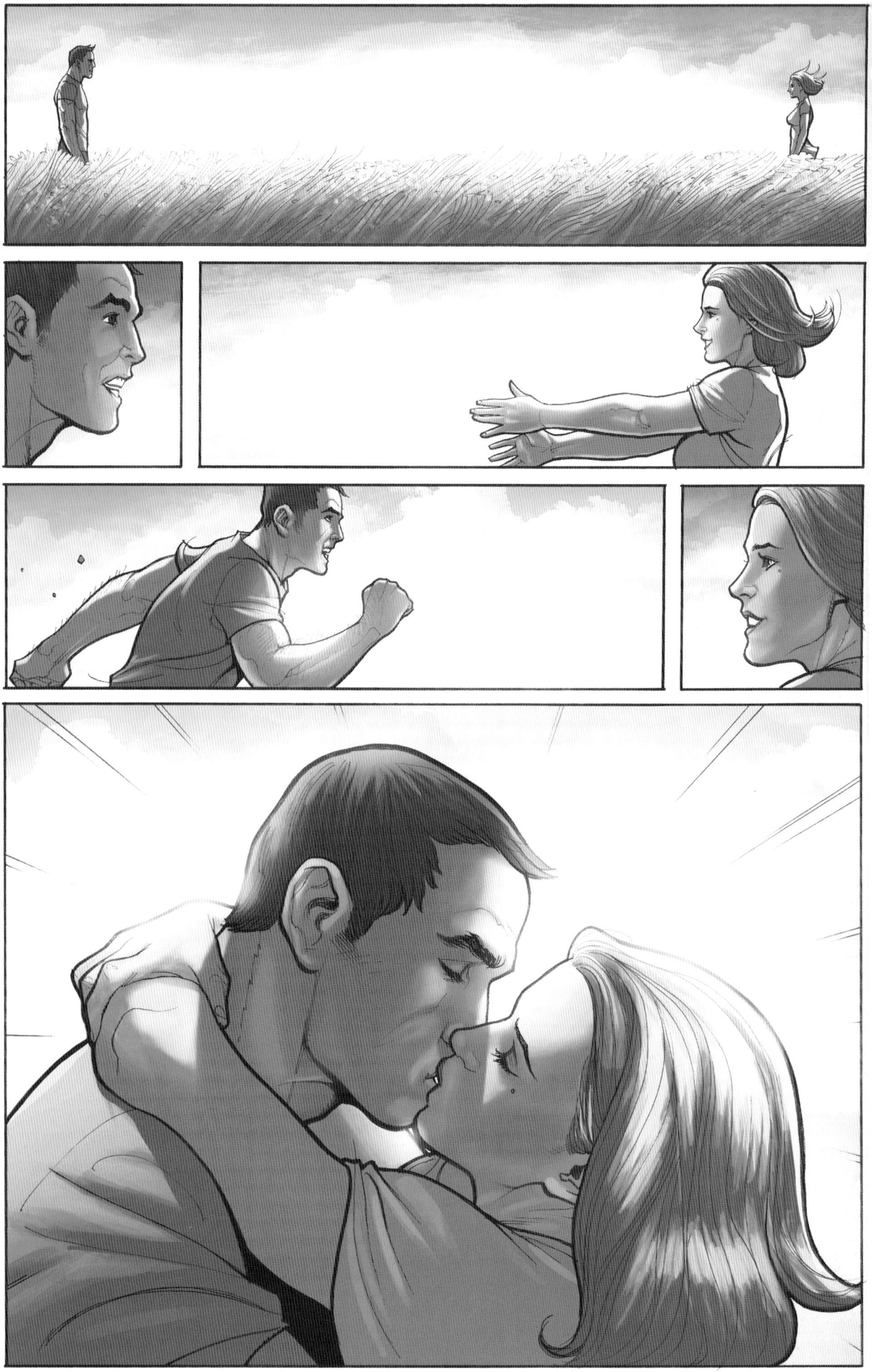

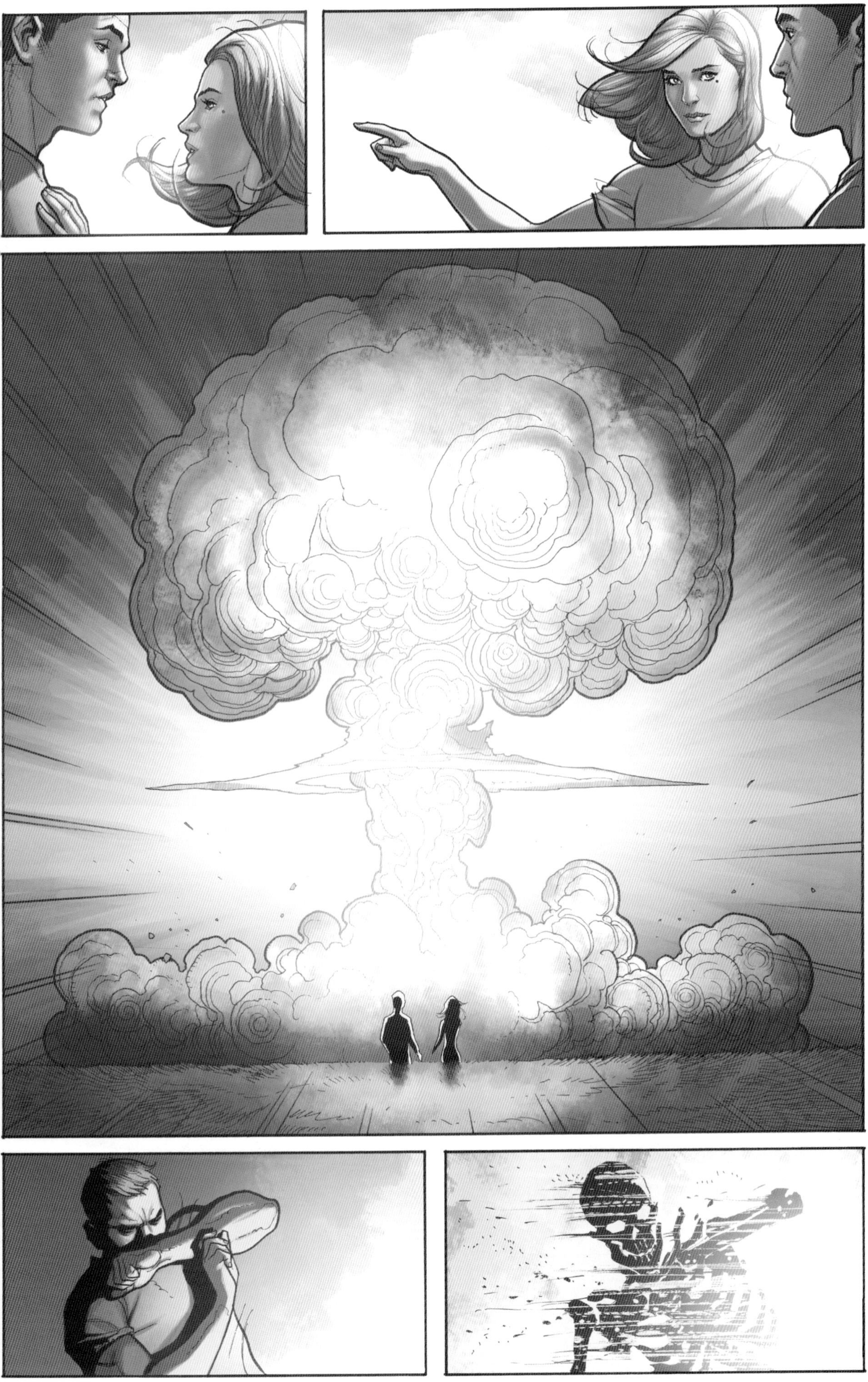

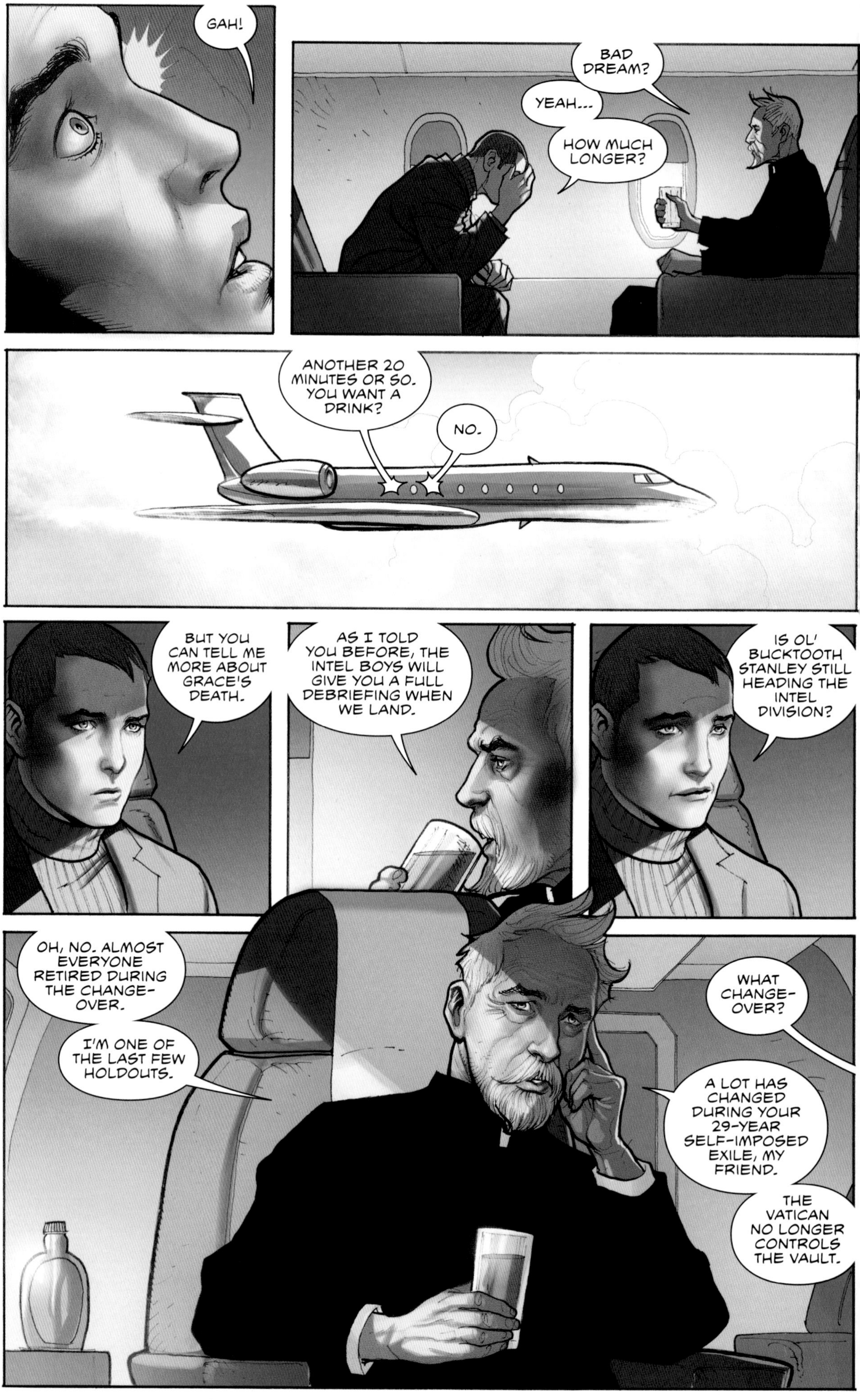
GAH!
BAD DREAM?
YEAH...
HOW MUCH LONGER?
ANOTHER 20 MINUTES OR SO. YOU WANT A DRINK?
NO.
BUT YOU CAN TELL ME MORE ABOUT GRACE'S DEATH.
AS I TOLD YOU BEFORE, THE INTEL BOYS WILL GIVE YOU A FULL DEBRIEFING WHEN WE LAND.
IS OL' BUCKTOOTH STANLEY STILL HEADING THE INTEL DIVISION?
OH, NO. ALMOST EVERYONE RETIRED DURING THE CHANGE-OVER.
I'M ONE OF THE LAST FEW HOLDOUTS.
WHAT CHANGE-OVER?
A LOT HAS CHANGED DURING YOUR 29-YEAR SELF-IMPOSED EXILE, MY FRIEND.
THE VATICAN NO LONGER CONTROLS THE VAULT.

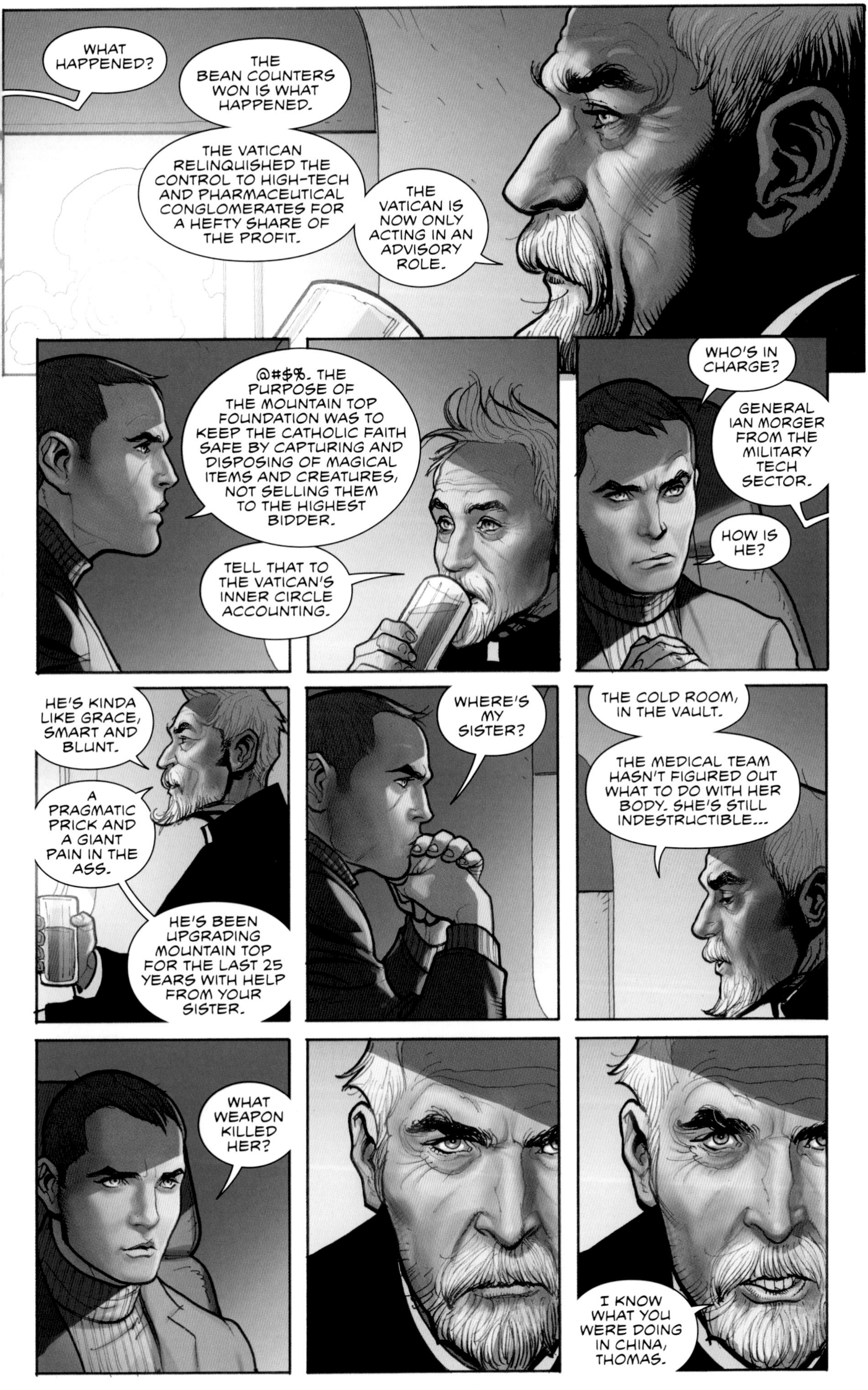
WHAT HAPPENED?
THE BEAN COUNTERS WON IS WHAT HAPPENED.
THE VATICAN RELINQUISHED THE CONTROL TO HIGH-TECH AND PHARMACEUTICAL CONGLOMERATES FOR A HEFTY SHARE OF THE PROFIT.
THE VATICAN IS NOW ONLY ACTING IN AN ADVISORY ROLE.
@#$%. THE PURPOSE OF THE MOUNTAIN TOP FOUNDATION WAS TO KEEP THE CATHOLIC FAITH SAFE BY CAPTURING AND DISPOSING OF MAGICAL ITEMS AND CREATURES, NOT SELLING THEM TO THE HIGHEST BIDDER.
TELL THAT TO THE VATICAN'S INNER CIRCLE ACCOUNTING.
WHO'S IN CHARGE?
GENERAL IAN MORGER FROM THE MILITARY TECH SECTOR.
HOW IS HE?
HE'S KINDA LIKE GRACE, SMART AND BLUNT.
A PRAGMATIC PRICK AND A GIANT PAIN IN THE ASS.
HE'S BEEN UPGRADING MOUNTAIN TOP FOR THE LAST 25 YEARS WITH HELP FROM YOUR SISTER.
WHERE'S MY SISTER?
THE COLD ROOM, IN THE VAULT.
THE MEDICAL TEAM HASN'T FIGURED OUT WHAT TO DO WITH HER BODY. SHE'S STILL INDESTRUCTIBLE...
WHAT WEAPON KILLED HER?
I KNOW WHAT YOU WERE DOING IN CHINA, THOMAS.

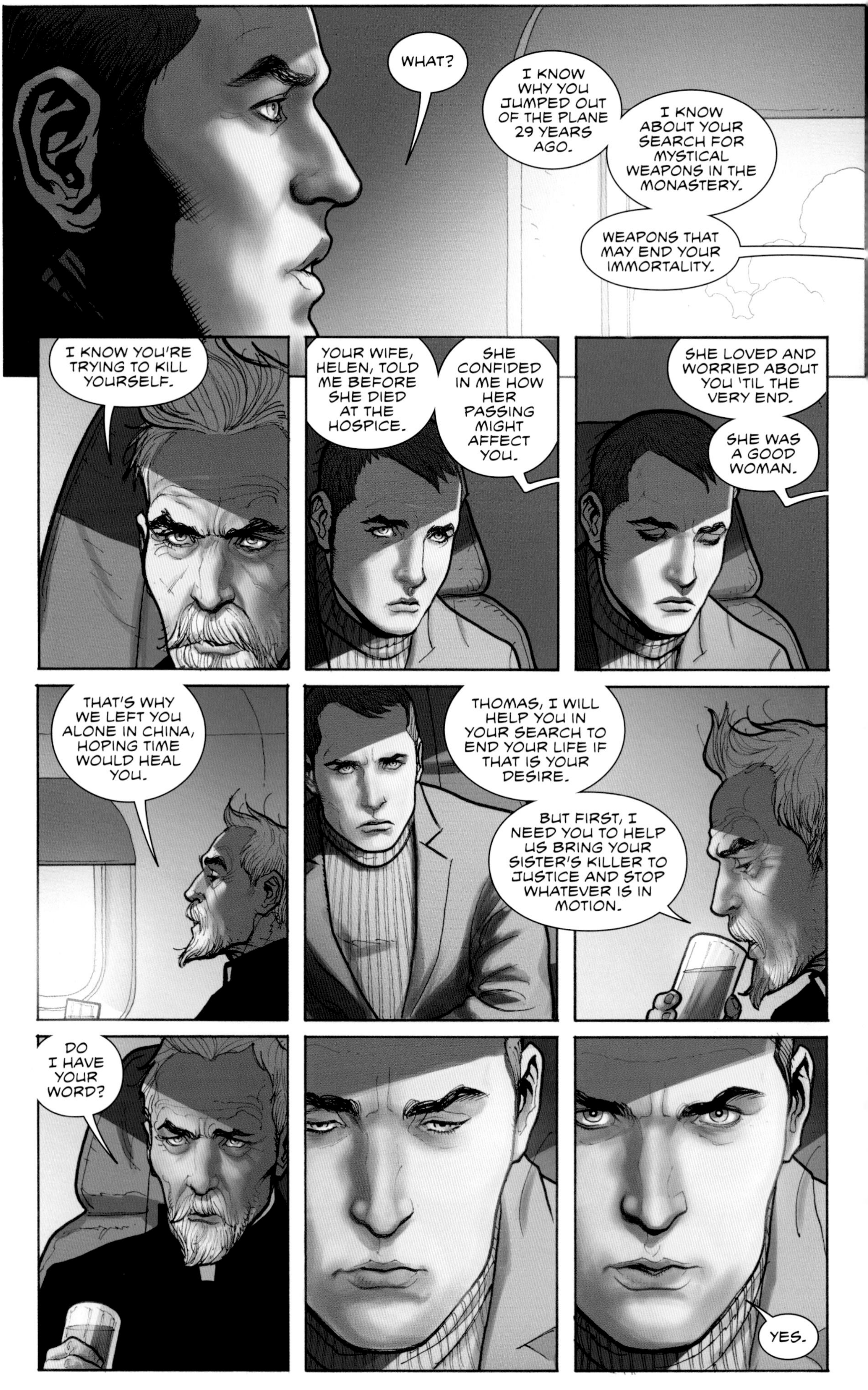
WHAT?
I KNOW WHY YOU JUMPED OUT OF THE PLANE 29 YEARS AGO.
I KNOW ABOUT YOUR SEARCH FOR MYSTICAL WEAPONS IN THE MONASTERY.
WEAPONS THAT MAY END YOUR IMMORTALITY.
I KNOW YOU'RE TRYING TO KILL YOURSELF.
YOUR WIFE, HELEN, TOLD ME BEFORE SHE DIED AT THE HOSPICE.
SHE CONFIDED IN ME HOW HER PASSING MIGHT AFFECT YOU.
SHE LOVED AND WORRIED ABOUT YOU 'TIL THE VERY END.
SHE WAS A GOOD WOMAN.
THAT'S WHY WE LEFT YOU ALONE IN CHINA, HOPING TIME WOULD HEAL YOU.
THOMAS, I WILL HELP YOU IN YOUR SEARCH TO END YOUR LIFE IF THAT IS YOUR DESIRE.
BUT FIRST, I NEED YOU TO HELP US BRING YOUR SISTER'S KILLER TO JUSTICE AND STOP WHATEVER IS IN MOTION.
DO I HAVE YOUR WORD?
YES.

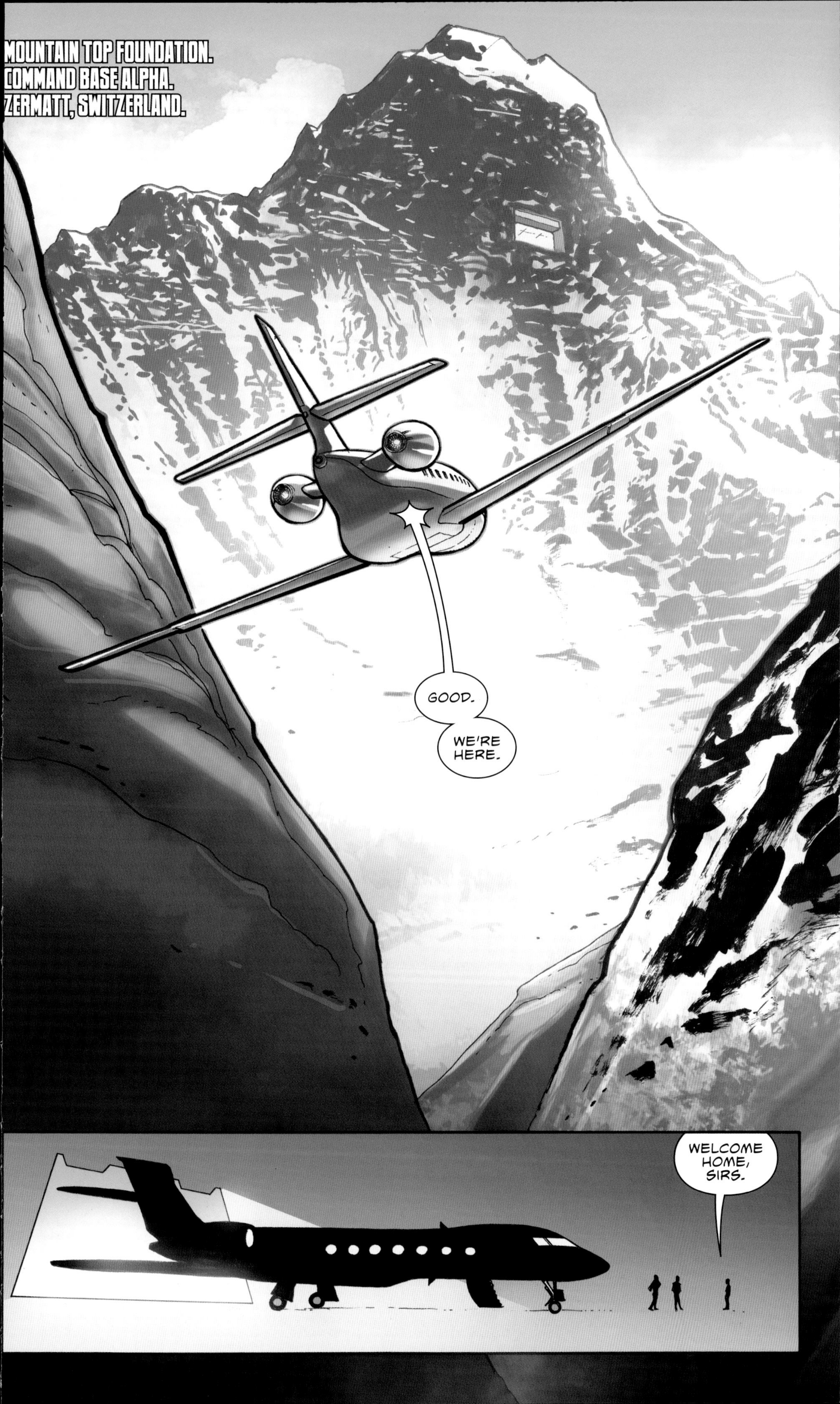
MOUNTAIN TOP FOUNDATION.
COMMAND BASE ALPHA.
ZERMATT, SWITZERLAND.
GOOD.
WE'RE HERE.
WELCOME HOME, SIRS.

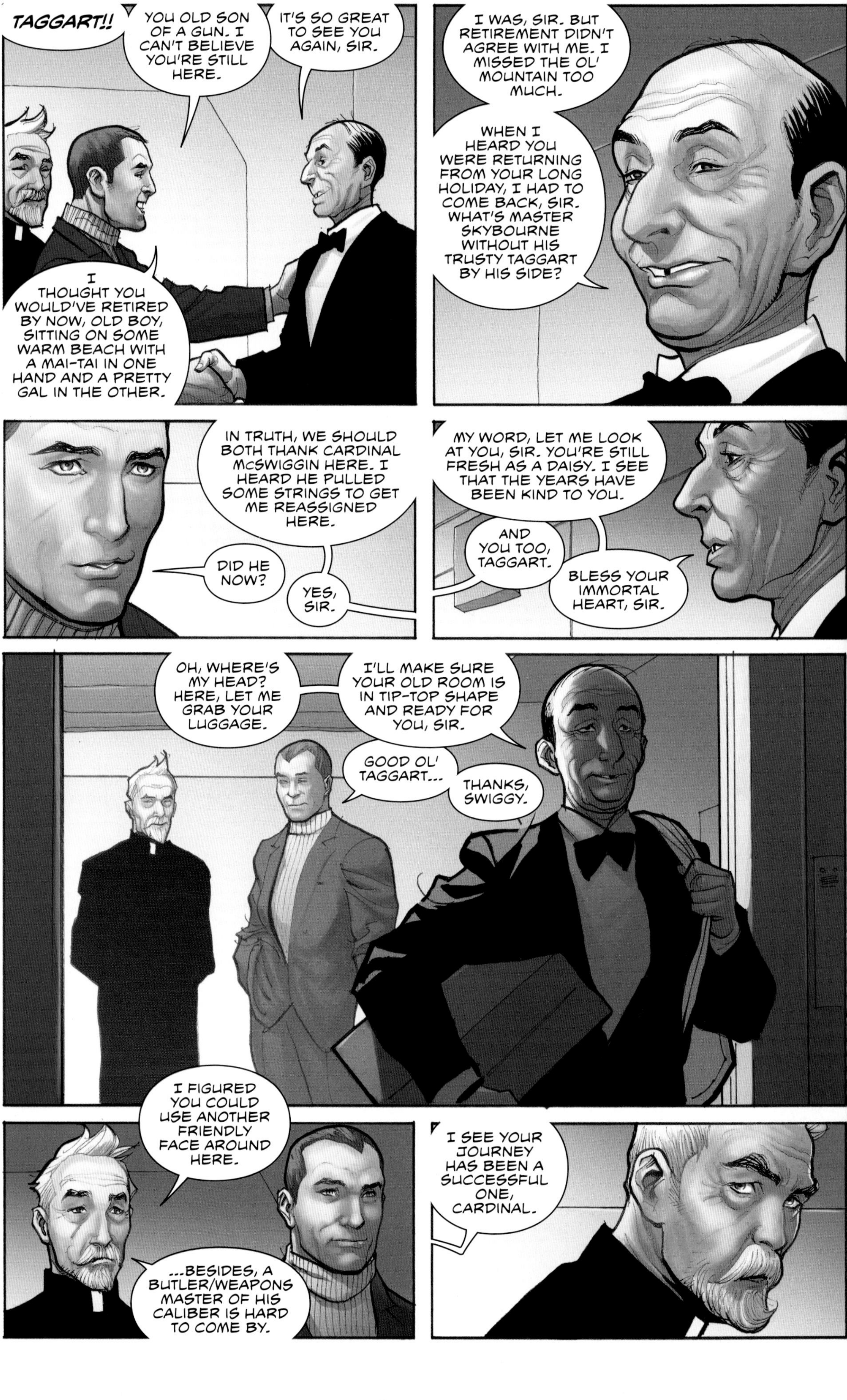
TAGGART!!
YOU OLD SON OF A GUN. I CAN'T BELIEVE YOU'RE STILL HERE.
IT'S SO GREAT TO SEE YOU AGAIN, SIR.
I THOUGHT YOU WOULD'VE RETIRED BY NOW, OLD BOY, SITTING ON SOME WARM BEACH WITH A MAI-TAI IN ONE HAND AND A PRETTY GAL IN THE OTHER.
I WAS, SIR. BUT RETIREMENT DIDN'T AGREE WITH ME. I MISSED THE OL' MOUNTAIN TOO MUCH.
WHEN I HEARD YOU WERE RETURNING FROM YOUR LONG HOLIDAY, I HAD TO COME BACK, SIR. WHAT'S MASTER SKYBOURNE WITHOUT HIS TRUSTY TAGGART BY HIS SIDE?
IN TRUTH, WE SHOULD BOTH THANK CARDINAL McSWIGGIN HERE. I HEARD HE PULLED SOME STRINGS TO GET ME REASSIGNED HERE.
DID HE NOW?
YES, SIR.
MY WORD, LET ME LOOK AT YOU, SIR. YOU'RE STILL FRESH AS A DAISY. I SEE THAT THE YEARS HAVE BEEN KIND TO YOU.
AND YOU TOO, TAGGART.
BLESS YOUR IMMORTAL HEART, SIR.
OH, WHERE'S MY HEAD? HERE, LET ME GRAB YOUR LUGGAGE.
I'LL MAKE SURE YOUR OLD ROOM IS IN TIP-TOP SHAPE AND READY FOR YOU, SIR.
GOOD OL' TAGGART...
THANKS, SWIGGY.
I FIGURED YOU COULD USE ANOTHER FRIENDLY FACE AROUND HERE.
...BESIDES, A BUTLER/WEAPONS MASTER OF HIS CALIBER IS HARD TO COME BY.
I SEE YOUR JOURNEY HAS BEEN A SUCCESSFUL ONE, CARDINAL.

AHH. THOMAS SKYBOURNE, THIS IS GENERAL IAN MORGER, THE PRIME DIRECTOR OF THE MOUNTAIN TOP FOUNDATION. GENERAL MORGER, THIS IS THOMAS SKYBOURNE.

PLEASED TO MEET YOU, GENERAL.

LIKEWISE.

AND HIS COLORFUL ASSESSMENT OF ME...

"DOUCHEBAG" OR "#$%HOLE", CARDINAL?

I CALLED YOU A "PRAGMATIC PRICK", GENERAL.

OUTSTANDING.

I SEE THAT YOU'VE EXPANDED THE FLIGHT DECK HERE. I HARDLY RECOGNIZED THE PLACE.

YES, WE MADE MANY UPGRADES AND IMPROVEMENTS DURING YOUR LONG ABSENCE.

IT'S A VERY DIFFERENT PLACE NOW, WITH NEW IDEAS AND NEW PROTOCOLS.

I'M SURE CARDINAL HERE HAS FILLED YOU IN ON THE CURRENT ORGANIZATIONAL ADMINISTRATION HISTORY AND COMMAND STRUCTURE IN HIS MOST DESCRIPTIVE NARRATIVE.

I'M NOT IN THE BUSINESS OF MAKING FRIENDS. LET ME BE FRANK, THE VATICAN IS NO LONGER IN CHARGE.

OUR FOCUS IS NO LONGER A SPIRITUAL ONE. OUR PRIMARY MISSION IS THE BETTERMENT OF MANKIND THROUGH SCIENCE AND MAGIC.

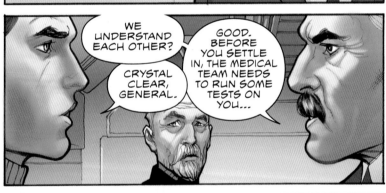

WE UNDERSTAND EACH OTHER?

CRYSTAL CLEAR, GENERAL.

GOOD. BEFORE YOU SETTLE IN, THE MEDICAL TEAM NEEDS TO RUN SOME TESTS ON YOU...

IF YOU EXCUSE ME, GENERAL, I WANT TO SEE MY SISTER FIRST.

YES, OF COURSE. SHE'S IN THE COLD ROOM IN DEEP STORAGE.

DO YOU NEED AN ESCORT?

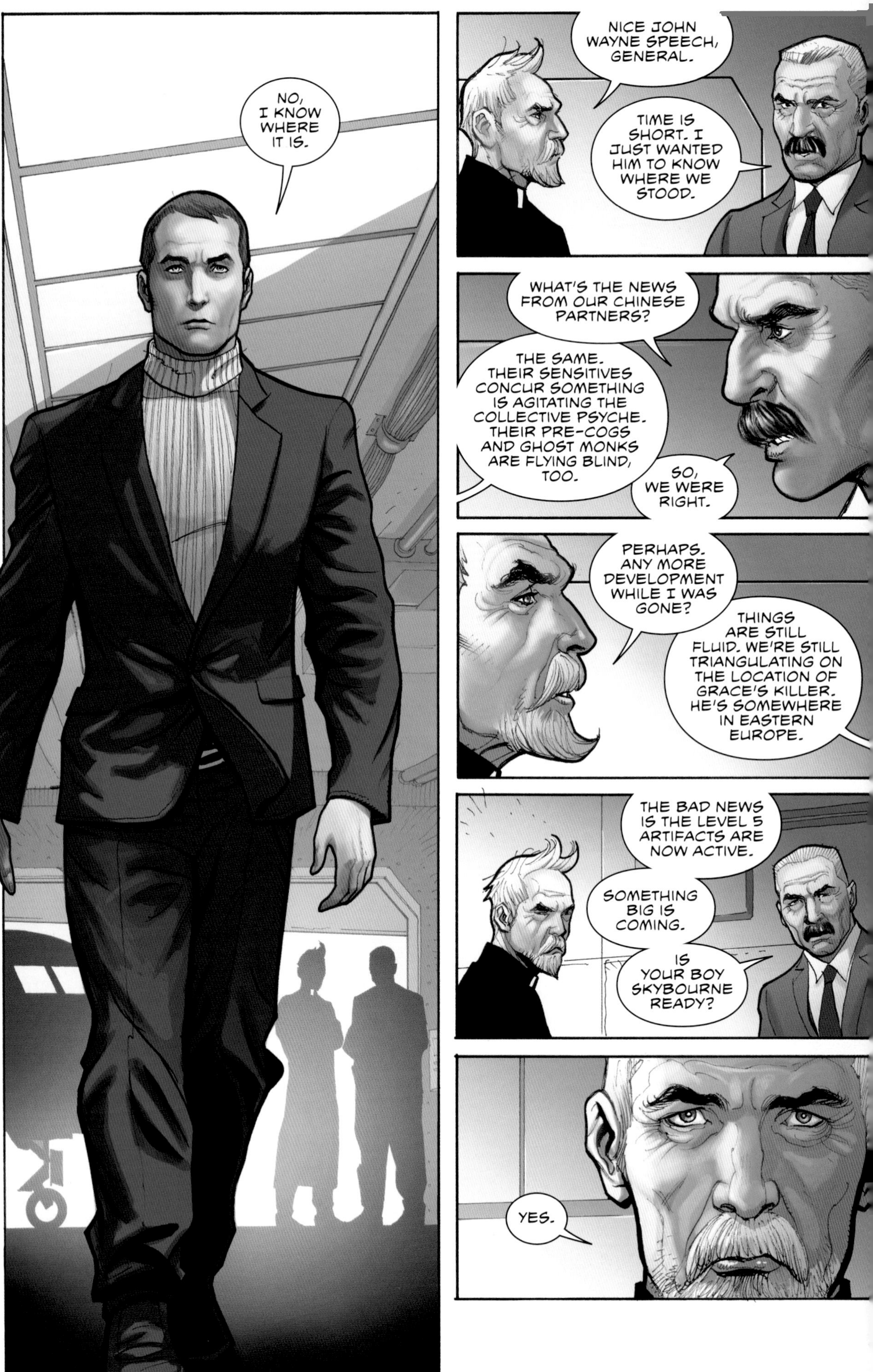

NO, I KNOW WHERE IT IS.
NICE JOHN WAYNE SPEECH, GENERAL.
TIME IS SHORT. I JUST WANTED HIM TO KNOW WHERE WE STOOD.
WHAT'S THE NEWS FROM OUR CHINESE PARTNERS?
THE SAME. THEIR SENSITIVES CONCUR SOMETHING IS AGITATING THE COLLECTIVE PSYCHE. THEIR PRE-COGS AND GHOST MONKS ARE FLYING BLIND, TOO.
SO, WE WERE RIGHT.
PERHAPS. ANY MORE DEVELOPMENT WHILE I WAS GONE?
THINGS ARE STILL FLUID. WE'RE STILL TRIANGULATING ON THE LOCATION OF GRACE'S KILLER. HE'S SOMEWHERE IN EASTERN EUROPE.
THE BAD NEWS IS THE LEVEL 5 ARTIFACTS ARE NOW ACTIVE.
SOMETHING BIG IS COMING.
IS YOUR BOY SKYBOURNE READY?
YES.

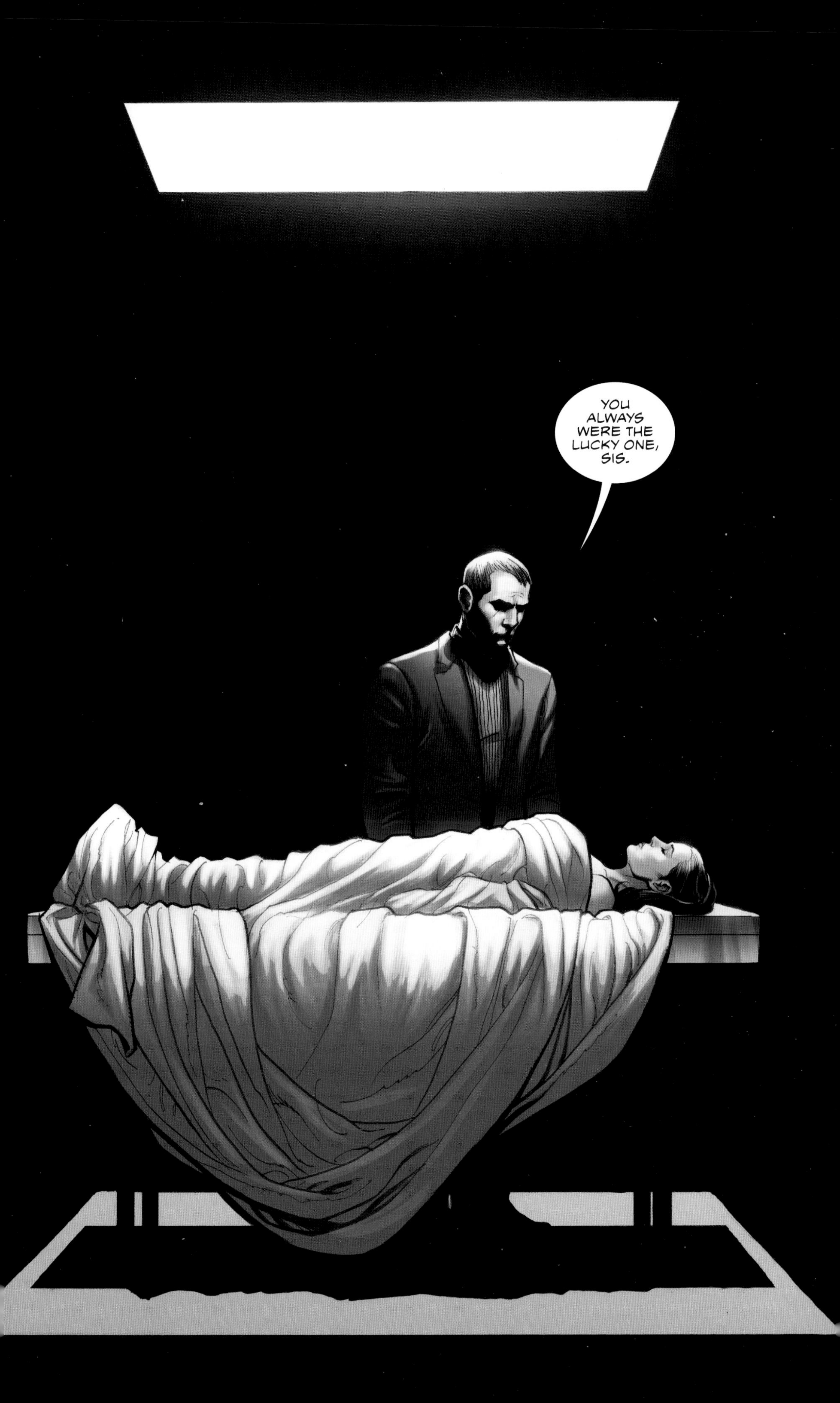
YOU ALWAYS WERE THE LUCKY ONE, SIS.

KHHHUUUURMM

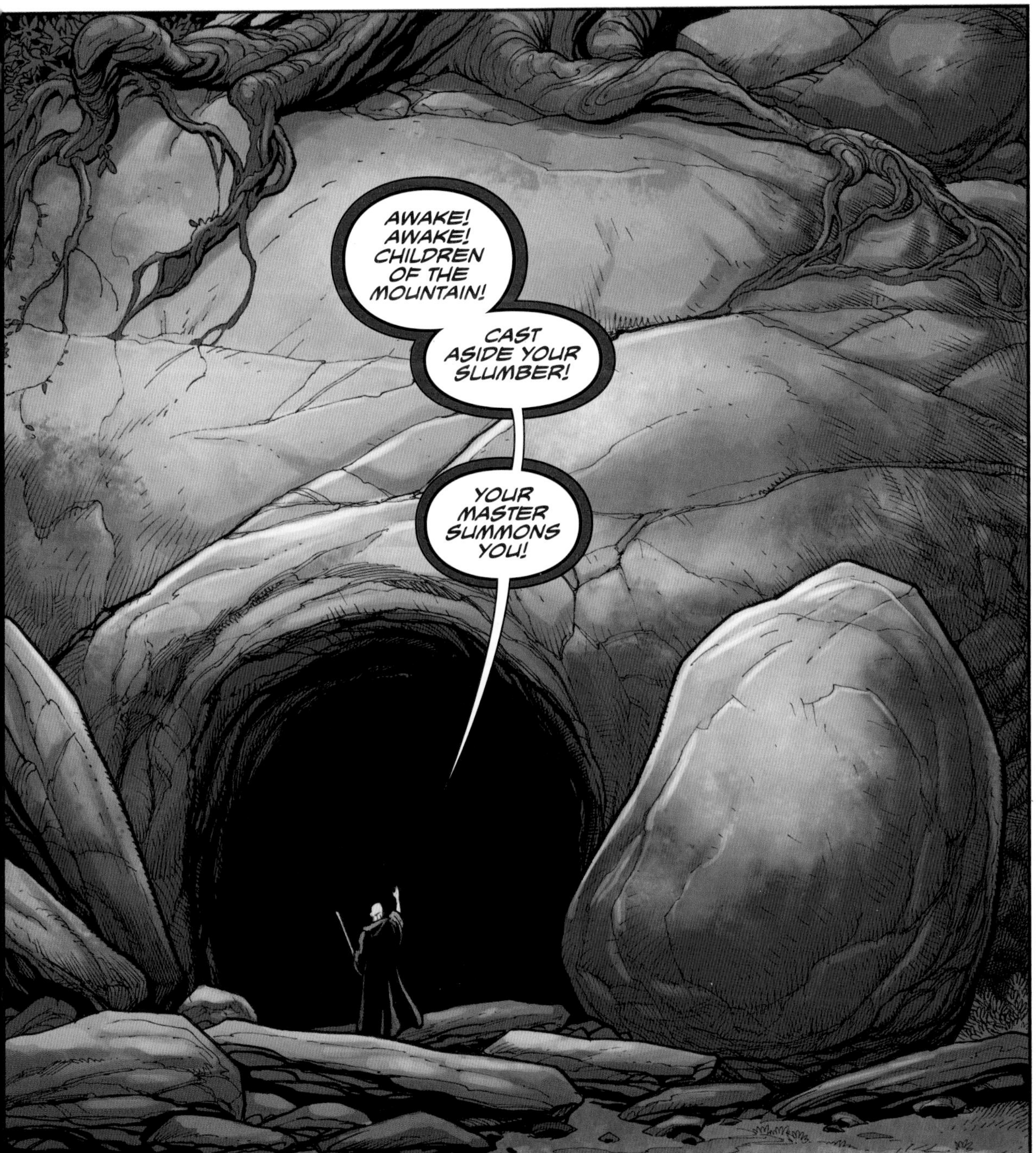
AWAKE! AWAKE! CHILDREN OF THE MOUNTAIN!
CAST ASIDE YOUR SLUMBER!
YOUR MASTER SUMMONS YOU!

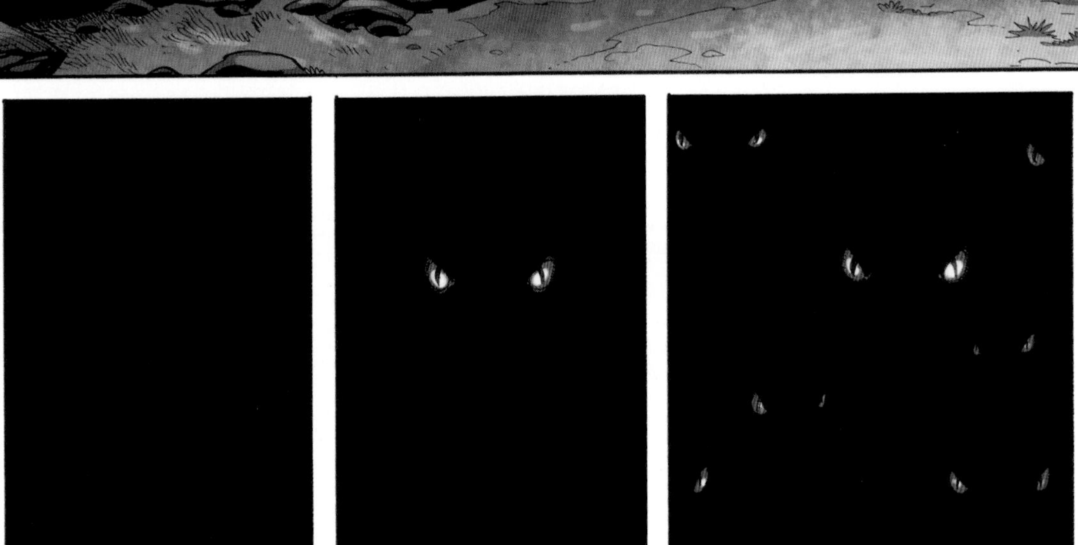

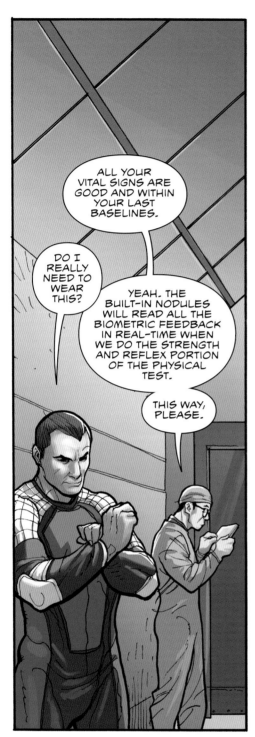

ALL YOUR VITAL SIGNS ARE GOOD AND WITHIN YOUR LAST BASELINES.

DO I REALLY NEED TO WEAR THIS?

YEAH. THE BUILT-IN NODULES WILL READ ALL THE BIOMETRIC FEEDBACK IN REAL-TIME WHEN WE DO THE STRENGTH AND REFLEX PORTION OF THE PHYSICAL TEST.

THIS WAY, PLEASE.

WOW.

WE MADE SOME MODIFICATIONS WHILE YOU WERE GONE. WE CARVED A NEW HUB AND COMMAND CENTER INTO THE MOUNTAIN.

ALL THE MYSTICAL OBJECTS AND MAGICAL CREATURES ARE HOUSED IN DIFFERENT LEVELS OF THE MOUNTAIN.

THIS IS THE SORTING STATION WHERE WE DETERMINE WHICH LEVEL WE PLACE THE CREATURES OR OBJECTS.

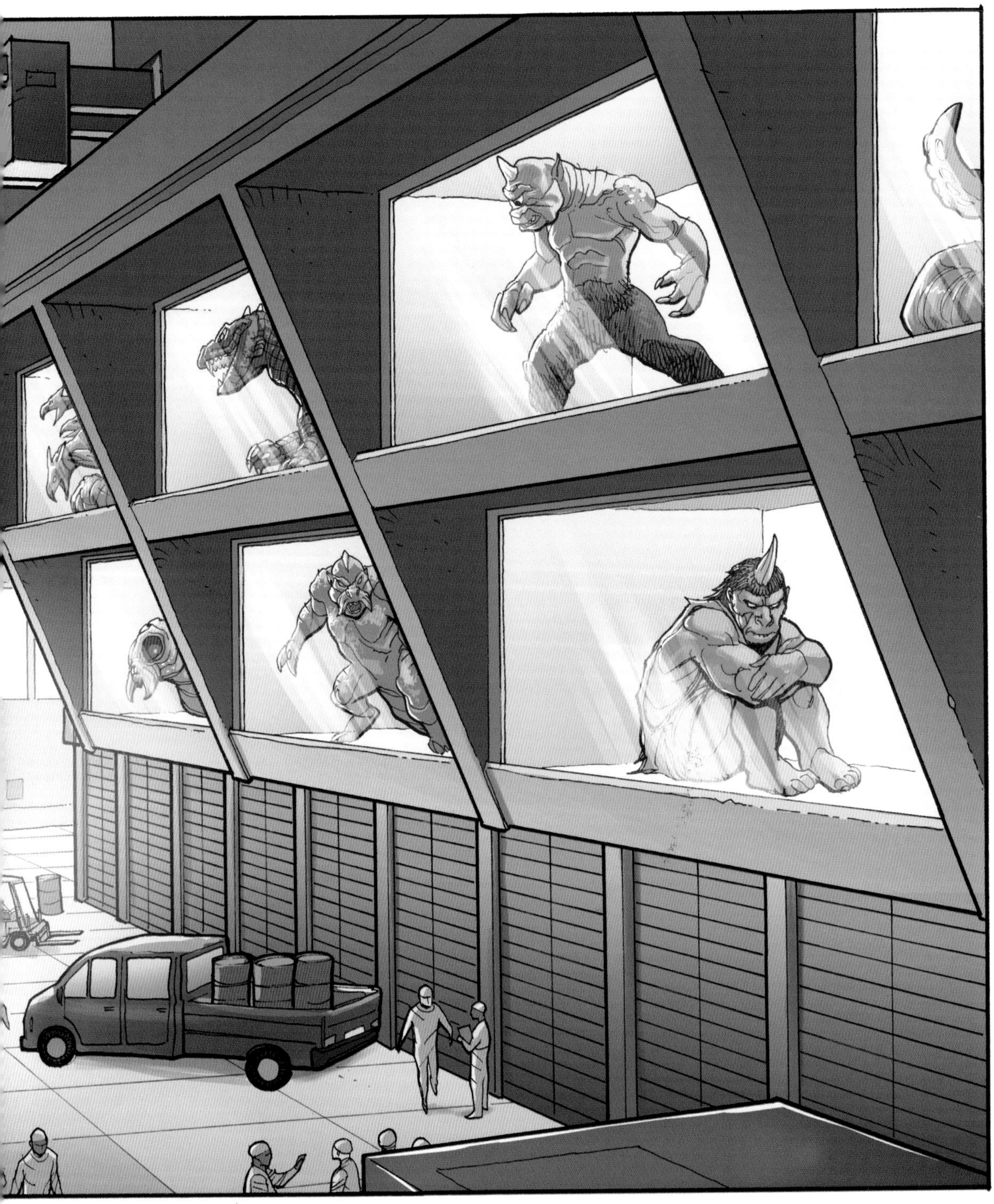

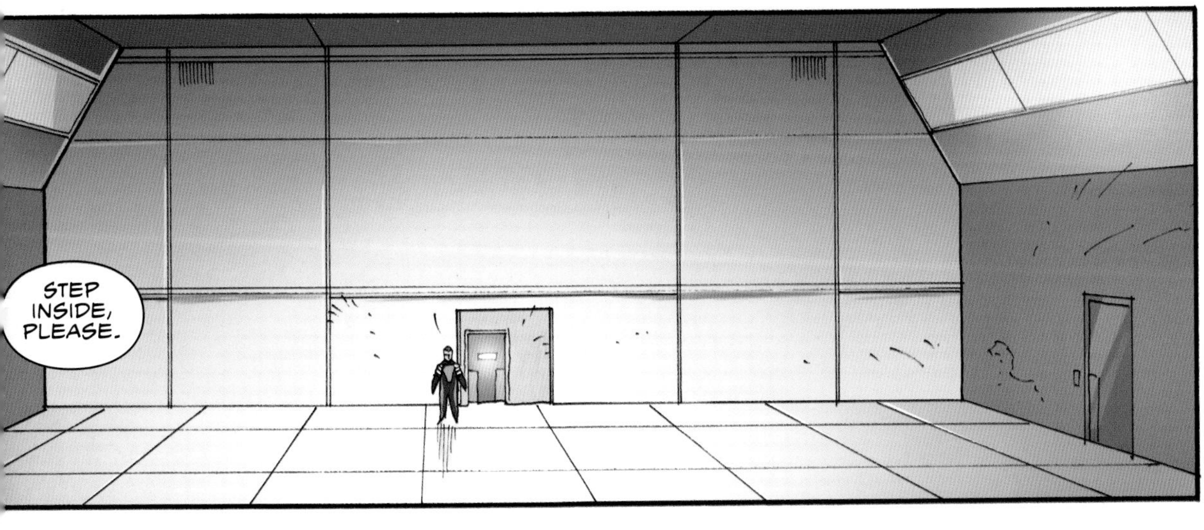
STEP INSIDE, PLEASE.

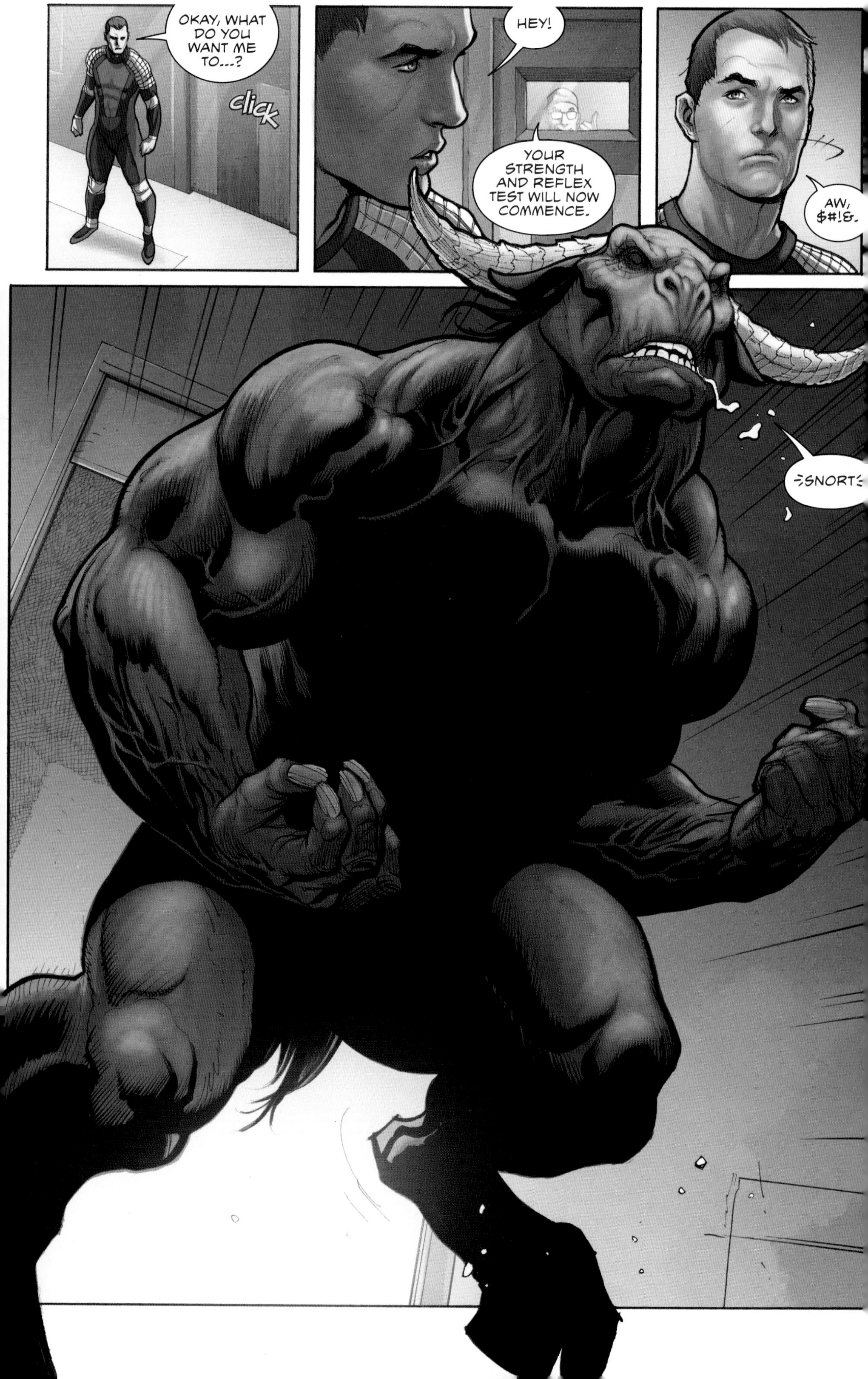
OKAY, WHAT DO YOU WANT ME TO...?
CLICK
HEY!
YOUR STRENGTH AND REFLEX TEST WILL NOW COMMENCE.
AW, $#!&.
=SNORT=

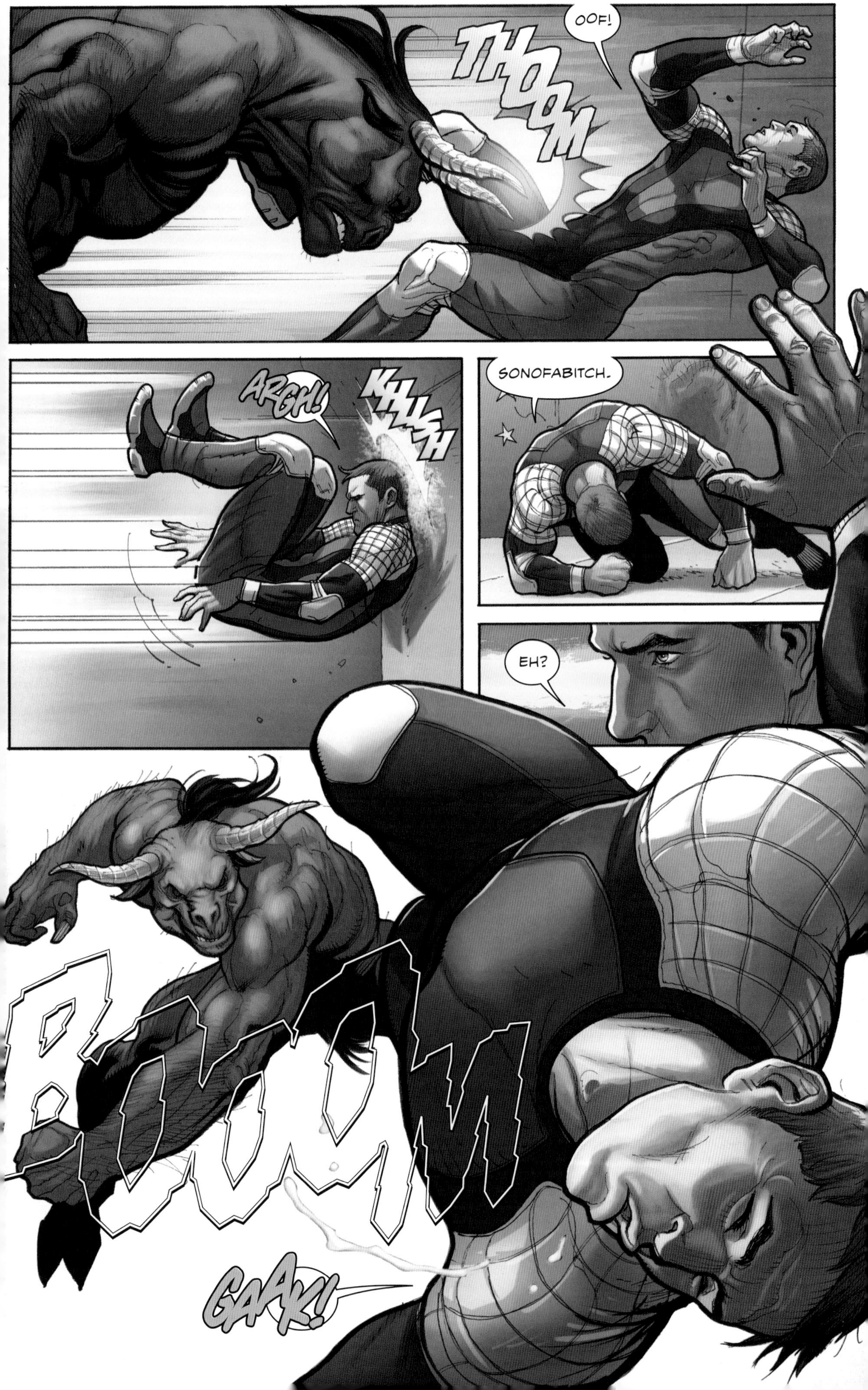

OOF!
THOOM
ARGH!
KHUSH
SONOFABITCH.
EH?
BOOOM
GAAK!

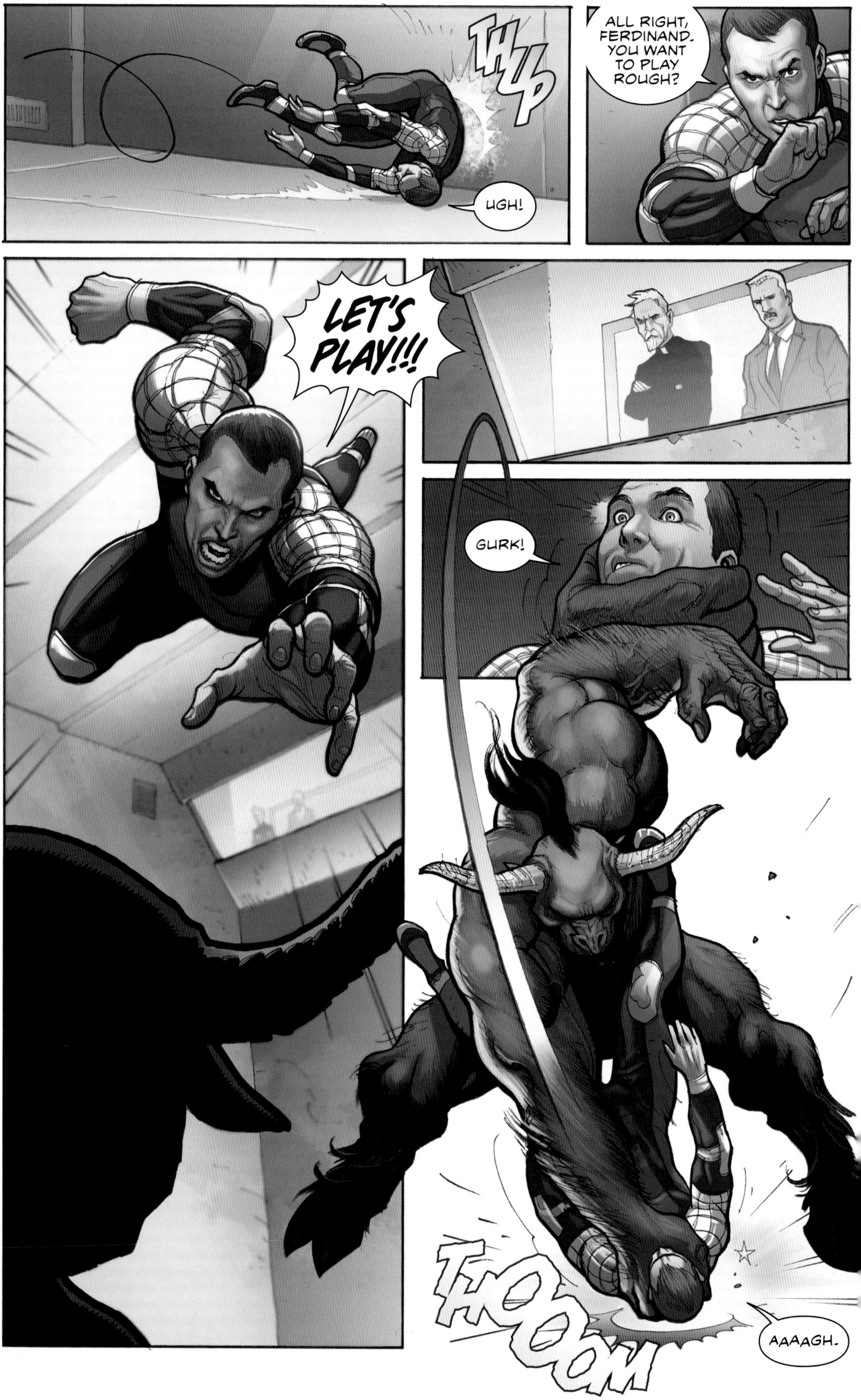
THUP
UGH!
ALL RIGHT, FERDINAND. YOU WANT TO PLAY ROUGH?
LET'S PLAY!!!
GURK!
THOOOOM
AAAAGH.

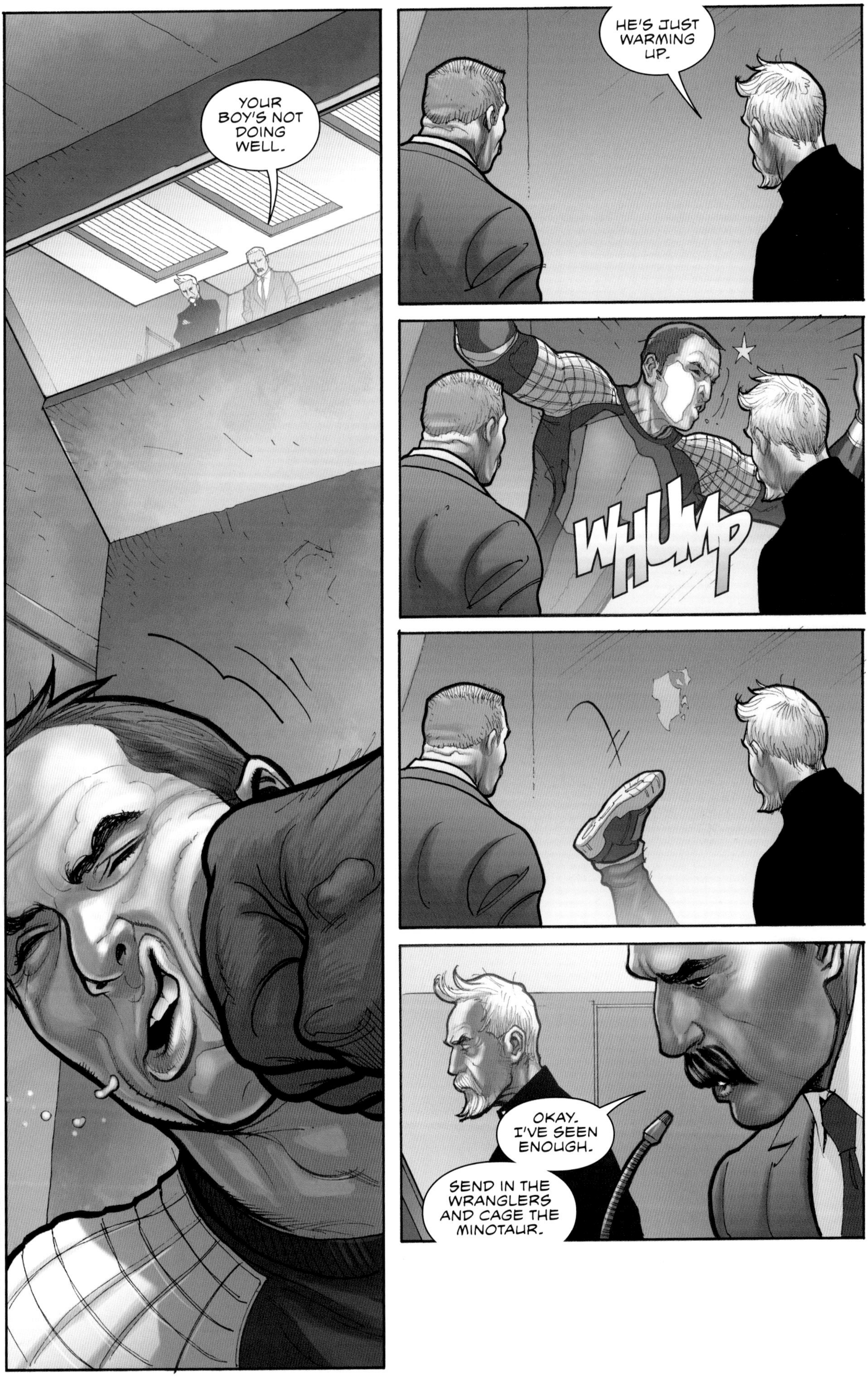
YOUR BOY'S NOT DOING WELL.
HE'S JUST WARMING UP.
WHUMP
OKAY. I'VE SEEN ENOUGH.
SEND IN THE WRANGLERS AND CAGE THE MINOTAUR.

"READY", MY ASS. I'M NOT IMPRESSED AT ALL, CARDINAL.

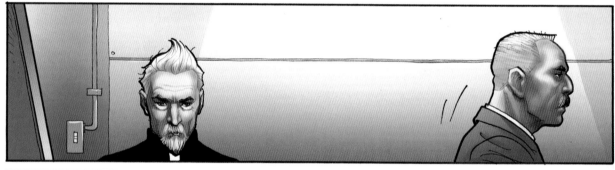

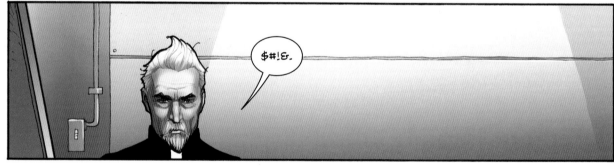

$#!&.

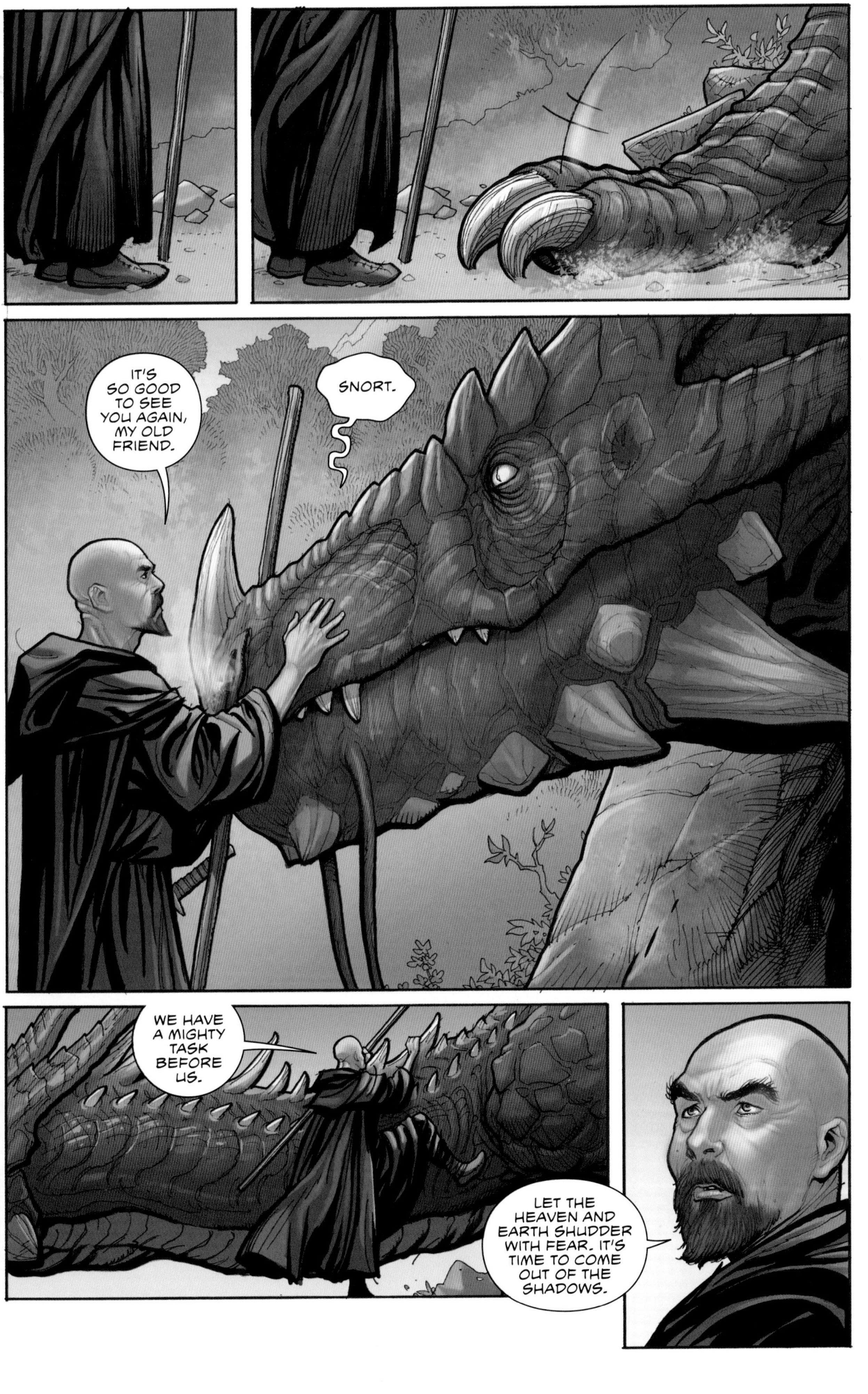
IT'S SO GOOD TO SEE YOU AGAIN, MY OLD FRIEND.
SNORT.
WE HAVE A MIGHTY TASK BEFORE US.
LET THE HEAVEN AND EARTH SHUDDER WITH FEAR. IT'S TIME TO COME OUT OF THE SHADOWS.

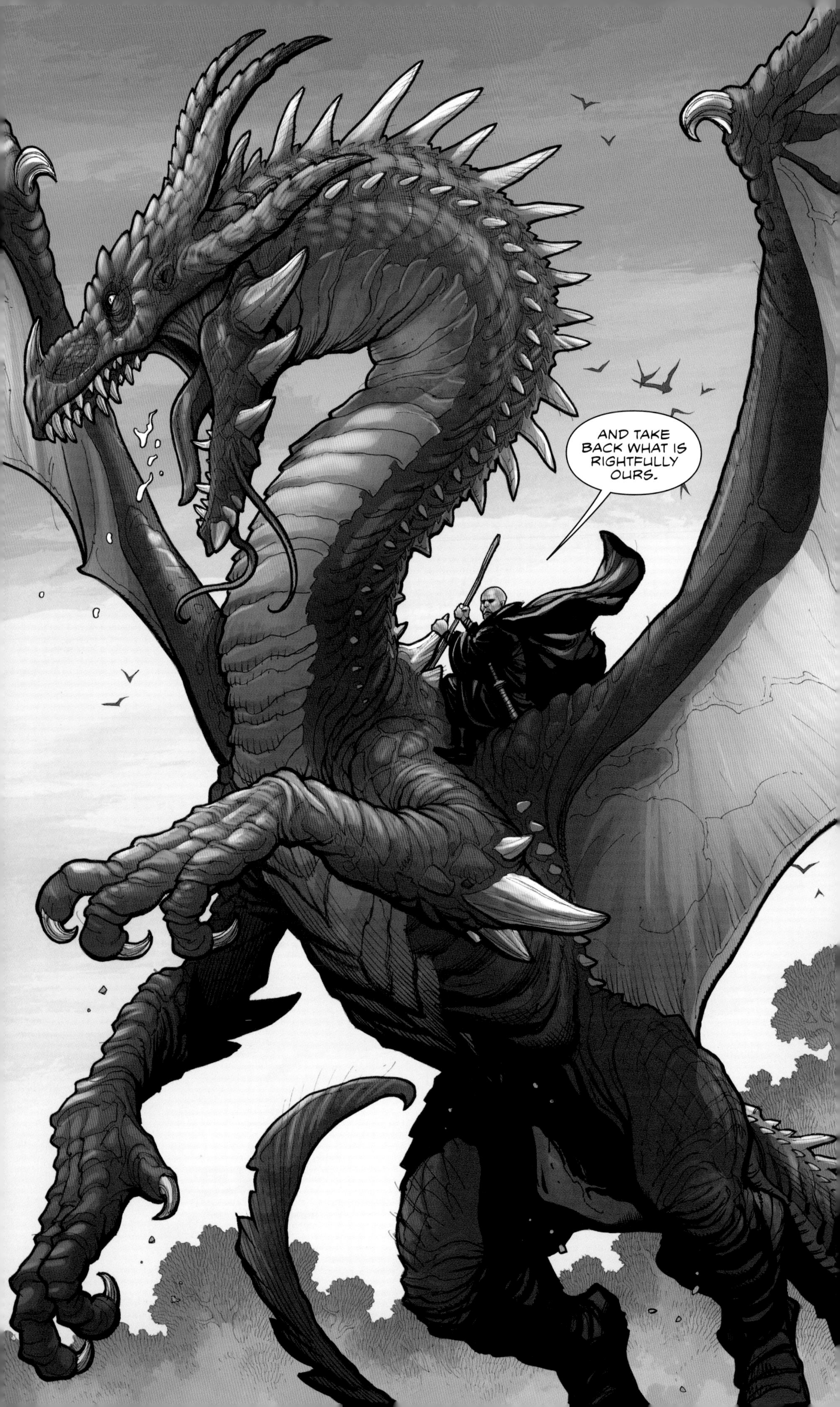
AND TAKE BACK WHAT IS RIGHTFULLY OURS.

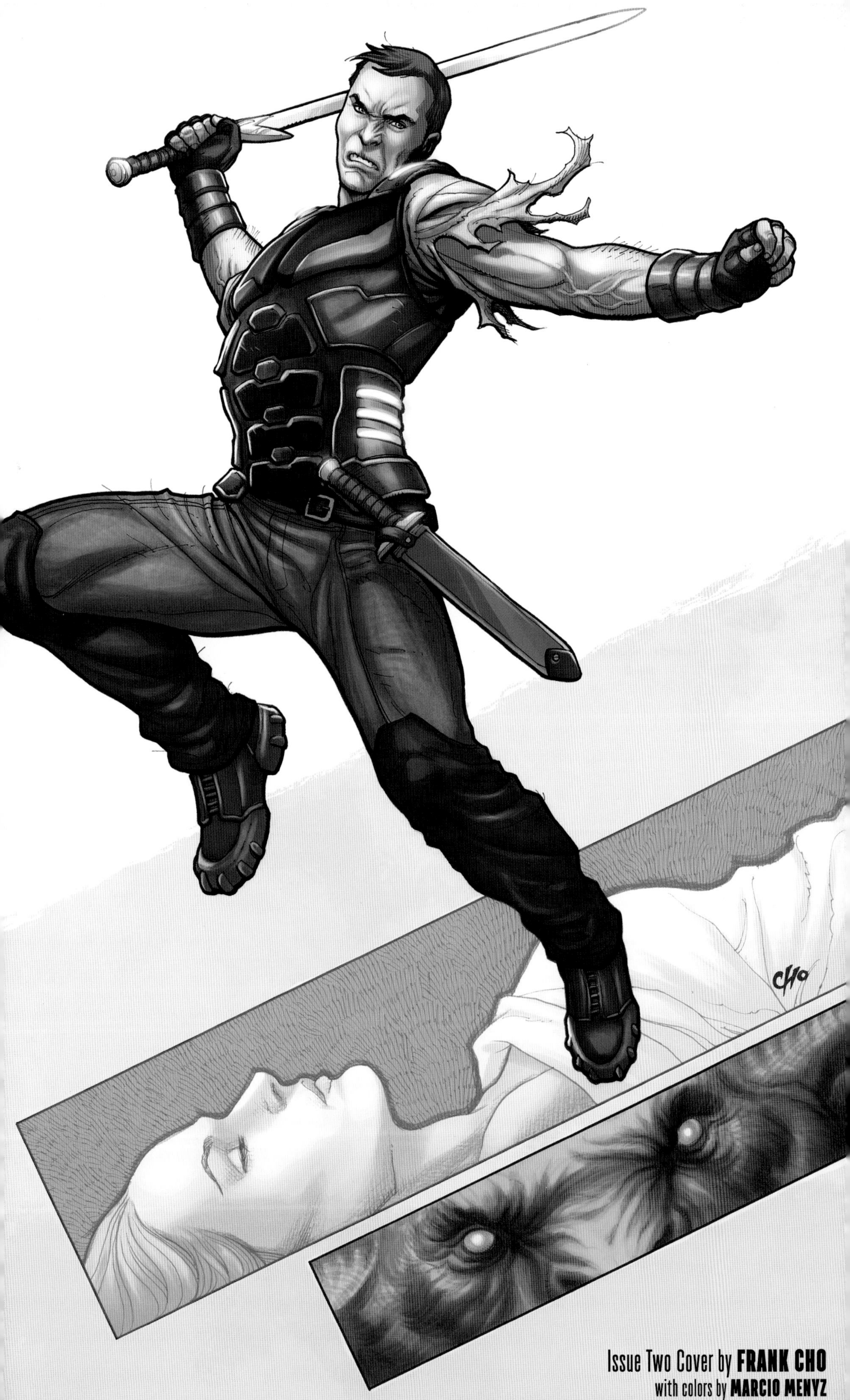
CHO

Issue Two Cover by **FRANK CHO**
with colors by **MARCIO MENYZ**

CHAPTER THREE

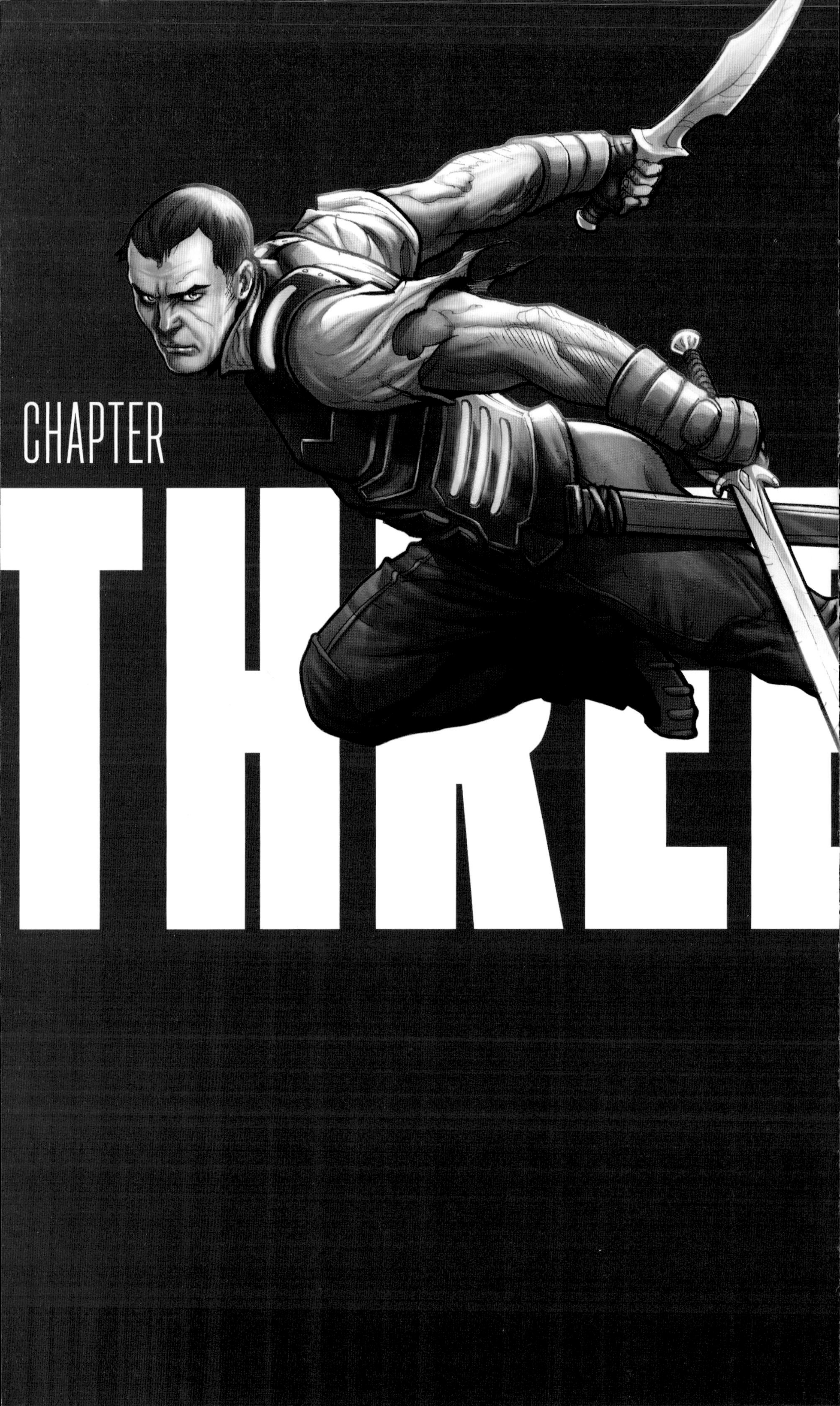

MITTENWALD, BAVARIAN REGION. PRESENT DAY.
WE HAVE A VISUAL ON THE TARGET.
CONFIRMED. DEADLY FORCE AUTHORIZED.
COPY.
WE'RE MOVING IN.
PHOOT PHOOT
VIP
VIP

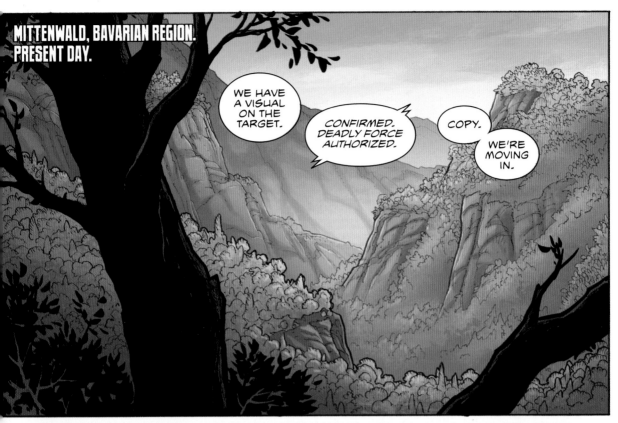

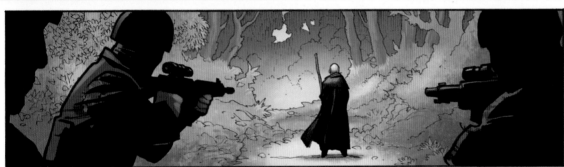

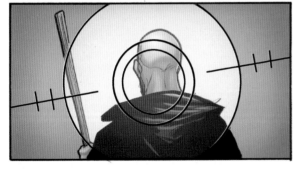

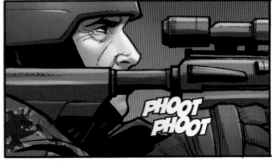

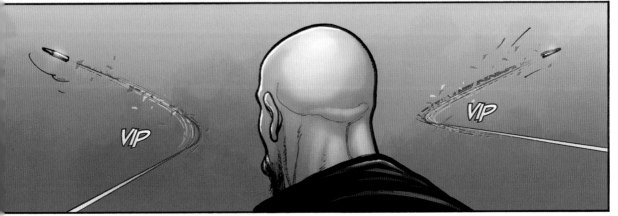

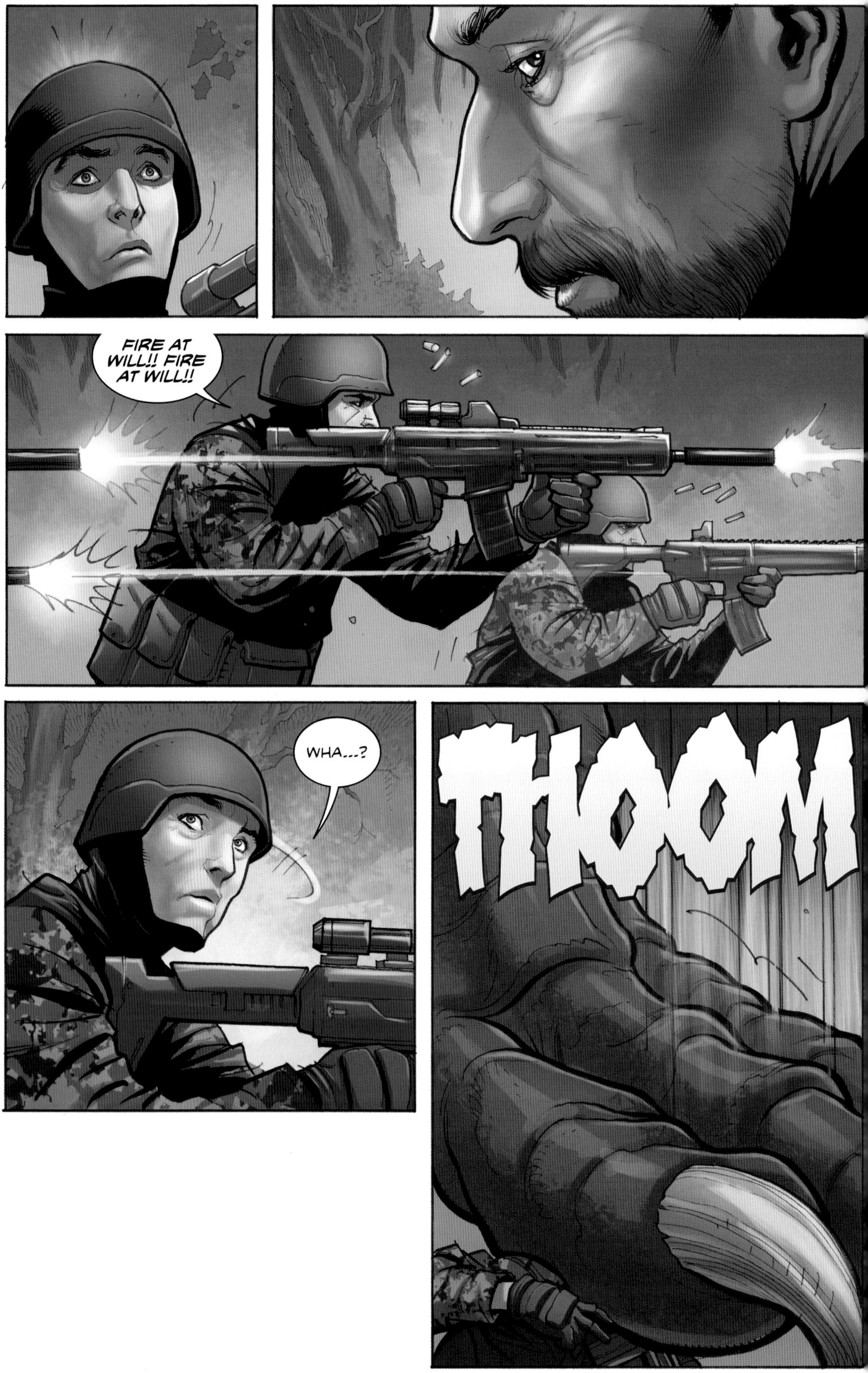
FIRE AT WILL!! FIRE AT WILL!!
WHA...?
THOOM

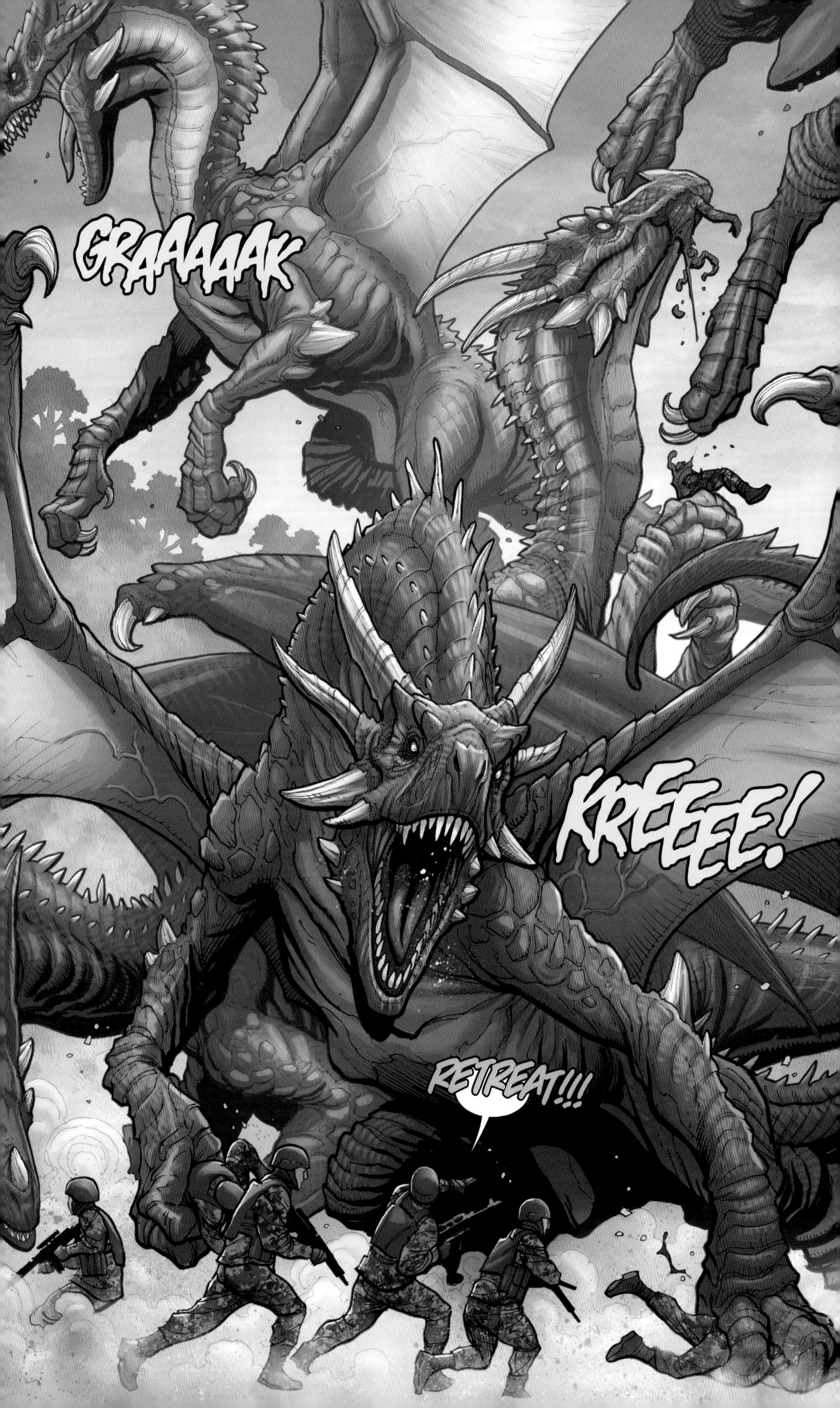
GRAAAAAK
KREEEEE!
RETREAT!!!

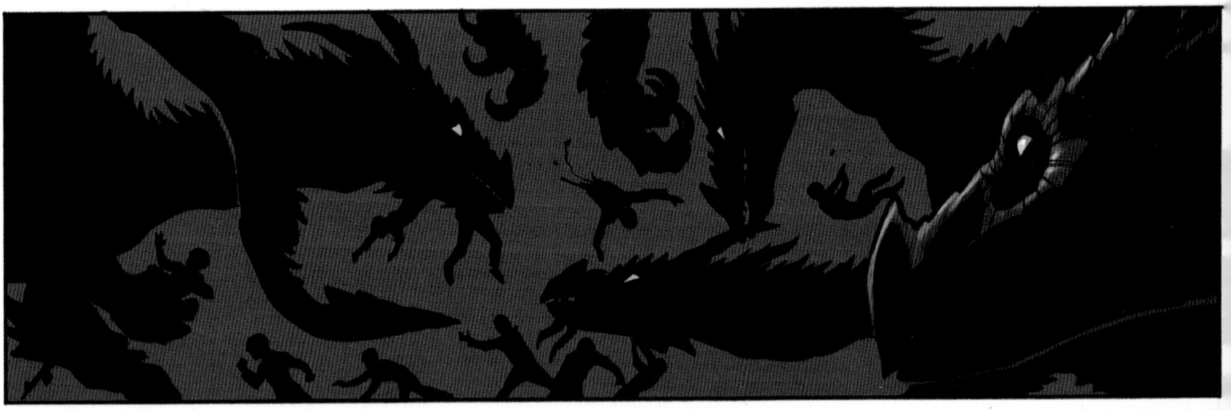
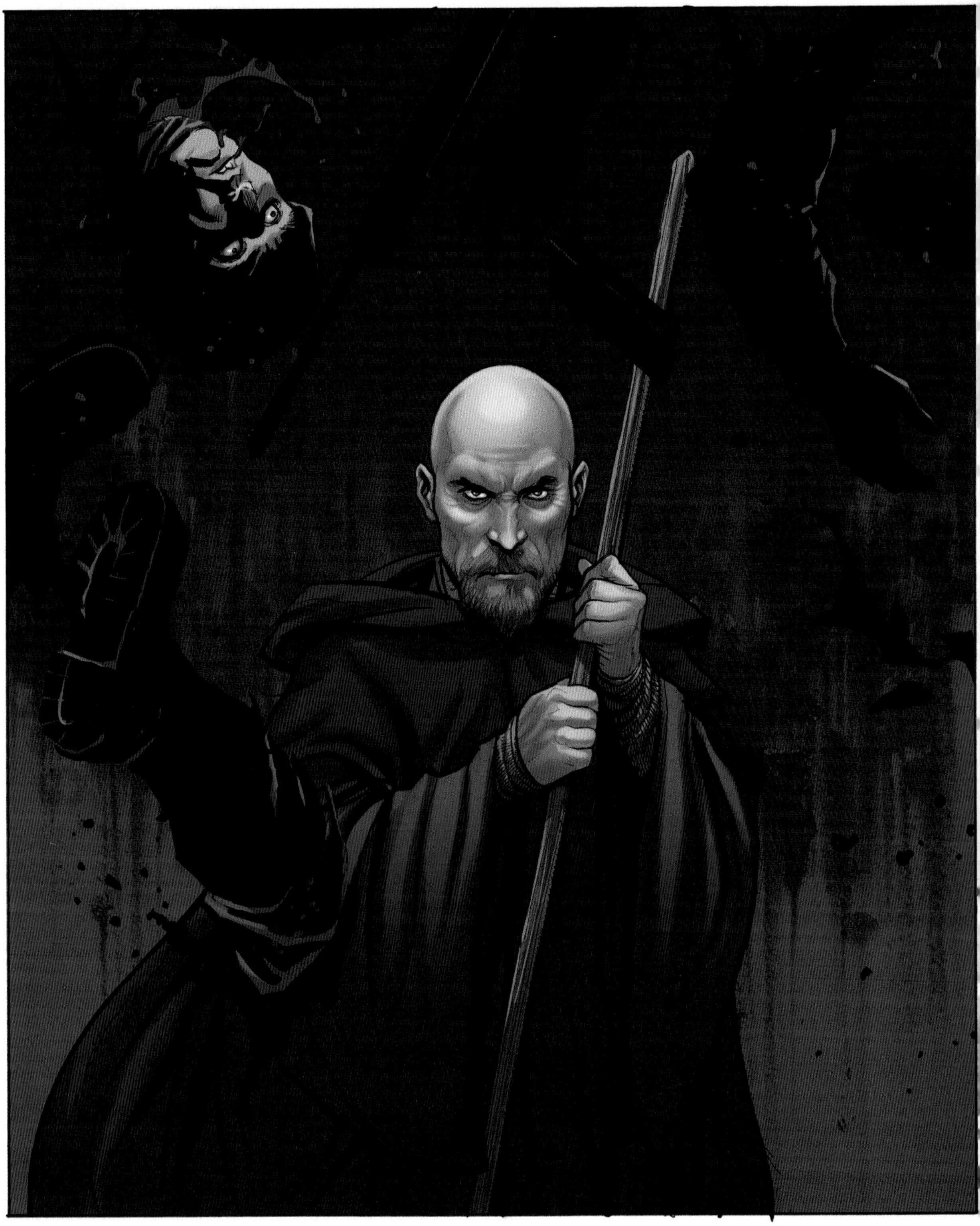

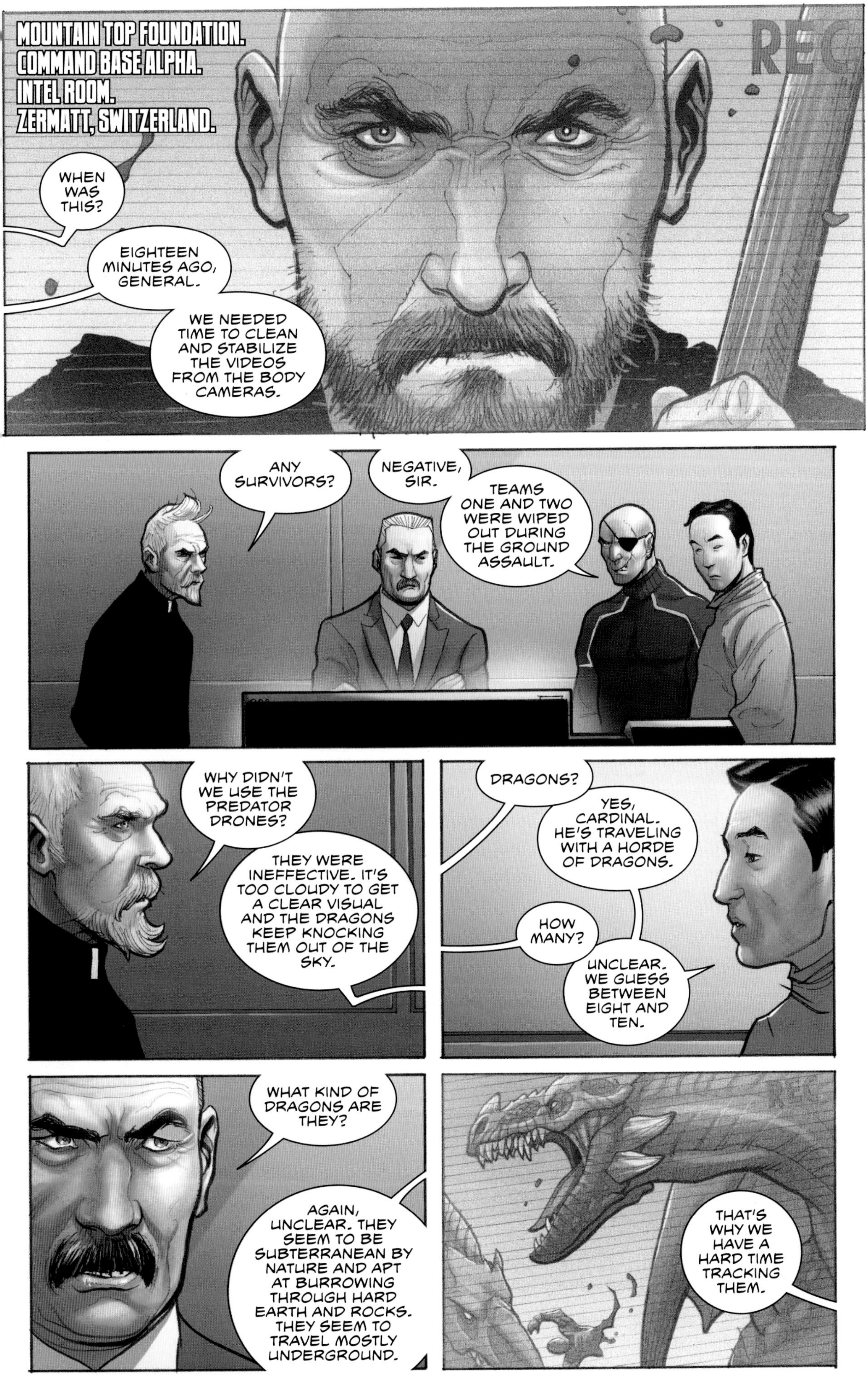

MOUNTAIN TOP FOUNDATION. COMMAND BASE ALPHA. INTEL ROOM. ZERMATT, SWITZERLAND.
REC
WHEN WAS THIS?
EIGHTEEN MINUTES AGO, GENERAL.
WE NEEDED TIME TO CLEAN AND STABILIZE THE VIDEOS FROM THE BODY CAMERAS.
ANY SURVIVORS?
NEGATIVE, SIR.
TEAMS ONE AND TWO WERE WIPED OUT DURING THE GROUND ASSAULT.
WHY DIDN'T WE USE THE PREDATOR DRONES?
THEY WERE INEFFECTIVE. IT'S TOO CLOUDY TO GET A CLEAR VISUAL AND THE DRAGONS KEEP KNOCKING THEM OUT OF THE SKY.
DRAGONS?
YES, CARDINAL. HE'S TRAVELING WITH A HORDE OF DRAGONS.
HOW MANY?
UNCLEAR. WE GUESS BETWEEN EIGHT AND TEN.
WHAT KIND OF DRAGONS ARE THEY?
AGAIN, UNCLEAR. THEY SEEM TO BE SUBTERRANEAN BY NATURE AND APT AT BURROWING THROUGH HARD EARTH AND ROCKS. THEY SEEM TO TRAVEL MOSTLY UNDERGROUND.
REC
THAT'S WHY WE HAVE A HARD TIME TRACKING THEM.

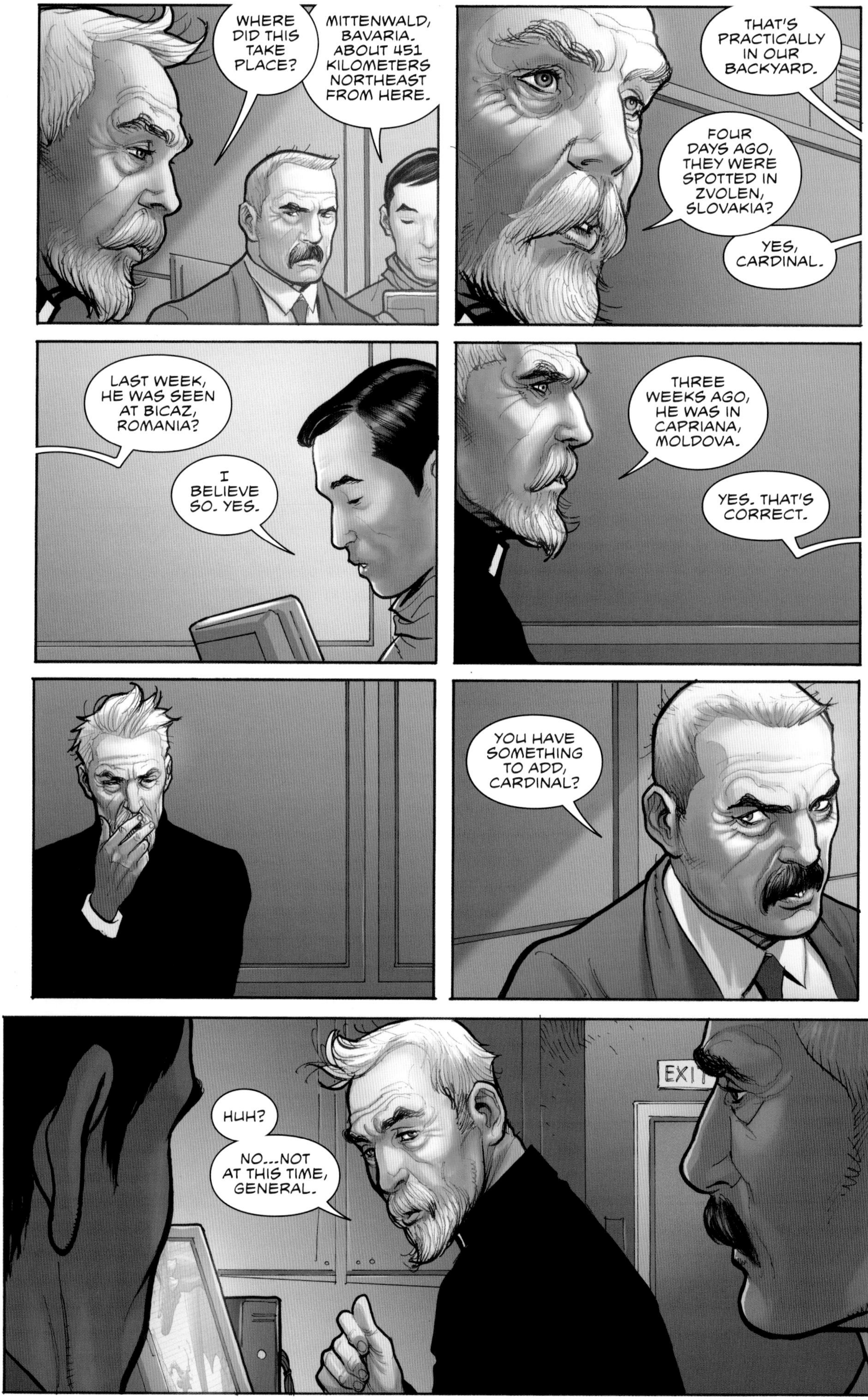
WHERE DID THIS TAKE PLACE?
MITTENWALD, BAVARIA. ABOUT 451 KILOMETERS NORTHEAST FROM HERE.
THAT'S PRACTICALLY IN OUR BACKYARD.
FOUR DAYS AGO, THEY WERE SPOTTED IN ZVOLEN, SLOVAKIA?
YES, CARDINAL.
LAST WEEK, HE WAS SEEN AT BICAZ, ROMANIA?
I BELIEVE SO. YES.
THREE WEEKS AGO, HE WAS IN CAPRIANA, MOLDOVA.
YES. THAT'S CORRECT.
YOU HAVE SOMETHING TO ADD, CARDINAL?
HUH?
NO...NOT AT THIS TIME, GENERAL.
EXIT

WHERE'S TEAM THREE?

EN ROUTE TO RETRIEVE THE BODIES.

I'VE CALLED UP THE RESERVE IN CASE WE DECIDE TO PRESS THE ATTACK AGAIN.

HOLD OFF ON THE ATTACK, CAPTAIN.

CARDINAL McSWIGGIN. IT'S TIME TO PUT YOUR BOY SKYBOURNE INTO PLAY. HOW SOON CAN HE BE READY?

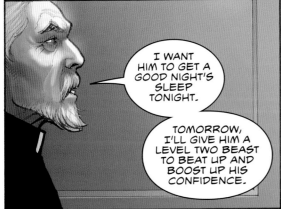

I WANT HIM TO GET A GOOD NIGHT'S SLEEP TONIGHT.

TOMORROW, I'LL GIVE HIM A LEVEL TWO BEAST TO BEAT UP AND BOOST UP HIS CONFIDENCE.

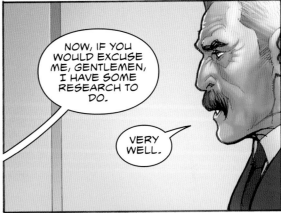

NOW, IF YOU WOULD EXCUSE ME, GENTLEMEN, I HAVE SOME RESEARCH TO DO.

VERY WELL.

CAPTAIN COLOMBO.

PREP THE NUKE.

IF THIS GOES SIDEWAYS, I WANT THE LAST WORD.

YES, GENERAL.

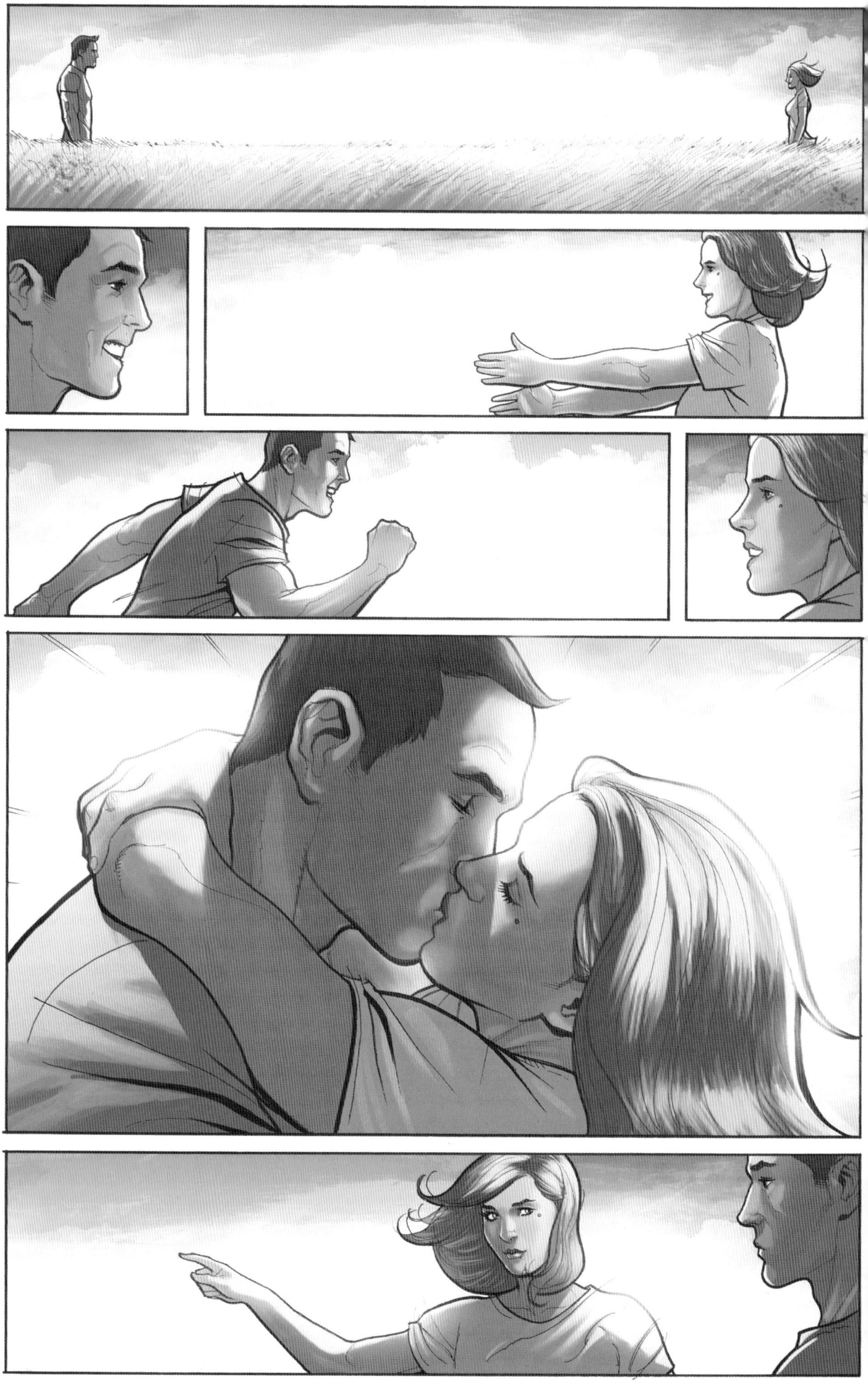

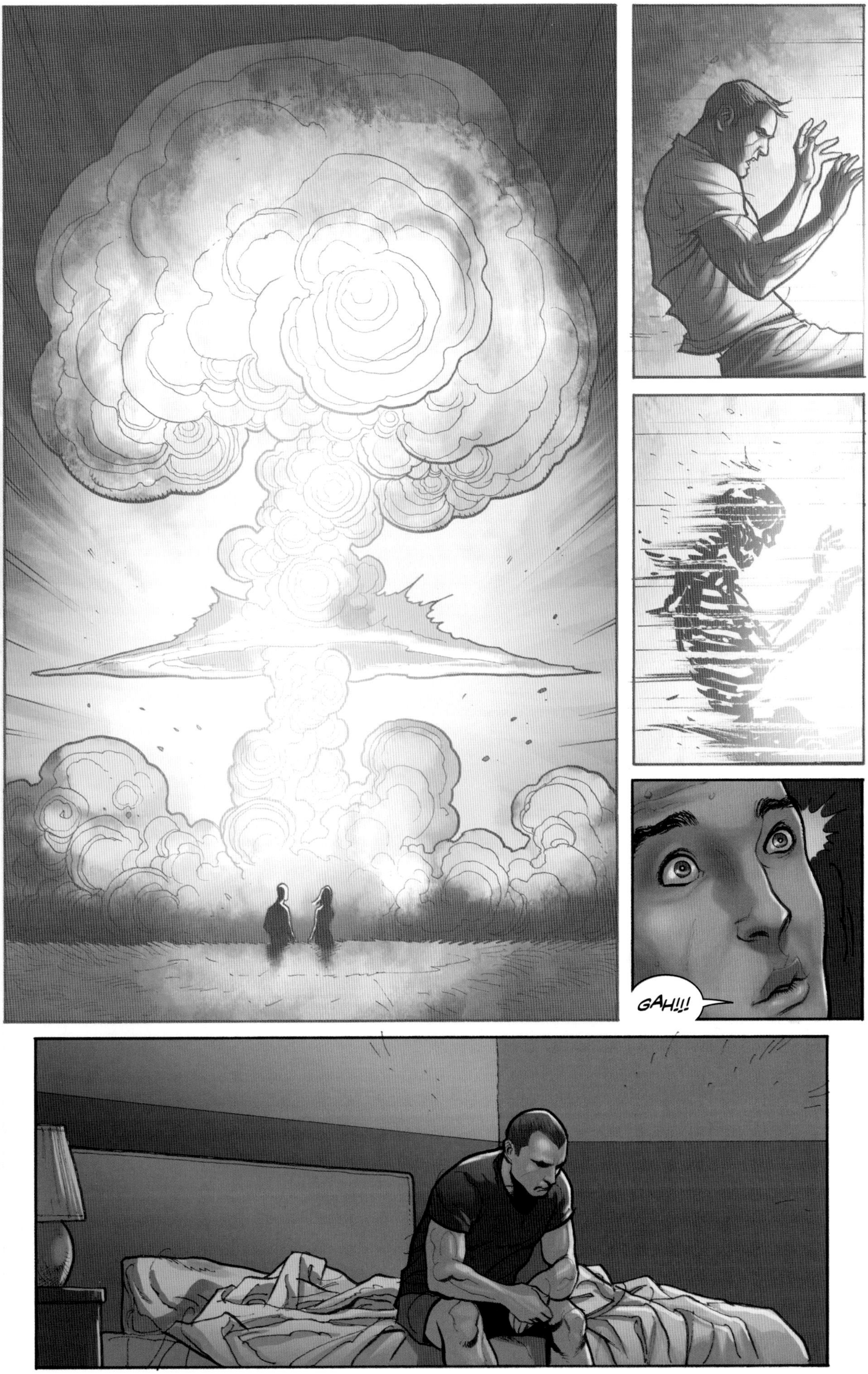
GAH!!!

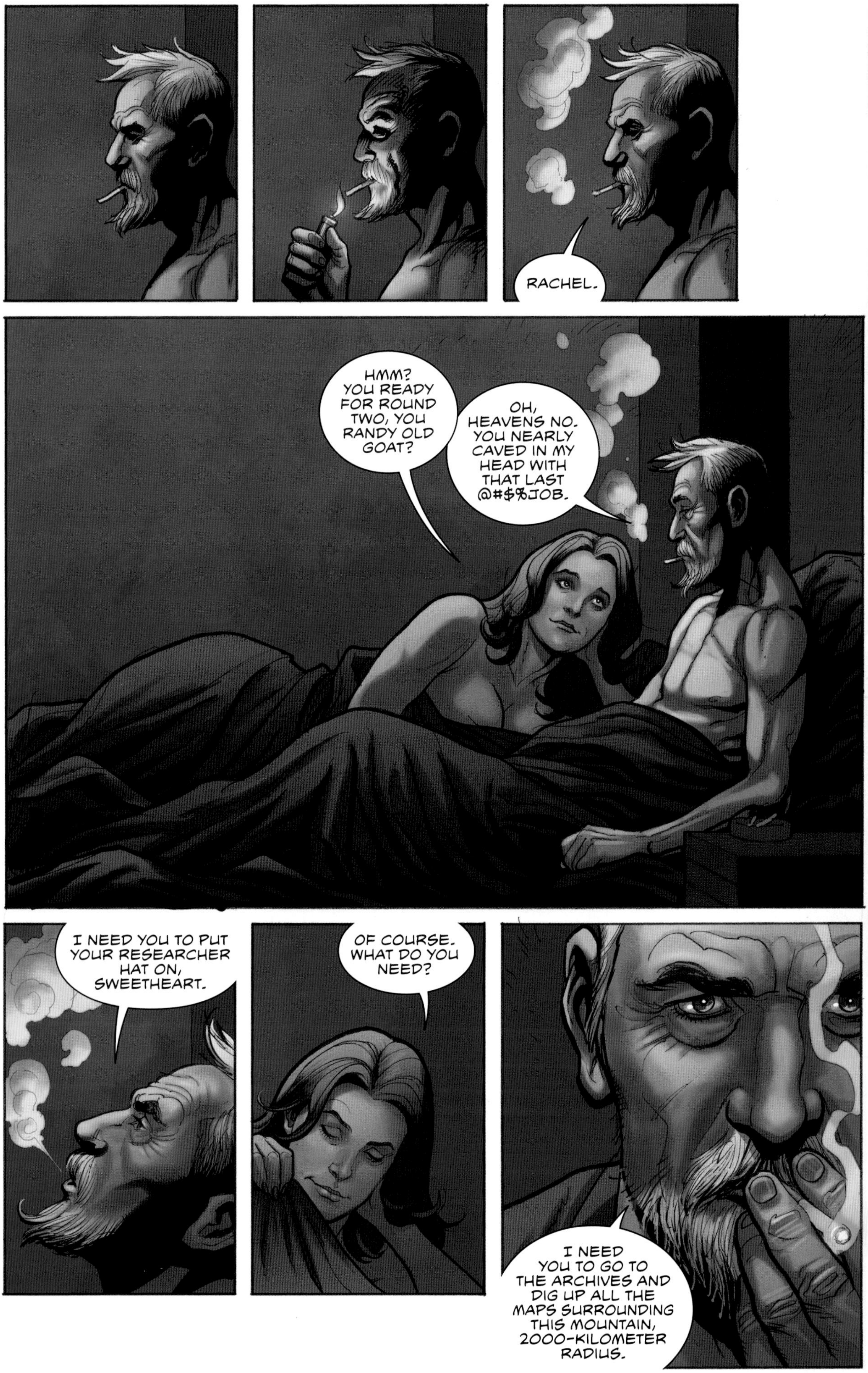
RACHEL.
HMM? YOU READY FOR ROUND TWO, YOU RANDY OLD GOAT?
OH, HEAVENS NO. YOU NEARLY CAVED IN MY HEAD WITH THAT LAST @#$%JOB.
I NEED YOU TO PUT YOUR RESEARCHER HAT ON, SWEETHEART.
OF COURSE. WHAT DO YOU NEED?
I NEED YOU TO GO TO THE ARCHIVES AND DIG UP ALL THE MAPS SURROUNDING THIS MOUNTAIN, 2000-KILOMETER RADIUS.

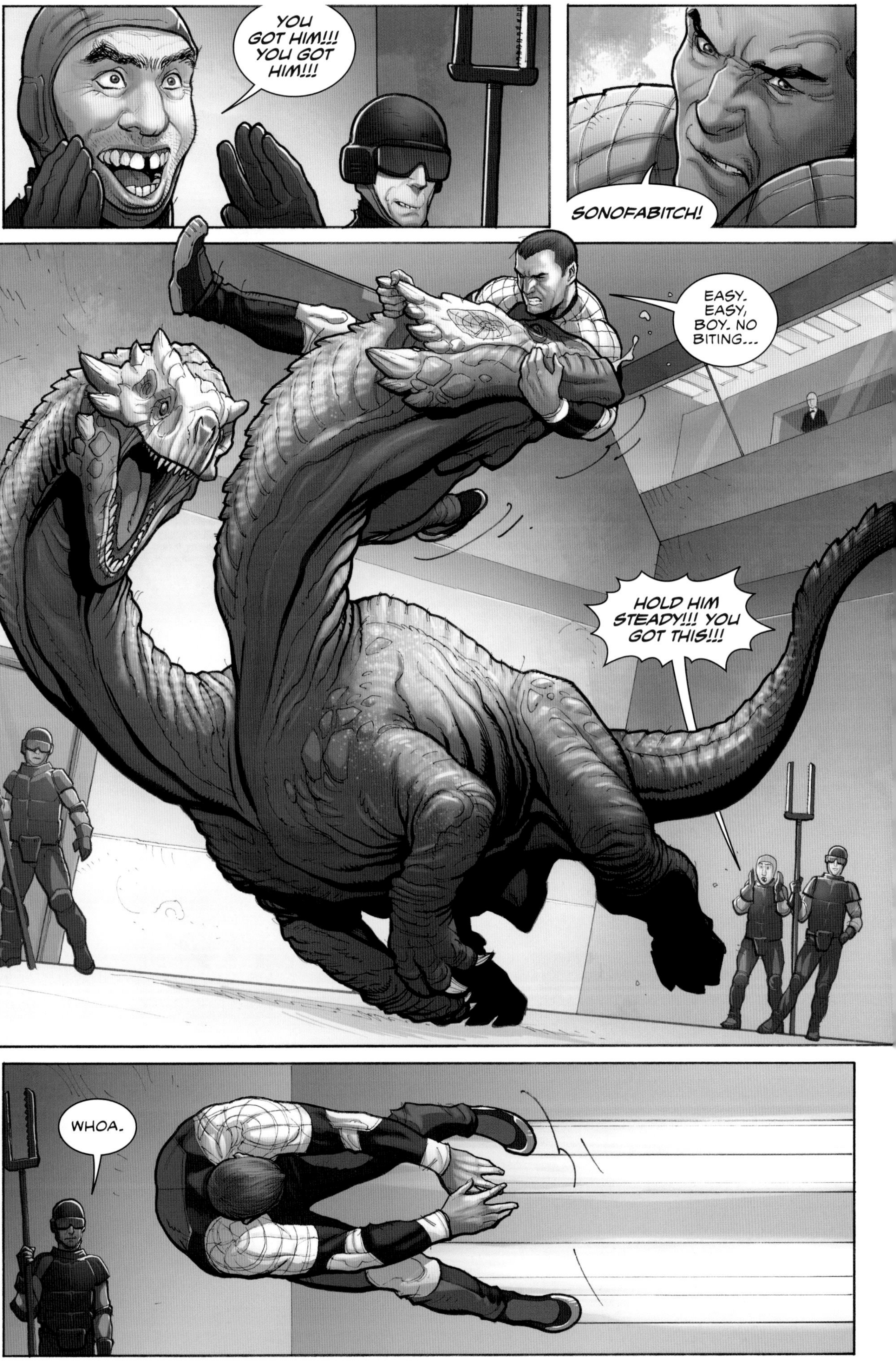
YOU GOT HIM!!! YOU GOT HIM!!!
SONOFABITCH!
EASY. EASY, BOY. NO BITING...
HOLD HIM STEADY!!! YOU GOT THIS!!!
WHOA.

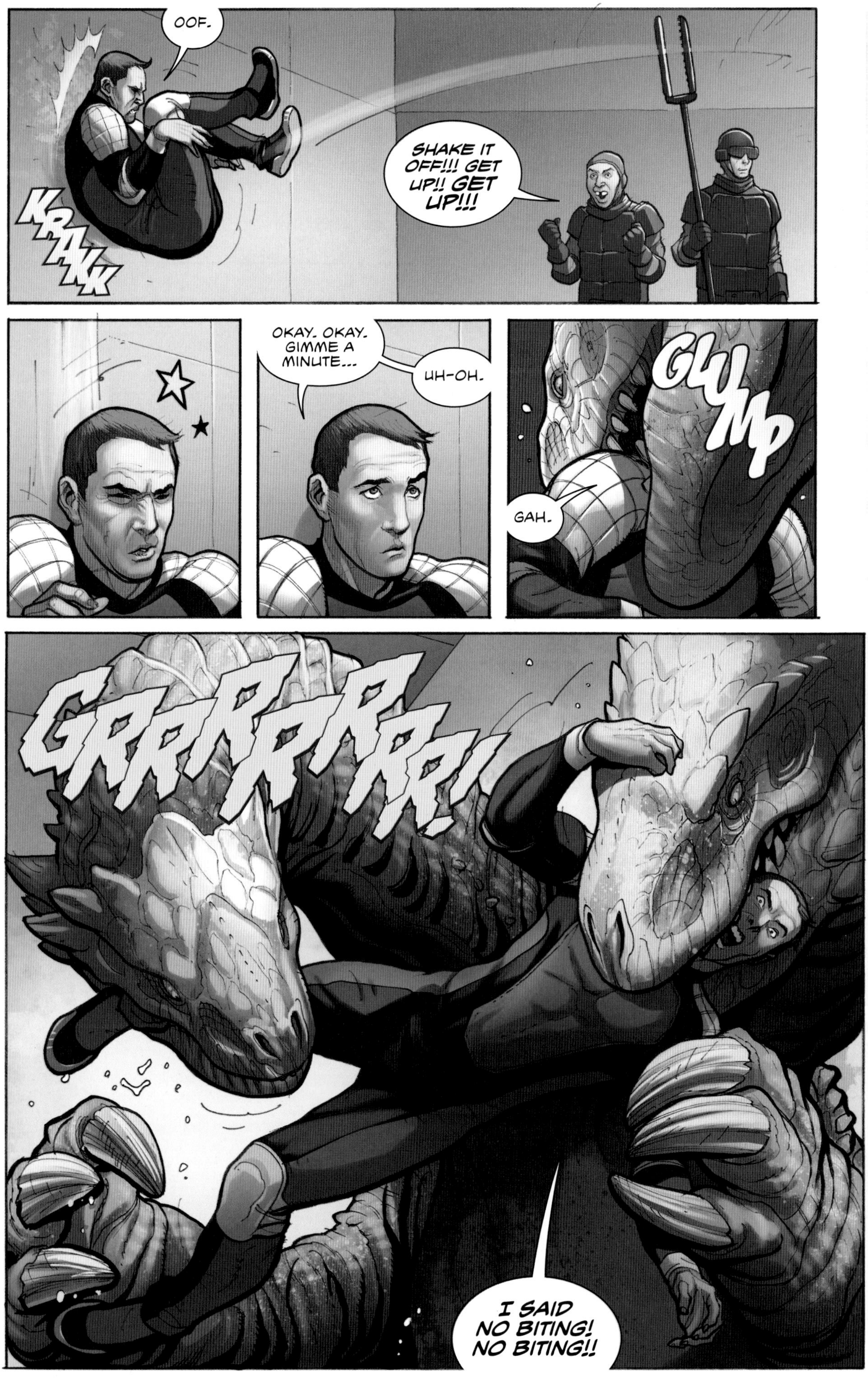
OOF.
KRAKK
SHAKE IT OFF!!! GET UP!! GET UP!!!
OKAY. OKAY. GIMME A MINUTE...
UH-OH.
GLUMP
GAH.
GRRRRRR!
I SAID NO BITING! NO BITING!!

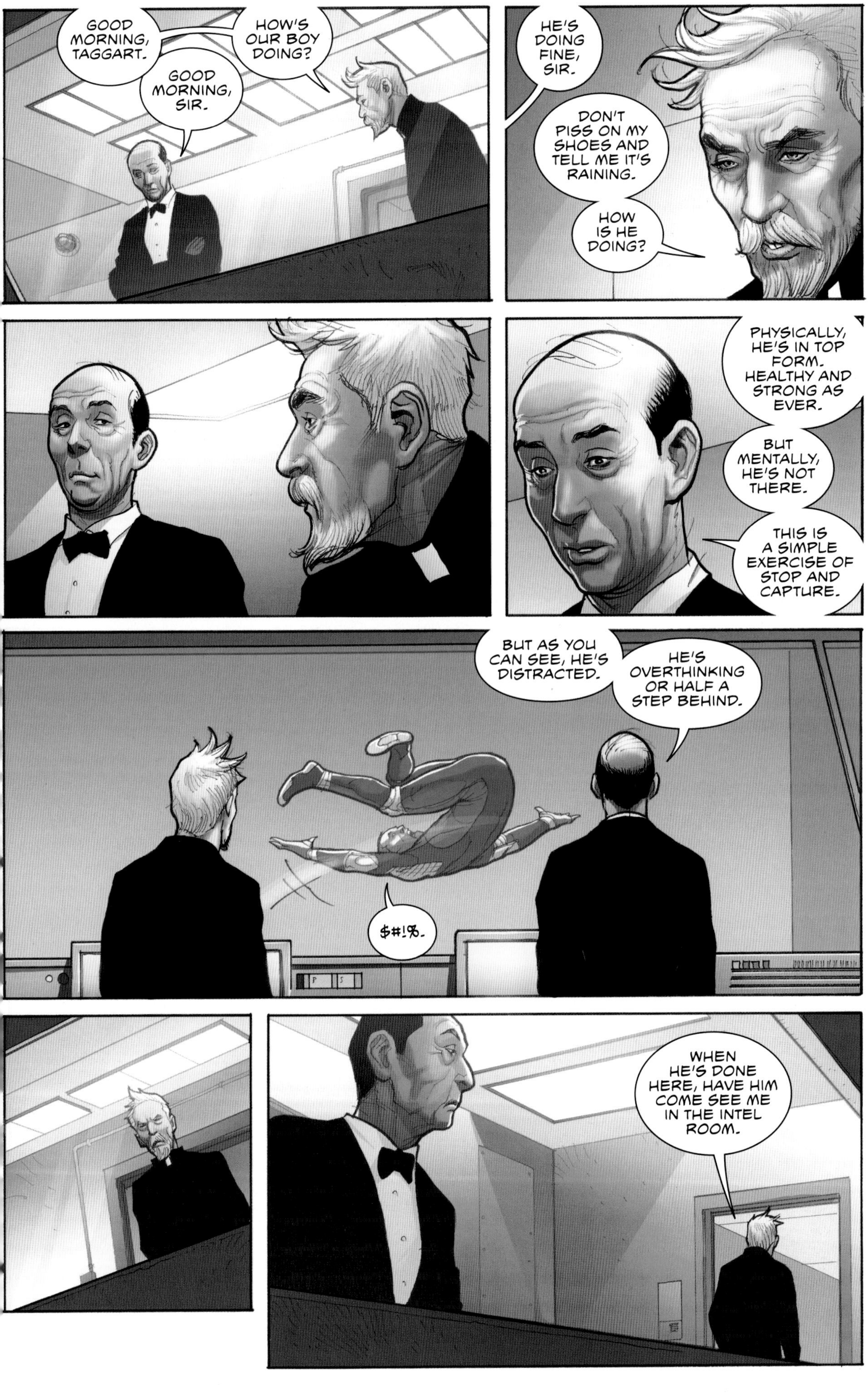
GOOD MORNING, TAGGART.
GOOD MORNING, SIR.
HOW'S OUR BOY DOING?
HE'S DOING FINE, SIR.
DON'T PISS ON MY SHOES AND TELL ME IT'S RAINING.
HOW IS HE DOING?
PHYSICALLY, HE'S IN TOP FORM. HEALTHY AND STRONG AS EVER.
BUT MENTALLY, HE'S NOT THERE.
THIS IS A SIMPLE EXERCISE OF STOP AND CAPTURE.
BUT AS YOU CAN SEE, HE'S DISTRACTED.
HE'S OVERTHINKING OR HALF A STEP BEHIND.
$#!%.
WHEN HE'S DONE HERE, HAVE HIM COME SEE ME IN THE INTEL ROOM.

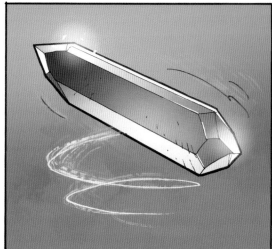

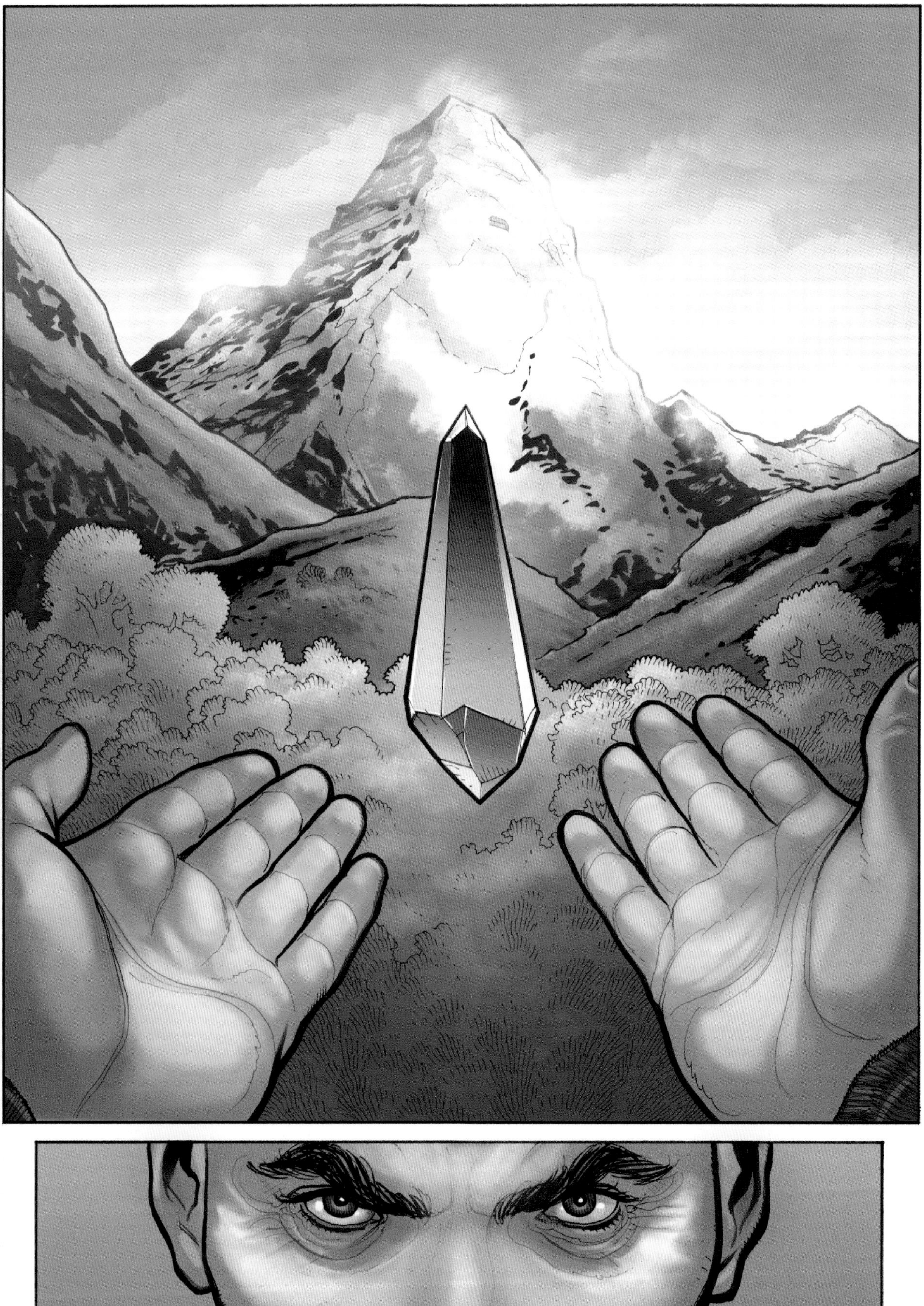

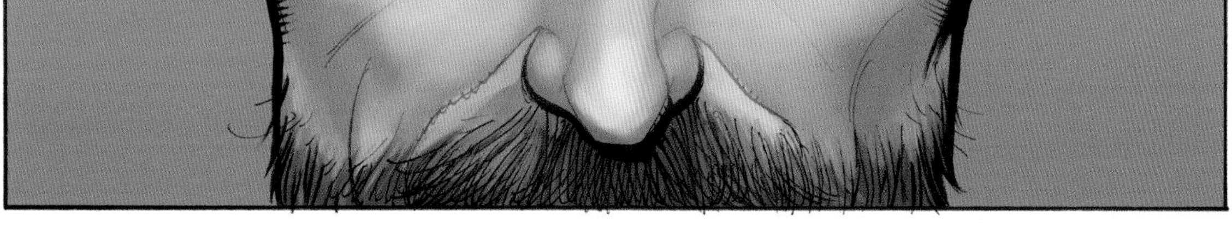

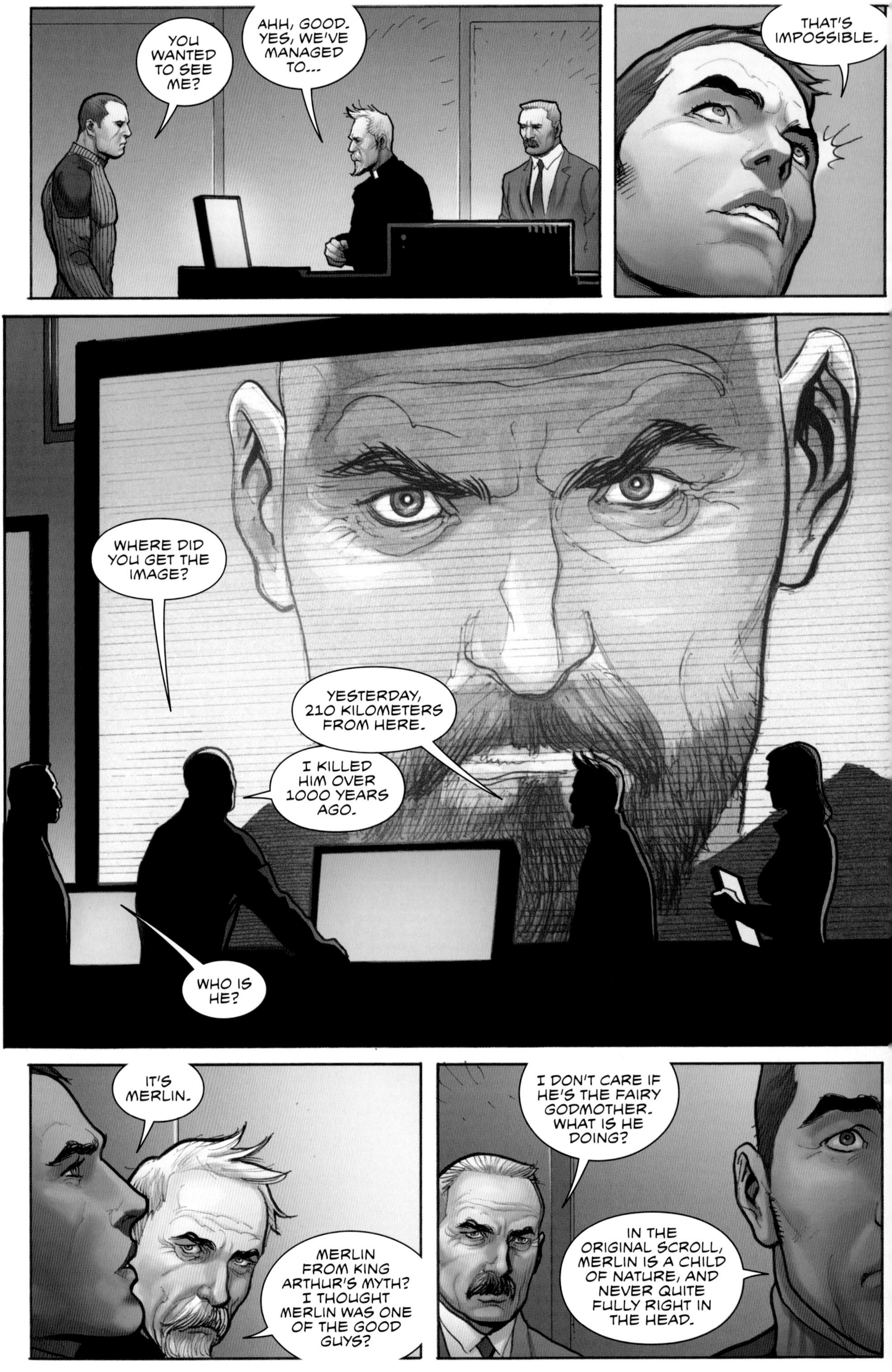
YOU WANTED TO SEE ME?
AHH, GOOD. YES, WE'VE MANAGED TO...
THAT'S IMPOSSIBLE.
WHERE DID YOU GET THE IMAGE?
YESTERDAY, 210 KILOMETERS FROM HERE.
I KILLED HIM OVER 1000 YEARS AGO.
WHO IS HE?
IT'S MERLIN.
MERLIN FROM KING ARTHUR'S MYTH? I THOUGHT MERLIN WAS ONE OF THE GOOD GUYS?
I DON'T CARE IF HE'S THE FAIRY GODMOTHER. WHAT IS HE DOING?
IN THE ORIGINAL SCROLL, MERLIN IS A CHILD OF NATURE, AND NEVER QUITE FULLY RIGHT IN THE HEAD.

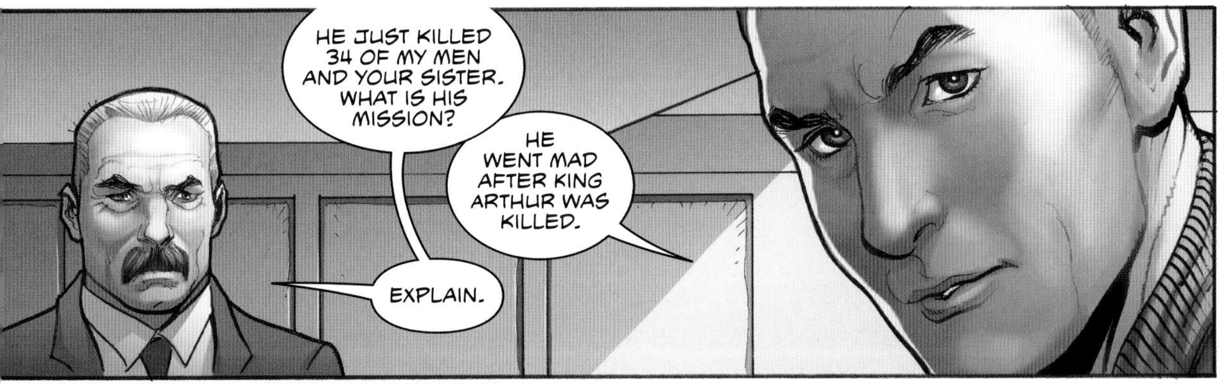
HE JUST KILLED 34 OF MY MEN AND YOUR SISTER. WHAT IS HIS MISSION?
HE WENT MAD AFTER KING ARTHUR WAS KILLED.
EXPLAIN.

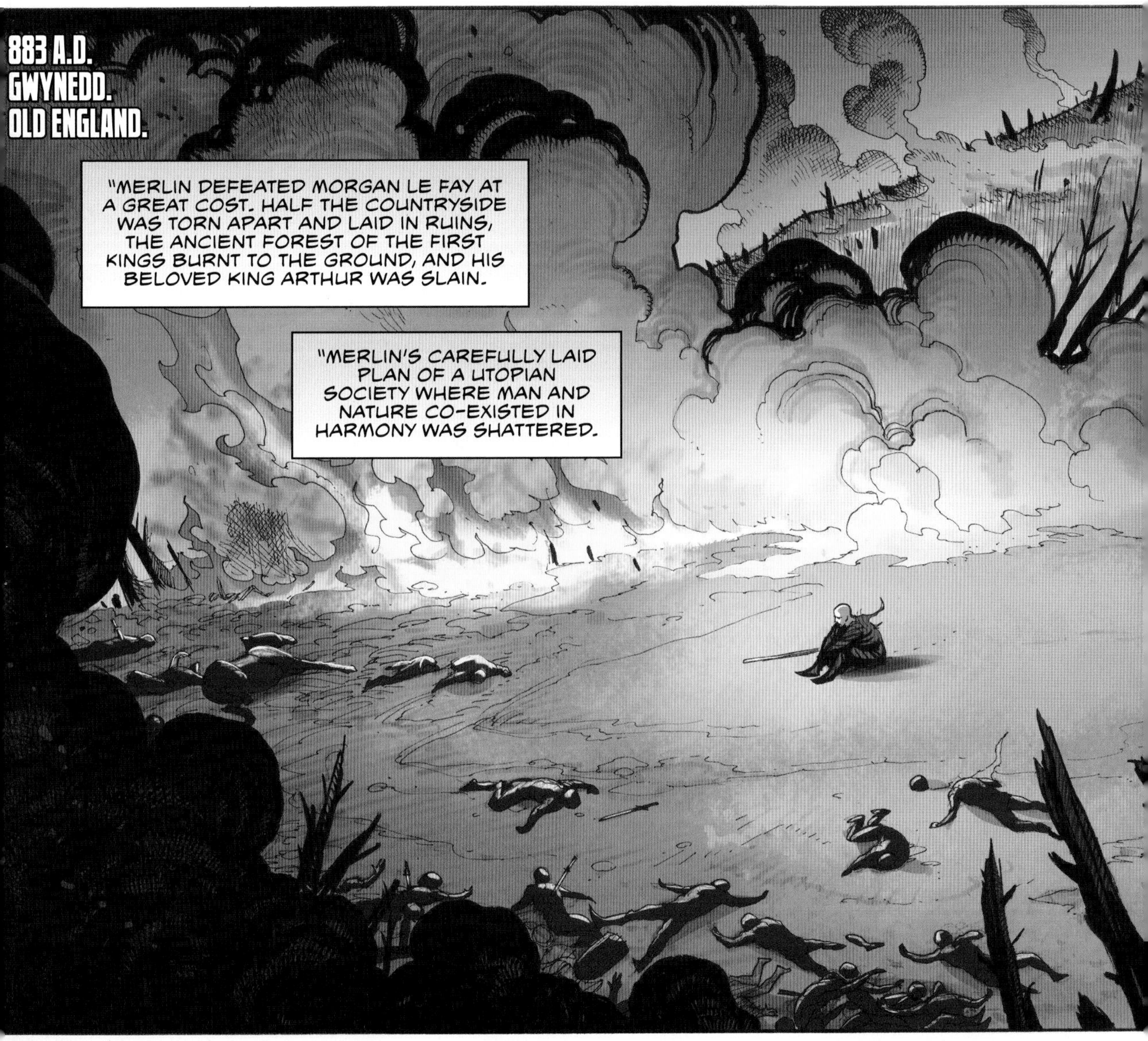
883 A.D. GWYNEDD. OLD ENGLAND.
"MERLIN DEFEATED MORGAN LE FAY AT A GREAT COST. HALF THE COUNTRYSIDE WAS TORN APART AND LAID IN RUINS, THE ANCIENT FOREST OF THE FIRST KINGS BURNT TO THE GROUND, AND HIS BELOVED KING ARTHUR WAS SLAIN.
"MERLIN'S CAREFULLY LAID PLAN OF A UTOPIAN SOCIETY WHERE MAN AND NATURE CO-EXISTED IN HARMONY WAS SHATTERED.

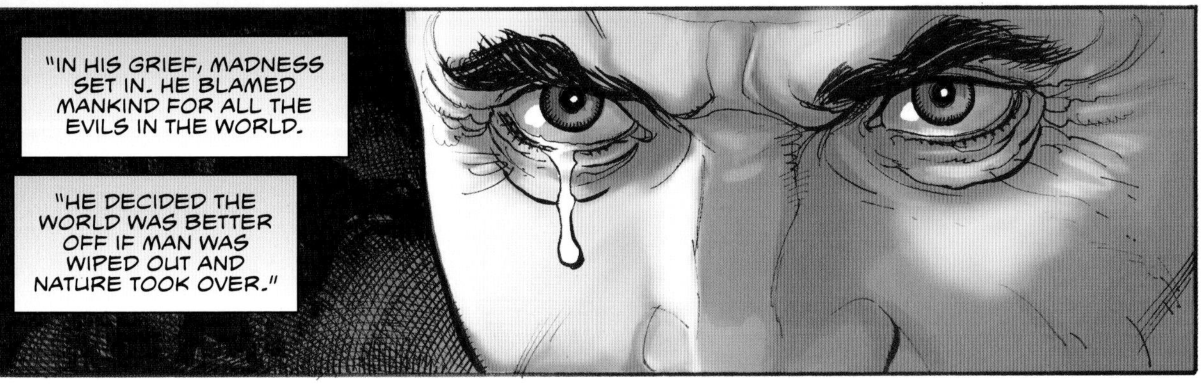
"IN HIS GRIEF, MADNESS SET IN. HE BLAMED MANKIND FOR ALL THE EVILS IN THE WORLD.
"HE DECIDED THE WORLD WAS BETTER OFF IF MAN WAS WIPED OUT AND NATURE TOOK OVER."

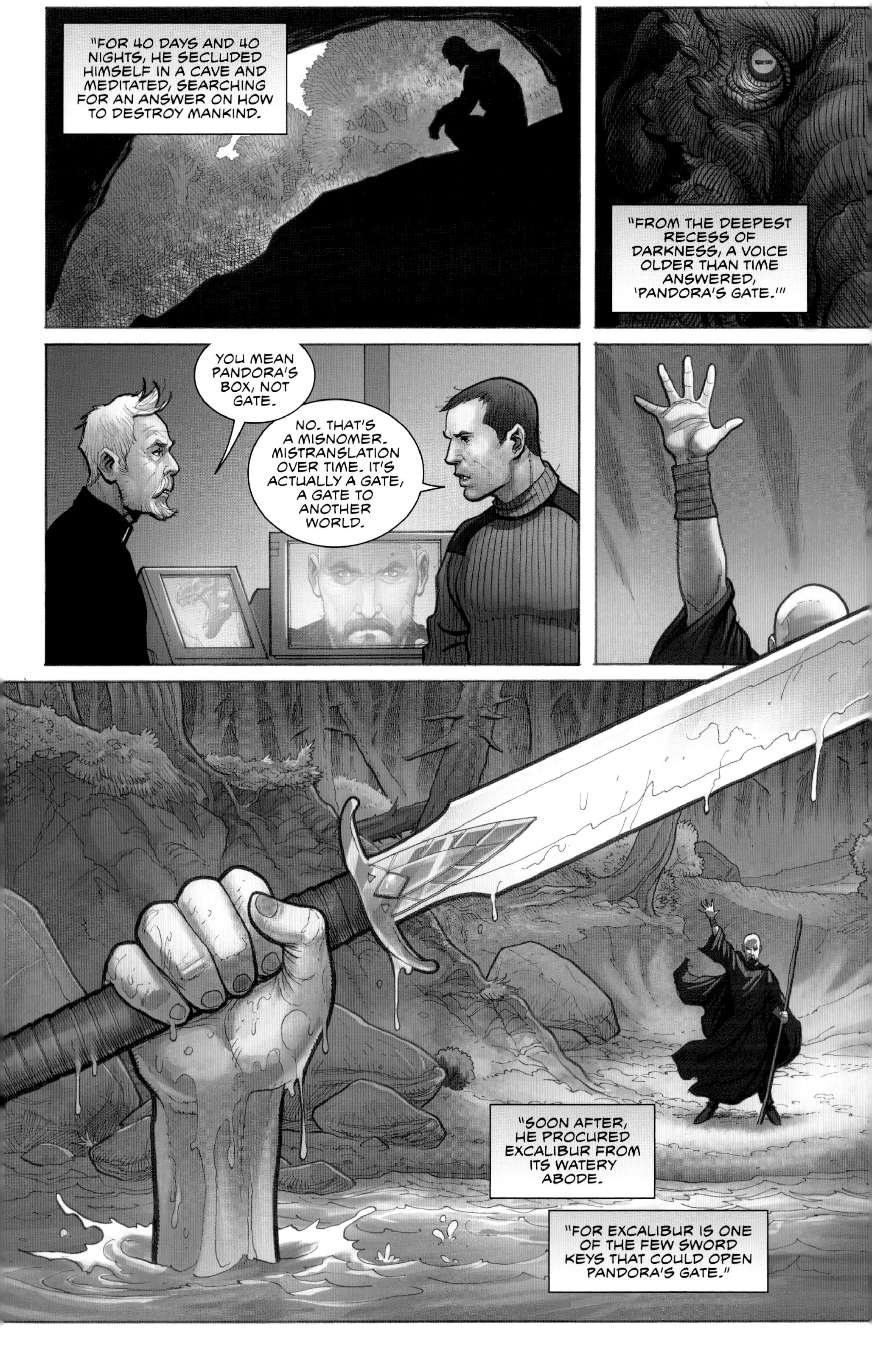
"FOR 40 DAYS AND 40 NIGHTS, HE SECLUDED HIMSELF IN A CAVE AND MEDITATED, SEARCHING FOR AN ANSWER ON HOW TO DESTROY MANKIND.
"FROM THE DEEPEST RECESS OF DARKNESS, A VOICE OLDER THAN TIME ANSWERED, 'PANDORA'S GATE.'"
YOU MEAN PANDORA'S BOX, NOT GATE.
NO. THAT'S A MISNOMER. MISTRANSLATION OVER TIME. IT'S ACTUALLY A GATE, A GATE TO ANOTHER WORLD.
"SOON AFTER, HE PROCURED EXCALIBUR FROM ITS WATERY ABODE.
"FOR EXCALIBUR IS ONE OF THE FEW SWORD KEYS THAT COULD OPEN PANDORA'S GATE."

HOW DO YOU KNOW ALL THIS?

HE TRIED TO RECRUIT ME IN DESTROYING MANKIND.

AND?

WHAT DO YOU MEAN "AND"?...I JOINED HIM. WE DESTROYED THE WORLD AND I SOLD T-SHIRTS ABOUT IT AFTERWARDS.

OF COURSE I REJECTED HIM. I RAISED AN ARMY AND STOPPED HIM INSTEAD.

OKAY. JUST MAKING SURE.

GENTLEMEN. PLEASE FOCUS ON THE CRISIS AT HAND.

RIGHT. RIGHT.

IS THAT WHY HE'S COMING HERE?

WHAT?!! IS THIS TRUE? WHY WASN'T I NOTIFIED OF THIS INFORMATION?

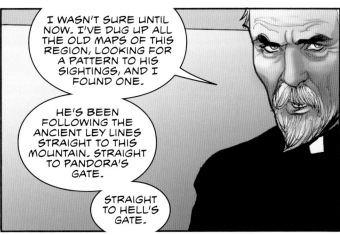

I WASN'T SURE UNTIL NOW. I'VE DUG UP ALL THE OLD MAPS OF THIS REGION, LOOKING FOR A PATTERN TO HIS SIGHTINGS, AND I FOUND ONE.

HE'S BEEN FOLLOWING THE ANCIENT LEY LINES STRAIGHT TO THIS MOUNTAIN. STRAIGHT TO PANDORA'S GATE.

STRAIGHT TO HELL'S GATE.

YES.

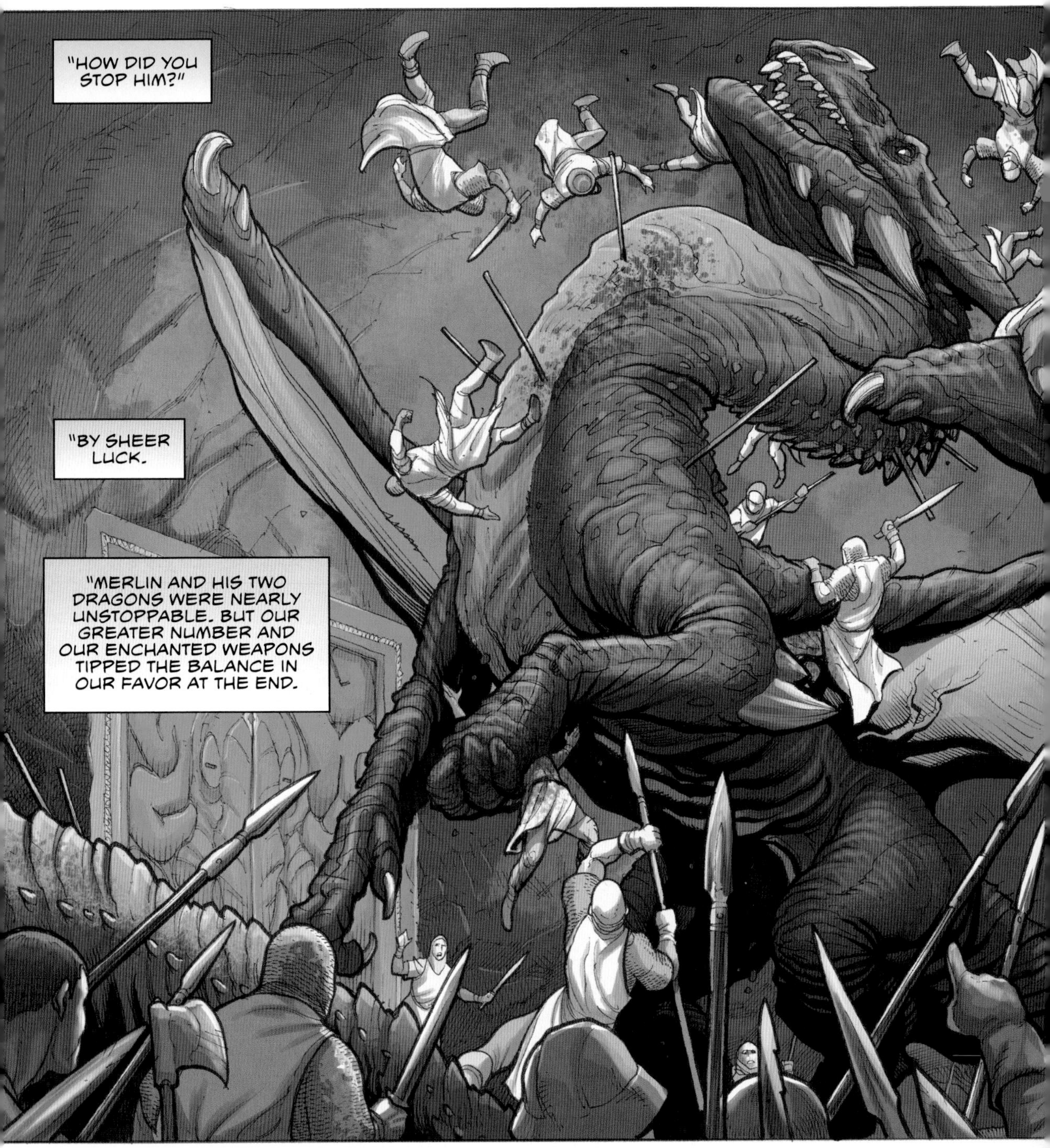
"HOW DID YOU STOP HIM?"
"BY SHEER LUCK.
"MERLIN AND HIS TWO DRAGONS WERE NEARLY UNSTOPPABLE. BUT OUR GREATER NUMBER AND OUR ENCHANTED WEAPONS TIPPED THE BALANCE IN OUR FAVOR AT THE END.

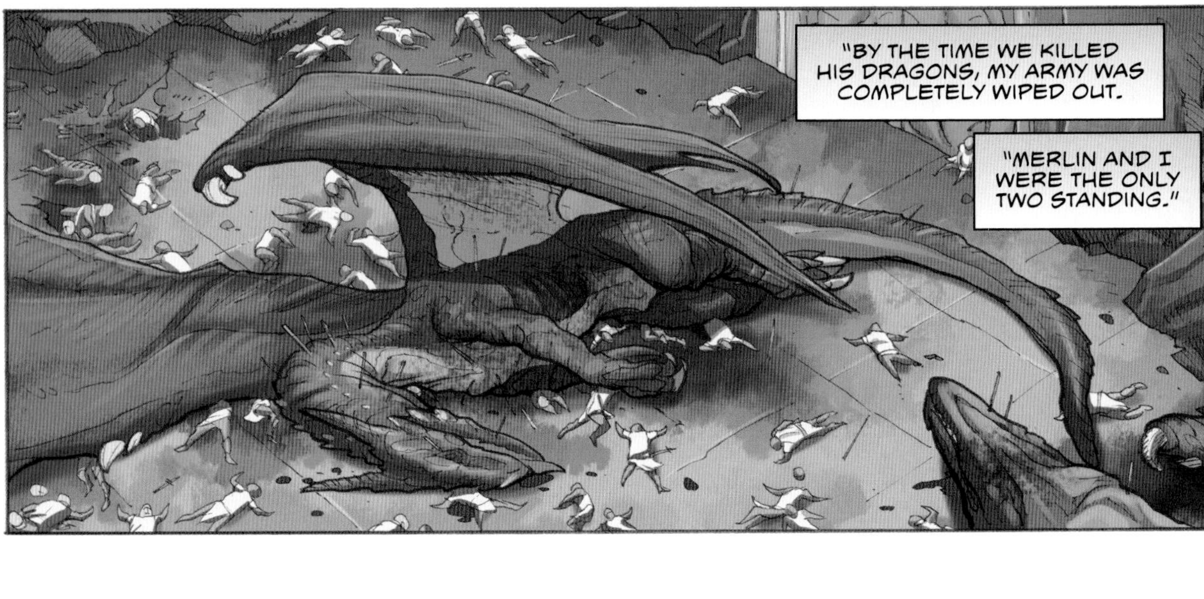
"BY THE TIME WE KILLED HIS DRAGONS, MY ARMY WAS COMPLETELY WIPED OUT.
"MERLIN AND I WERE THE ONLY TWO STANDING."

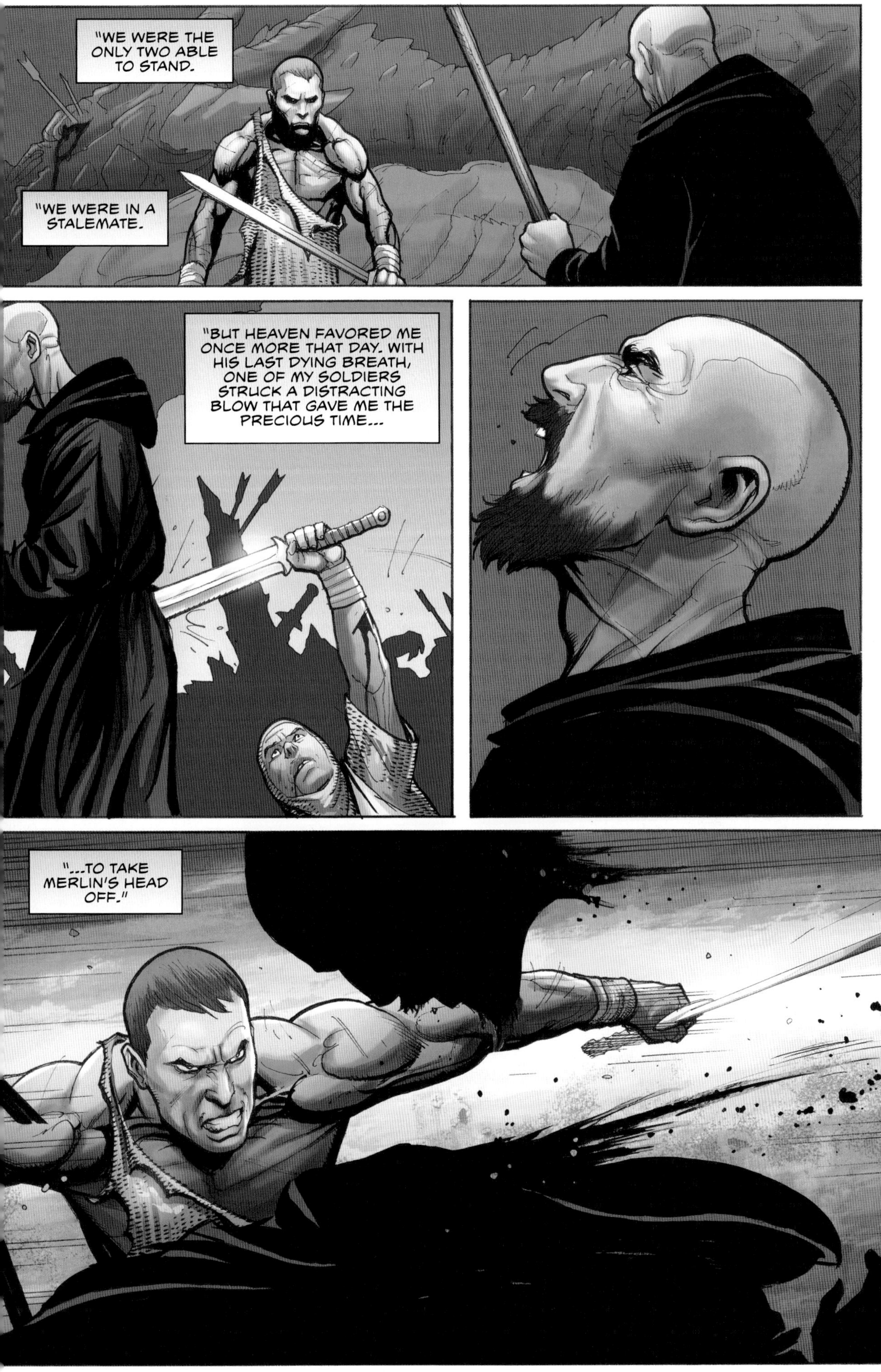
"WE WERE THE ONLY TWO ABLE TO STAND.
"WE WERE IN A STALEMATE.
"BUT HEAVEN FAVORED ME ONCE MORE THAT DAY. WITH HIS LAST DYING BREATH, ONE OF MY SOLDIERS STRUCK A DISTRACTING BLOW THAT GAVE ME THE PRECIOUS TIME...
"...TO TAKE MERLIN'S HEAD OFF."

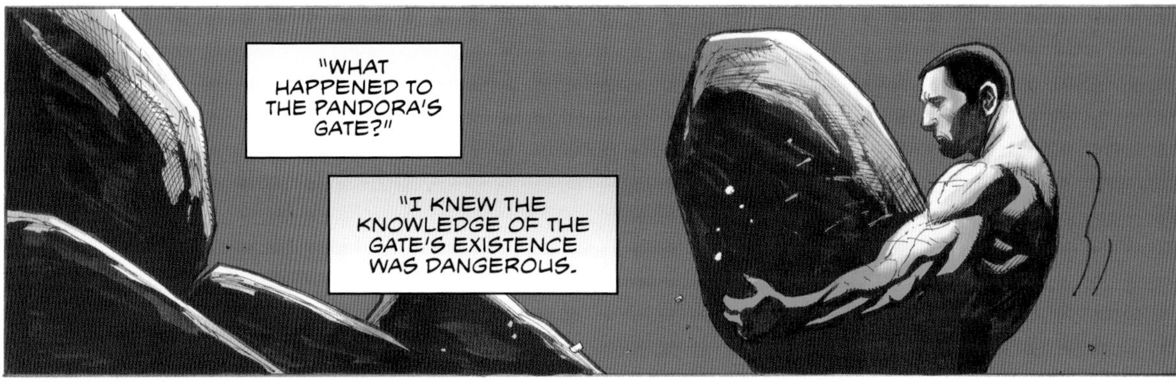
"WHAT HAPPENED TO THE PANDORA'S GATE?"
"I KNEW THE KNOWLEDGE OF THE GATE'S EXISTENCE WAS DANGEROUS.

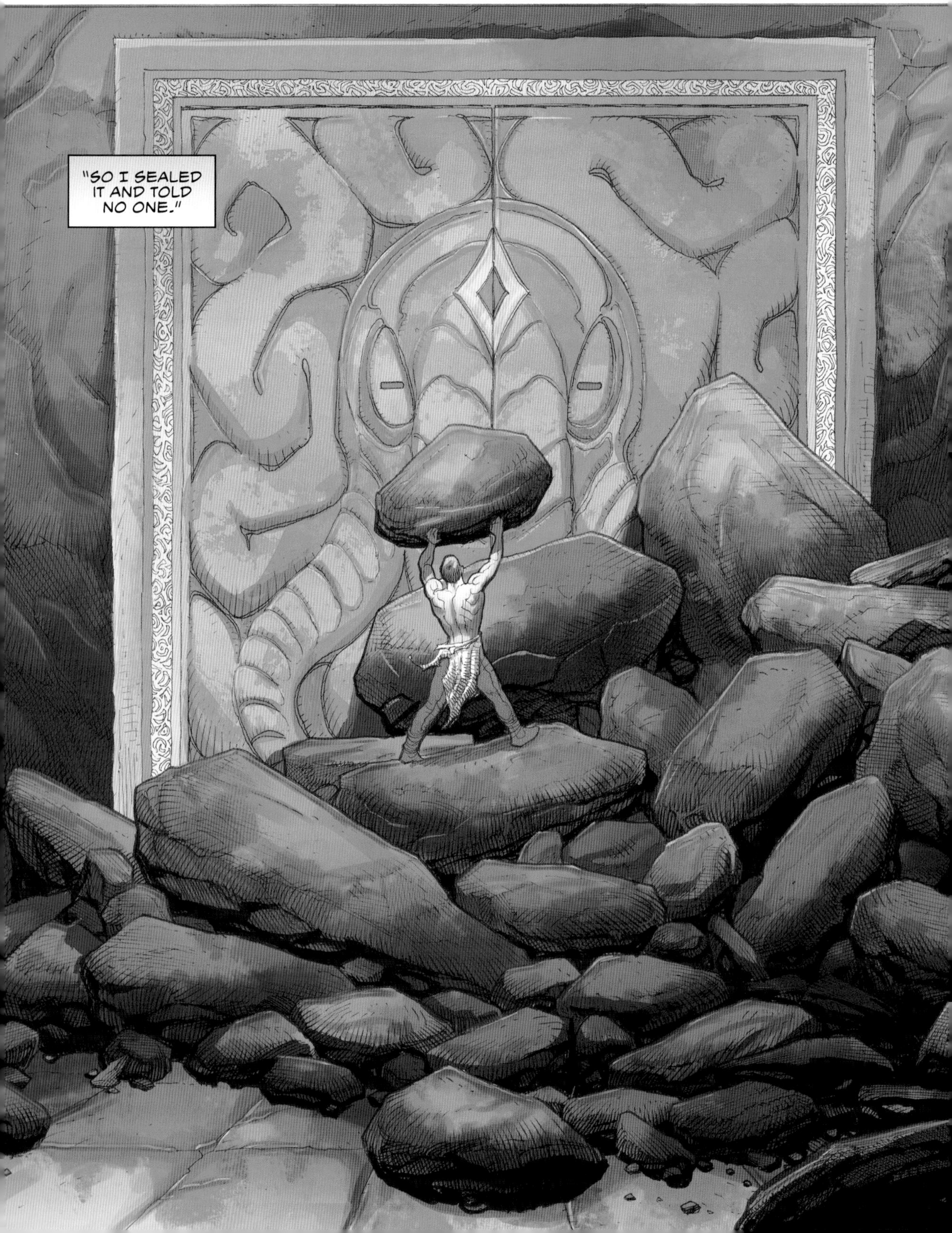
"SO I SEALED IT AND TOLD NO ONE."

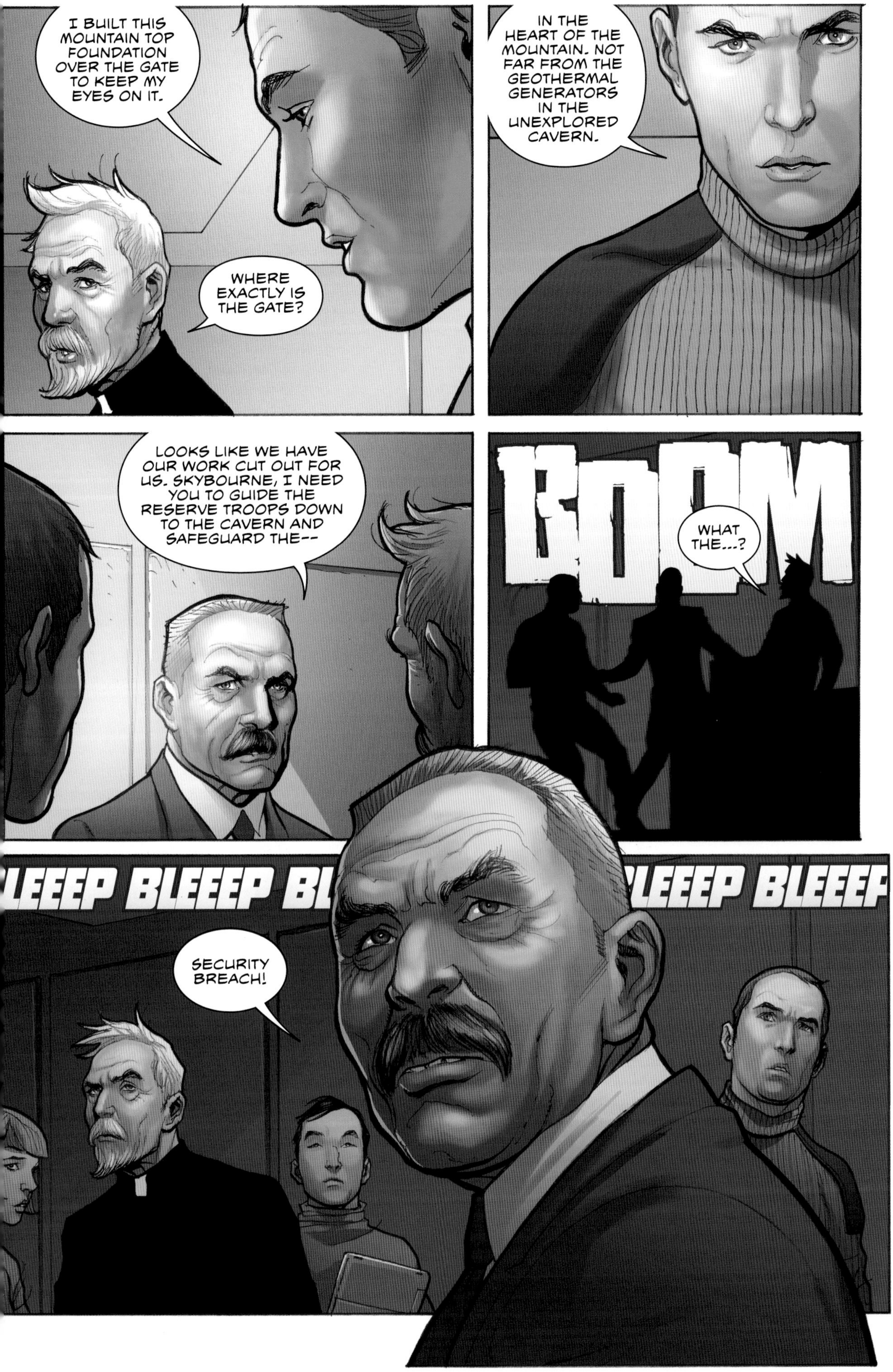
I BUILT THIS MOUNTAIN TOP FOUNDATION OVER THE GATE TO KEEP MY EYES ON IT.
WHERE EXACTLY IS THE GATE?
IN THE HEART OF THE MOUNTAIN. NOT FAR FROM THE GEOTHERMAL GENERATORS IN THE UNEXPLORED CAVERN.
LOOKS LIKE WE HAVE OUR WORK CUT OUT FOR US. SKYBOURNE, I NEED YOU TO GUIDE THE RESERVE TROOPS DOWN TO THE CAVERN AND SAFEGUARD THE--
BOOM
WHAT THE...?
BLEEEP BLEEEP BL
LEEEP BLEEEP
SECURITY BREACH!

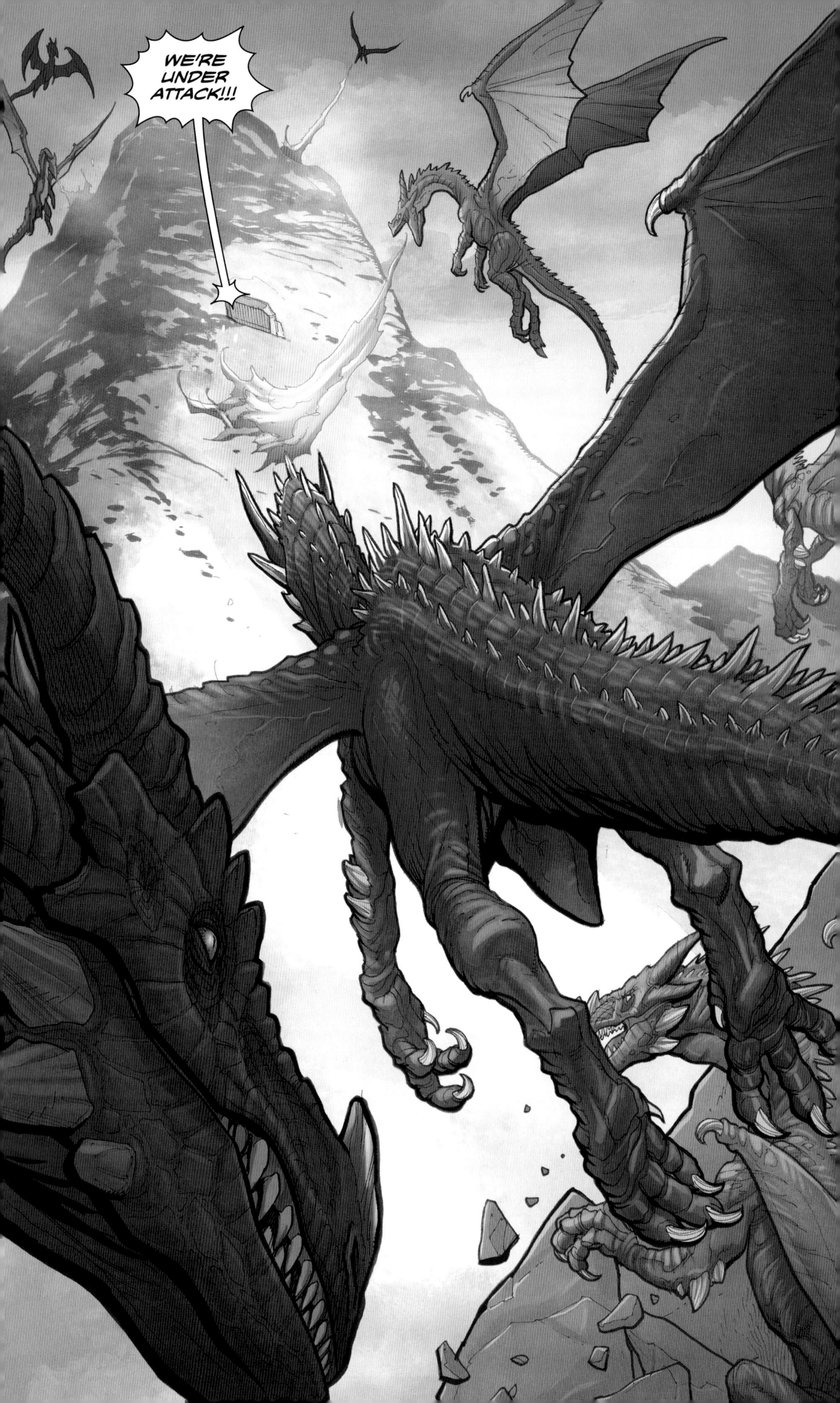
WE'RE UNDER ATTACK!!!

Issue Three Cover by **FRANK CHO**
with colors by **MARCIO MENYZ**

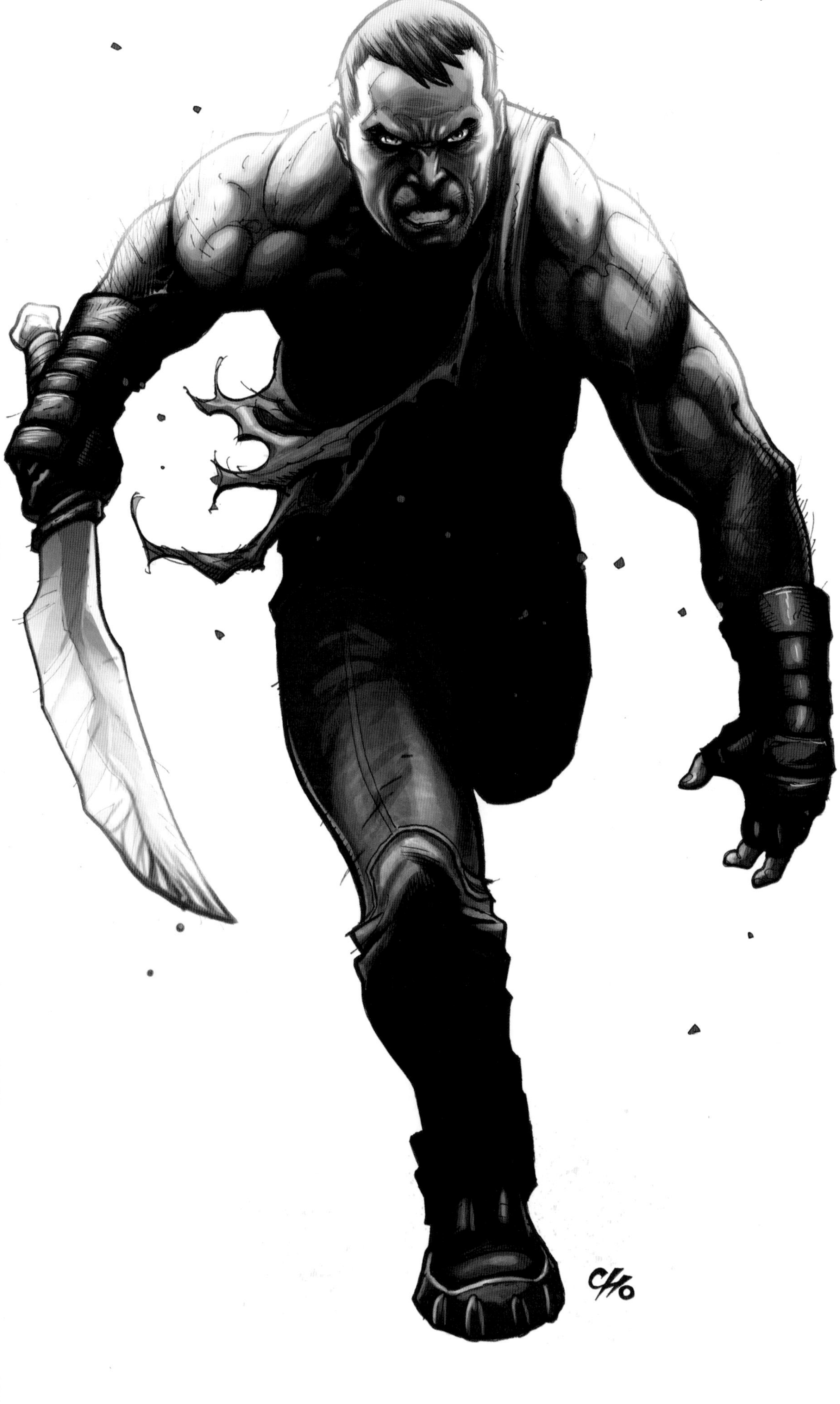
CHO

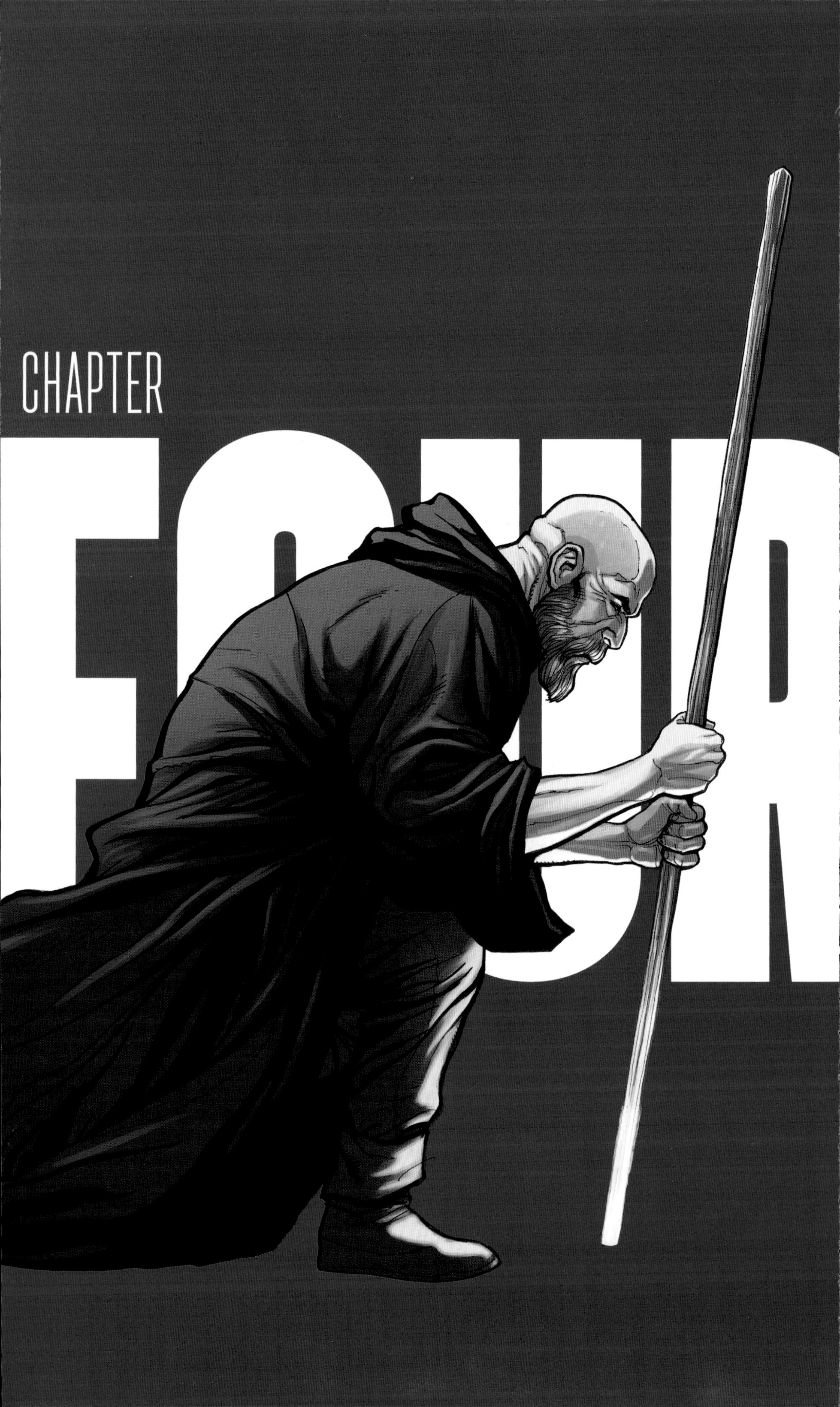
CHAPTER
FOUR

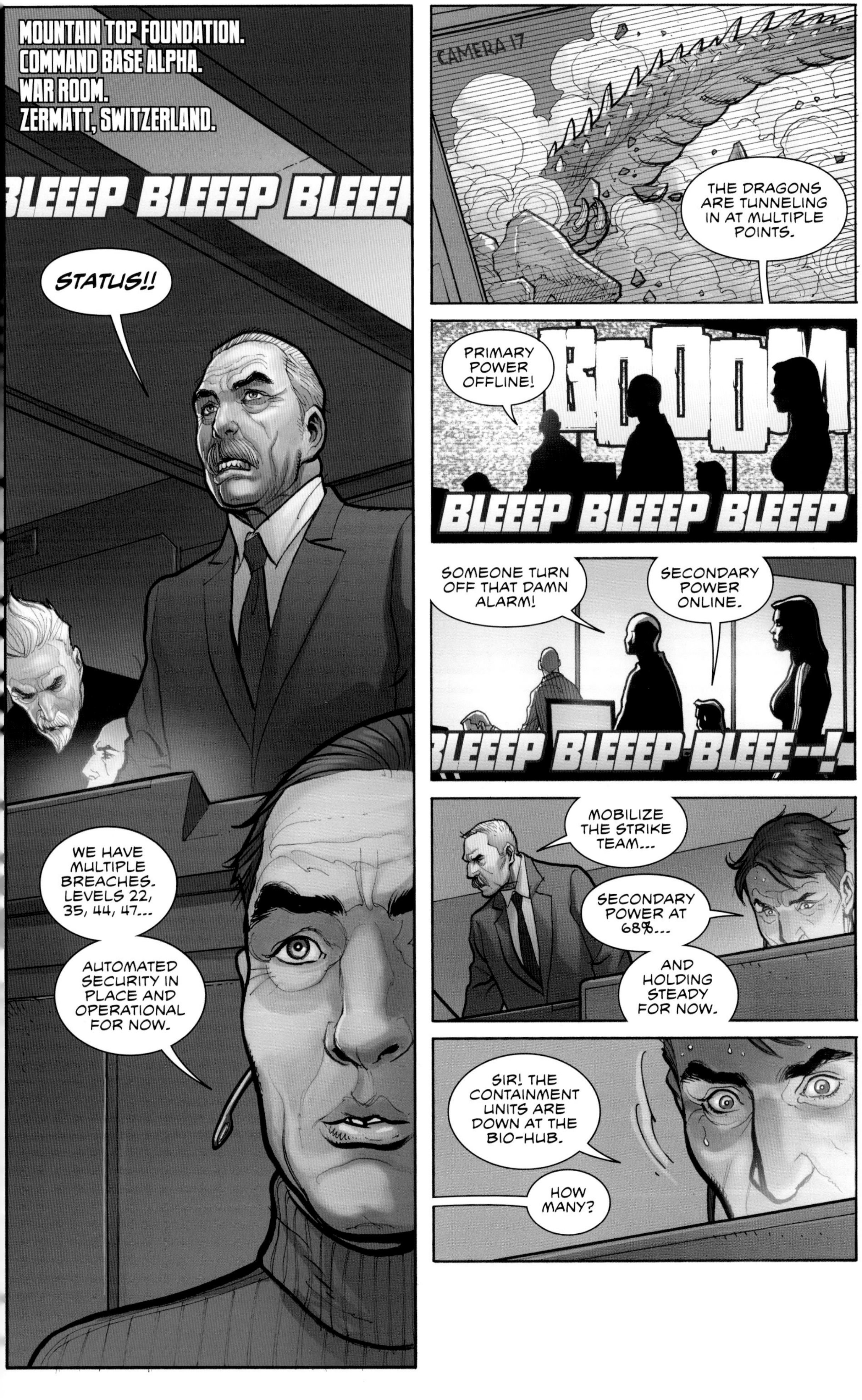
MOUNTAIN TOP FOUNDATION.
COMMAND BASE ALPHA.
WAR ROOM.
ZERMATT, SWITZERLAND.
BLEEEP BLEEEP BLEEE
STATUS!!
WE HAVE MULTIPLE BREACHES. LEVELS 22, 35, 44, 47...
AUTOMATED SECURITY IN PLACE AND OPERATIONAL FOR NOW.
CAMERA 17
THE DRAGONS ARE TUNNELING IN AT MULTIPLE POINTS.
BOOOM
PRIMARY POWER OFFLINE!
BLEEEP BLEEEP BLEEEP
SOMEONE TURN OFF THAT DAMN ALARM!
SECONDARY POWER ONLINE.
BLEEEP BLEEEP BLEEE--!
MOBILIZE THE STRIKE TEAM...
SECONDARY POWER AT 68%...
AND HOLDING STEADY FOR NOW.
SIR! THE CONTAINMENT UNITS ARE DOWN AT THE BIO-HUB.
HOW MANY?

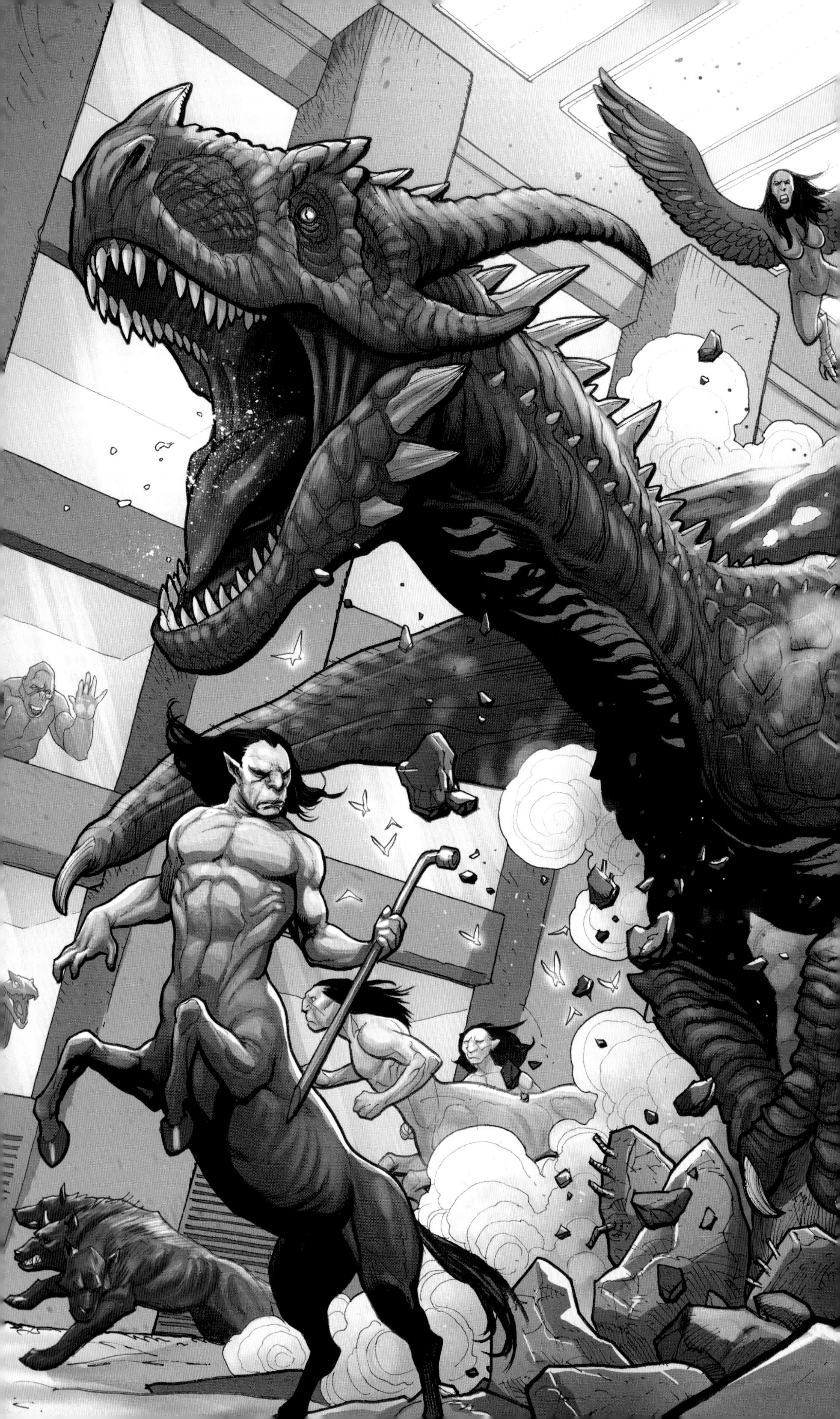

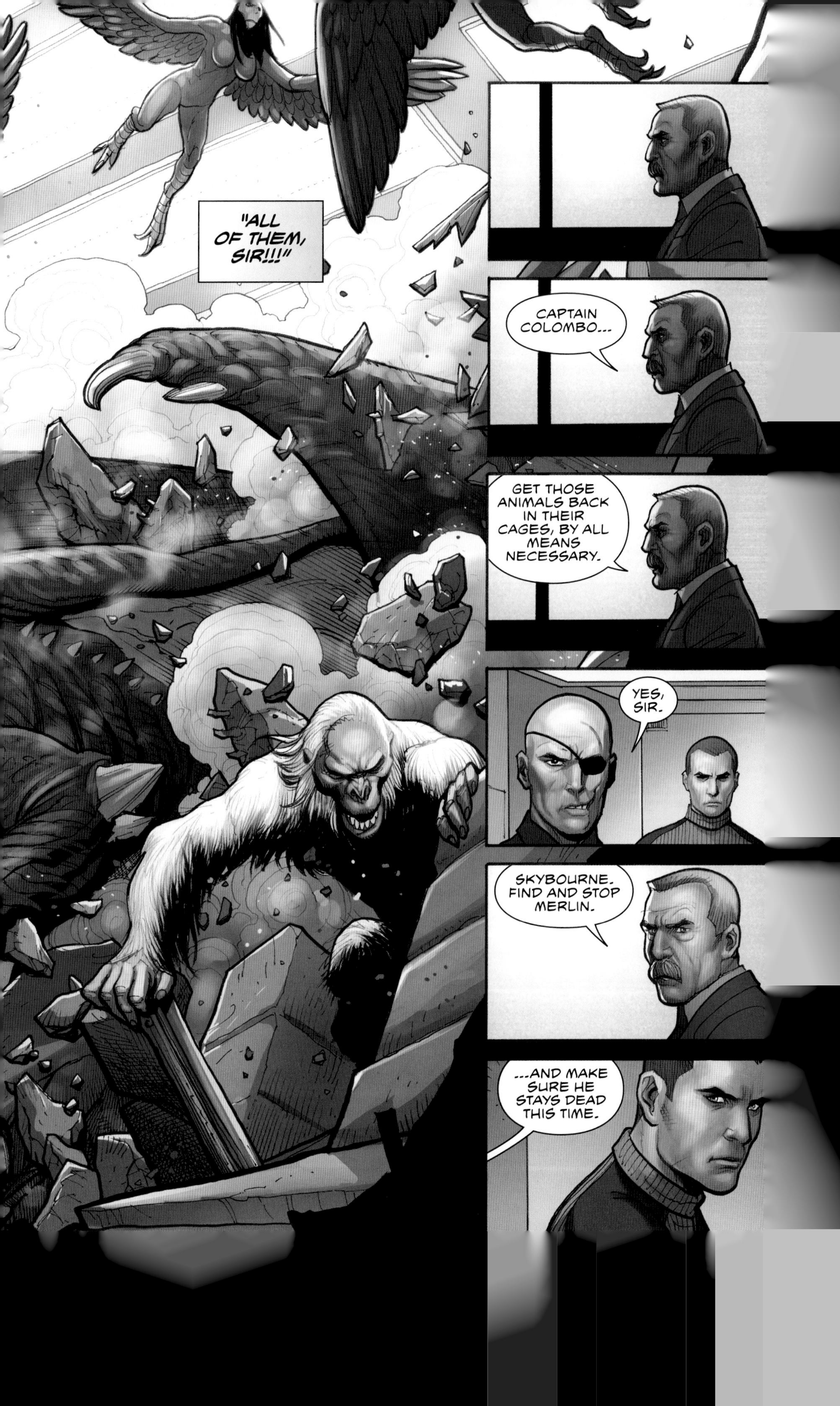
"ALL OF THEM, SIR!!!"
CAPTAIN COLOMBO...
GET THOSE ANIMALS BACK IN THEIR CAGES, BY ALL MEANS NECESSARY.
YES, SIR.
SKYBOURNE. FIND AND STOP MERLIN.
...AND MAKE SURE HE STAYS DEAD THIS TIME.

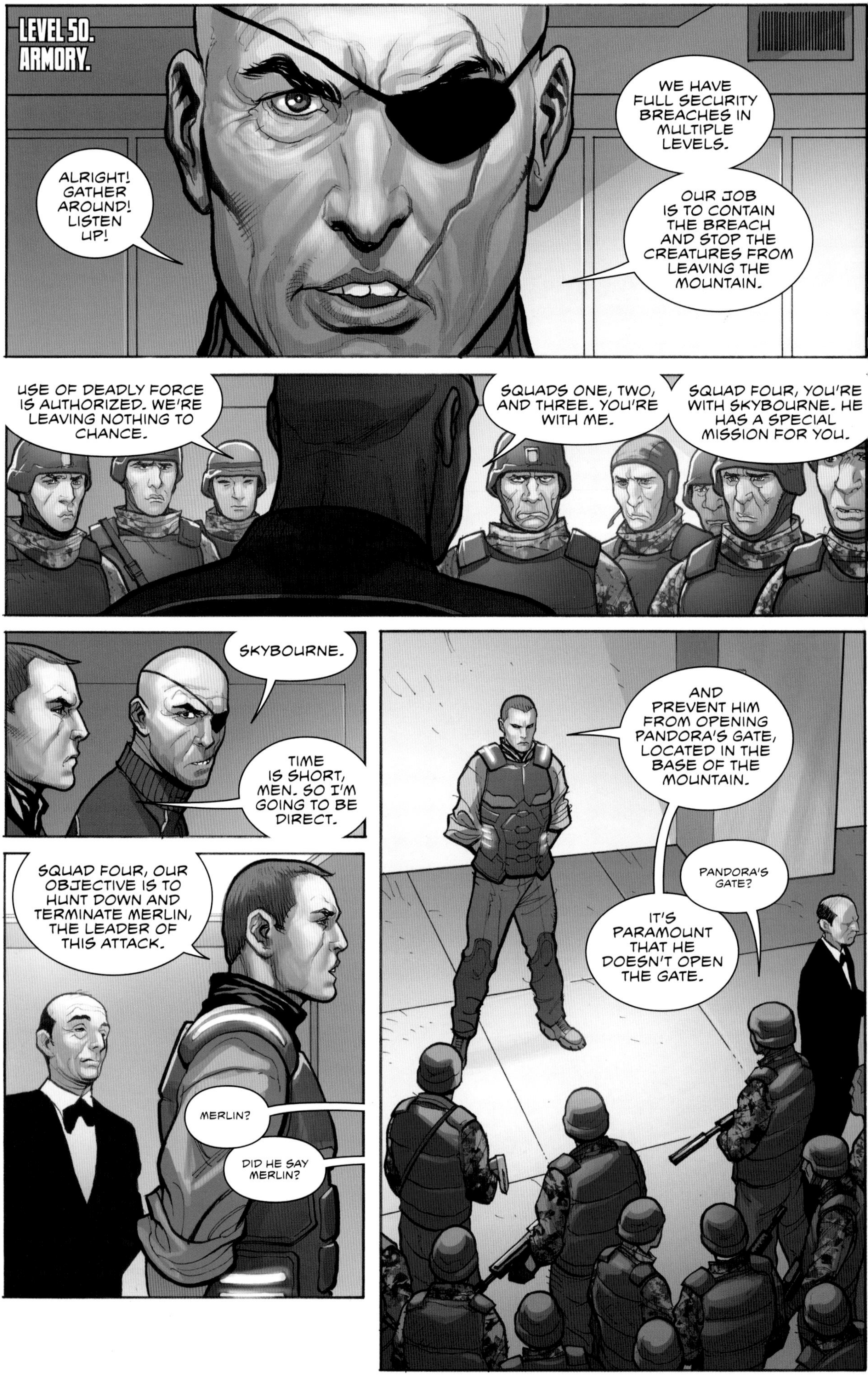
LEVEL 50. ARMORY.
ALRIGHT! GATHER AROUND! LISTEN UP!
WE HAVE FULL SECURITY BREACHES IN MULTIPLE LEVELS.
OUR JOB IS TO CONTAIN THE BREACH AND STOP THE CREATURES FROM LEAVING THE MOUNTAIN.
USE OF DEADLY FORCE IS AUTHORIZED. WE'RE LEAVING NOTHING TO CHANCE.
SQUADS ONE, TWO, AND THREE. YOU'RE WITH ME.
SQUAD FOUR, YOU'RE WITH SKYBOURNE. HE HAS A SPECIAL MISSION FOR YOU.
SKYBOURNE.
TIME IS SHORT, MEN. SO I'M GOING TO BE DIRECT.
SQUAD FOUR, OUR OBJECTIVE IS TO HUNT DOWN AND TERMINATE MERLIN, THE LEADER OF THIS ATTACK.
MERLIN?
DID HE SAY MERLIN?
AND PREVENT HIM FROM OPENING PANDORA'S GATE, LOCATED IN THE BASE OF THE MOUNTAIN.
PANDORA'S GATE?
IT'S PARAMOUNT THAT HE DOESN'T OPEN THE GATE.

MERLIN IS ARMED AND EXTREMELY DANGEROUS. SHOW HIM NO MERCY, FOR HE WILL HAVE NONE FOR YOU.

MERLIN HAS A PROTECTIVE SPELL THAT SHIELDS HIM FROM MOST CONVENTIONAL WEAPONS.

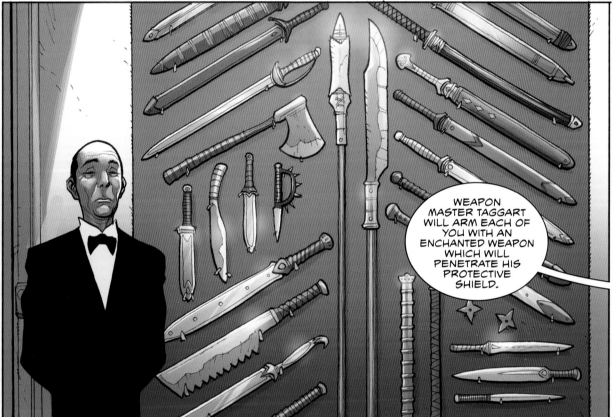

WEAPON MASTER TAGGART WILL ARM EACH OF YOU WITH AN ENCHANTED WEAPON WHICH WILL PENETRATE HIS PROTECTIVE SHIELD.

A WORD, THOMAS.

YOU CAN SAVE YOUR BREATH, SWIGGY. I GAVE YOU MY WORD.

I'LL TAKE CARE OF MERLIN, BRING HIM TO JUSTICE FOR WHAT HE DID TO GRACE AND SEE THIS THING TO THE BLOODY END.

THEN EXCALIBUR IS MINE.

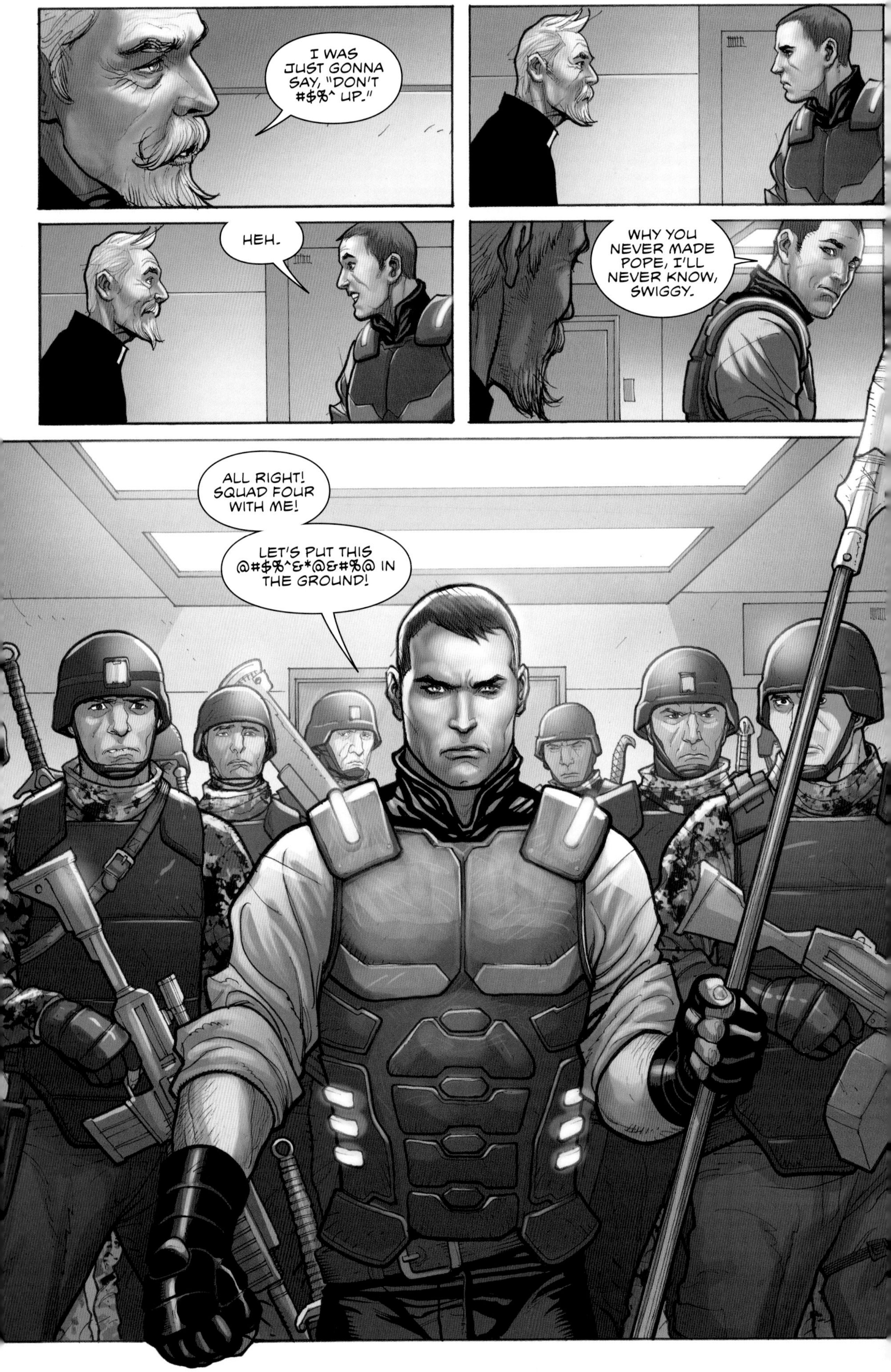
I WAS JUST GONNA SAY, "DON'T #$%^ UP."
HEH.
WHY YOU NEVER MADE POPE, I'LL NEVER KNOW, SWIGGY.
ALL RIGHT! SQUAD FOUR WITH ME!
LET'S PUT THIS @#$%^&*@&#%@ IN THE GROUND!

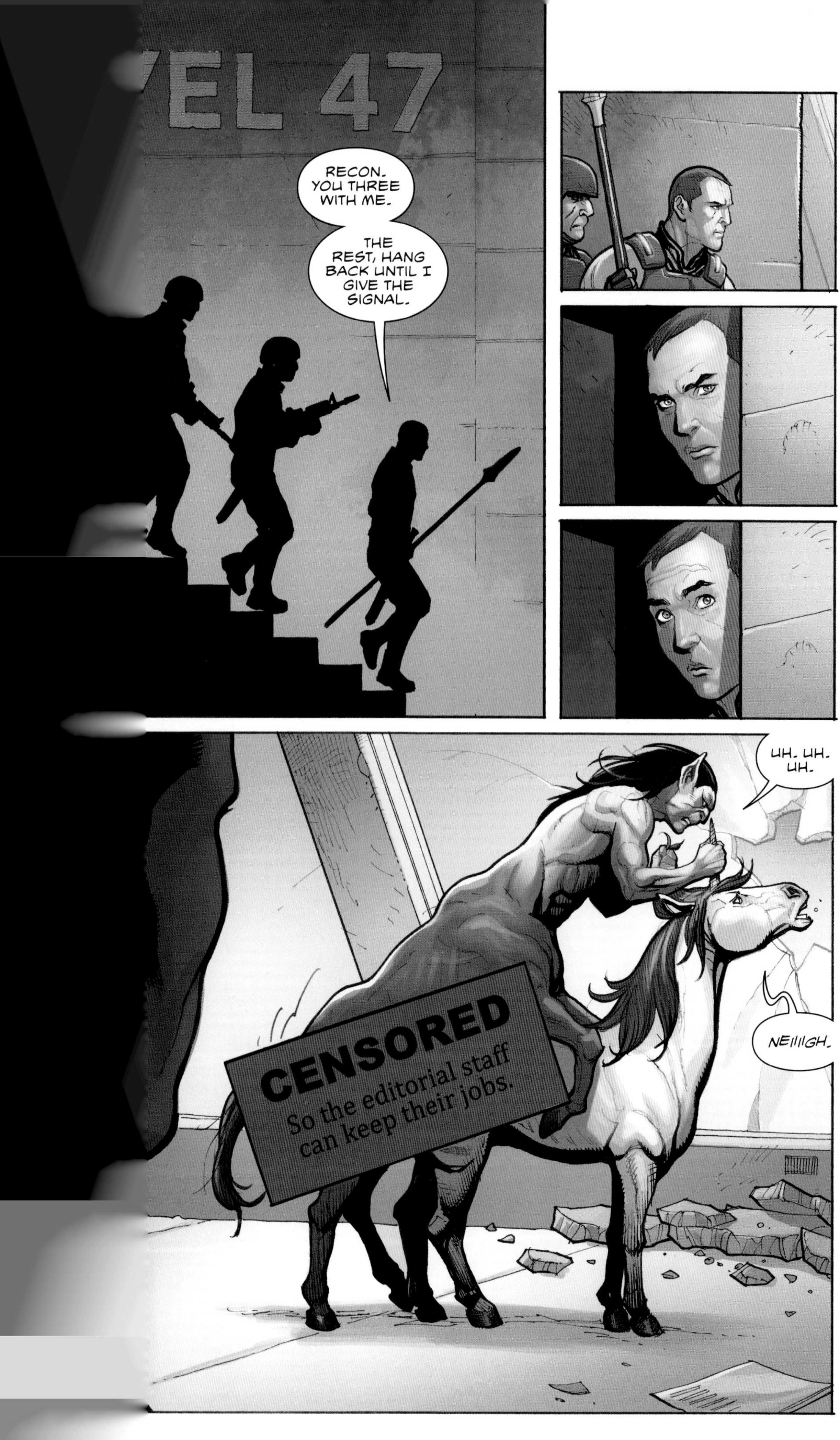

VEL 47
RECON. YOU THREE WITH ME.
THE REST, HANG BACK UNTIL I GIVE THE SIGNAL.
UH. UH. UH.
NEIIIIGH.
CENSORED
So the editorial staff can keep their jobs.

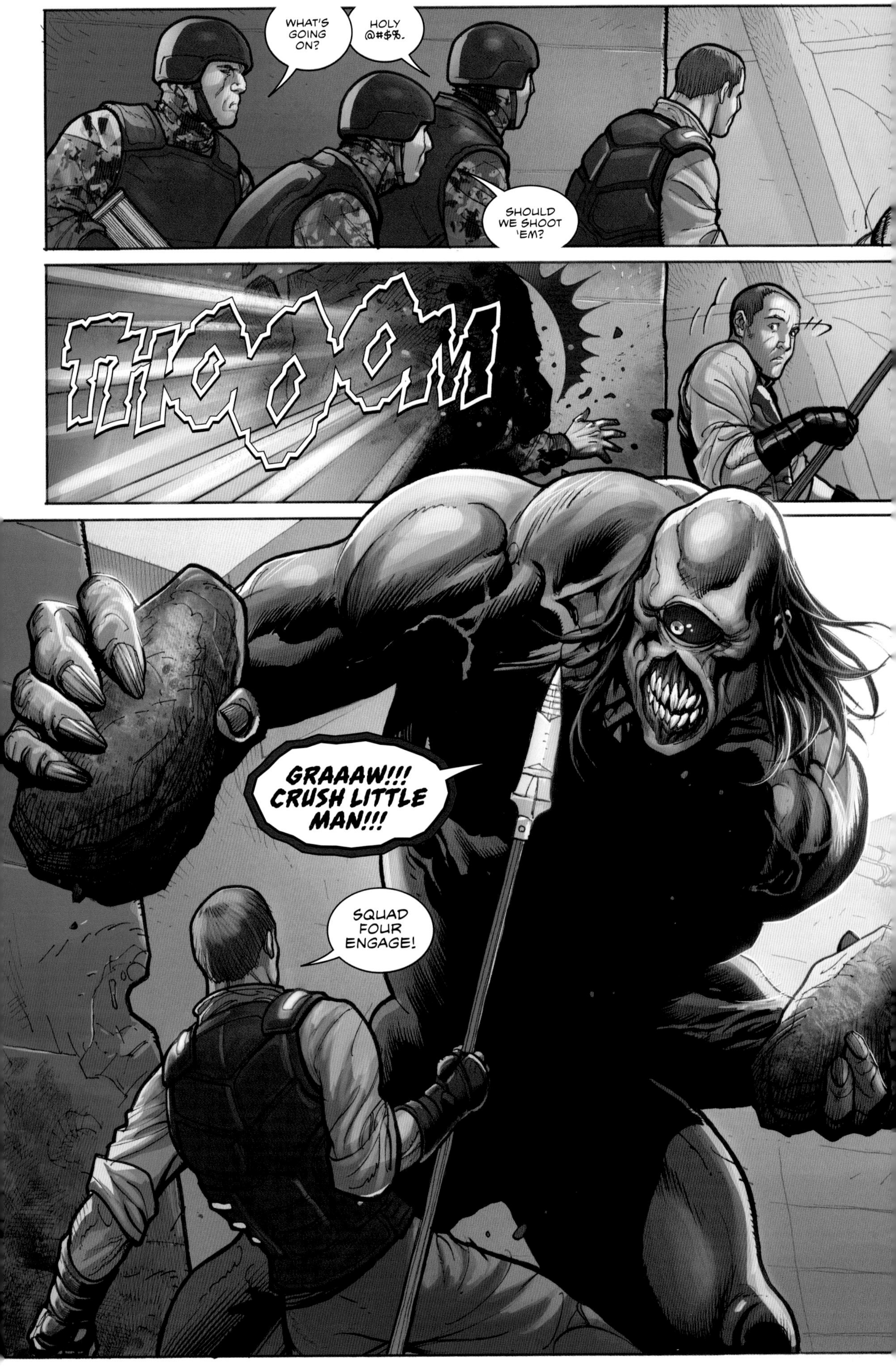
WHAT'S GOING ON?
HOLY @#$%.
SHOULD WE SHOOT 'EM?
THOOOM
GRAAAW!!! CRUSH LITTLE MAN!!!
SQUAD FOUR ENGAGE!

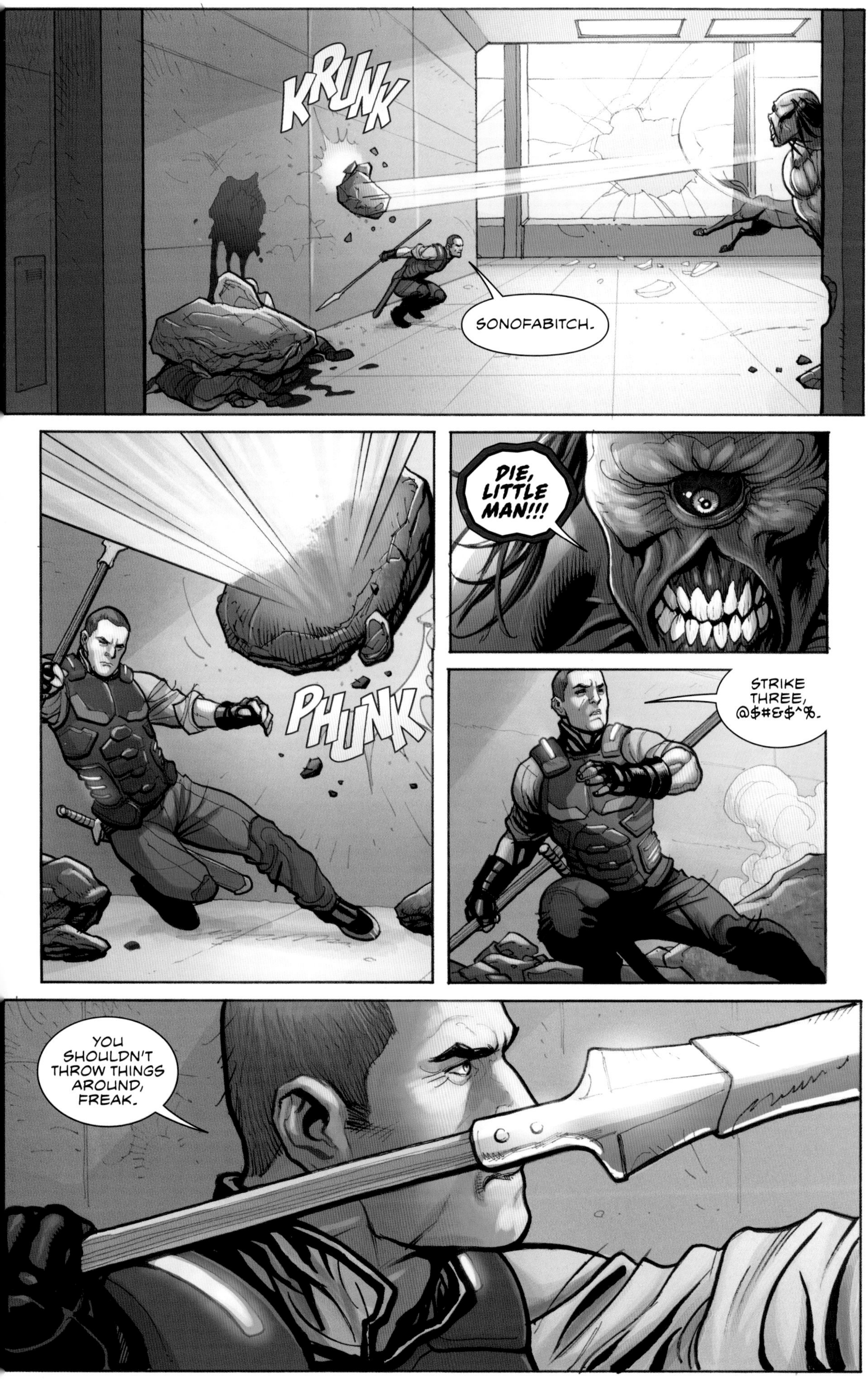
KRUNK
SONOFABITCH.
PHUNK
DIE, LITTLE MAN!!!
STRIKE THREE, @$#&$^%.
YOU SHOULDN'T THROW THINGS AROUND, FREAK.

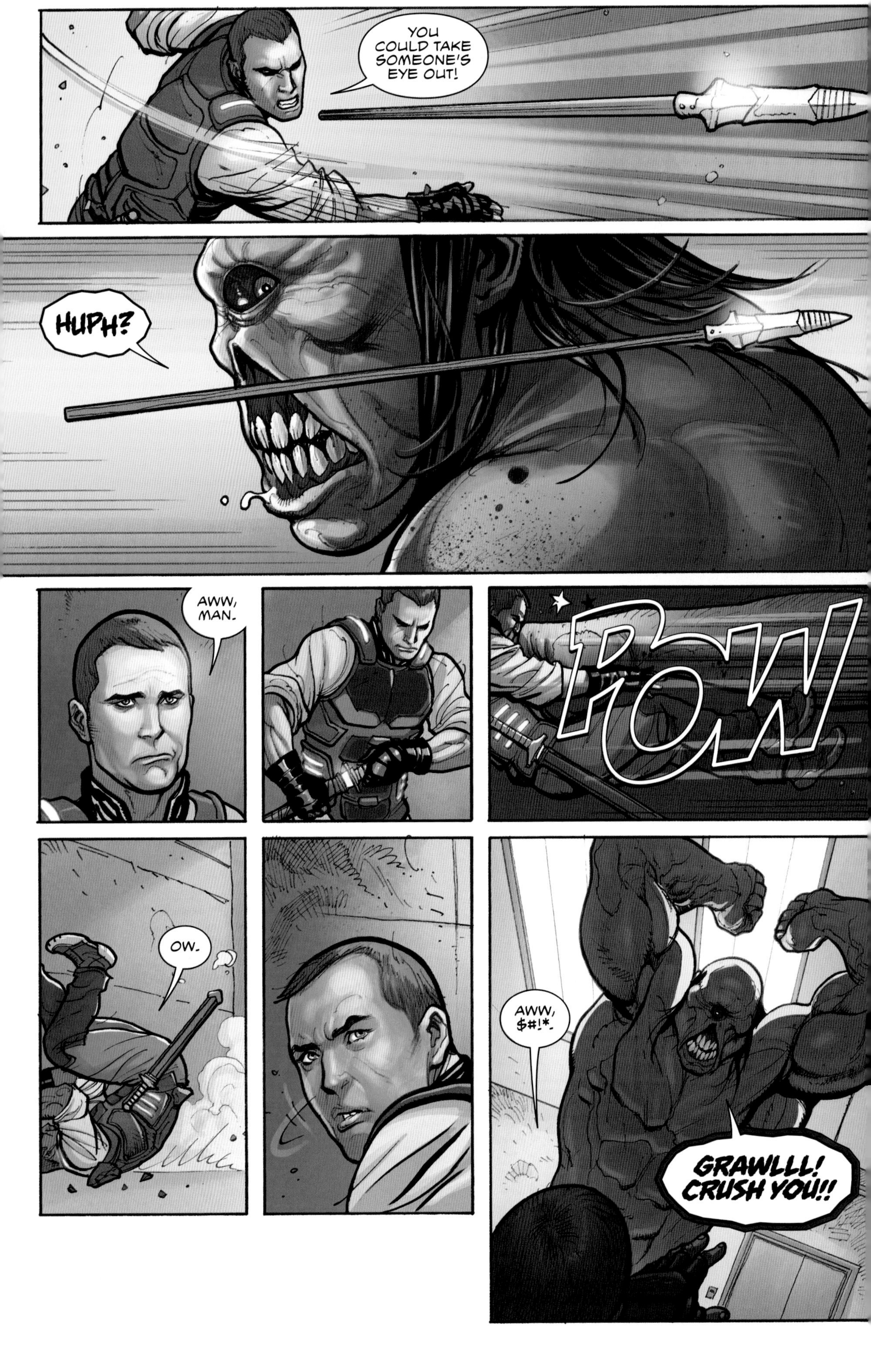
YOU COULD TAKE SOMEONE'S EYE OUT!
HUPH?
AWW, MAN.
POW
OW.
AWW, $#!*.
GRAWLLL! CRUSH YOU!!

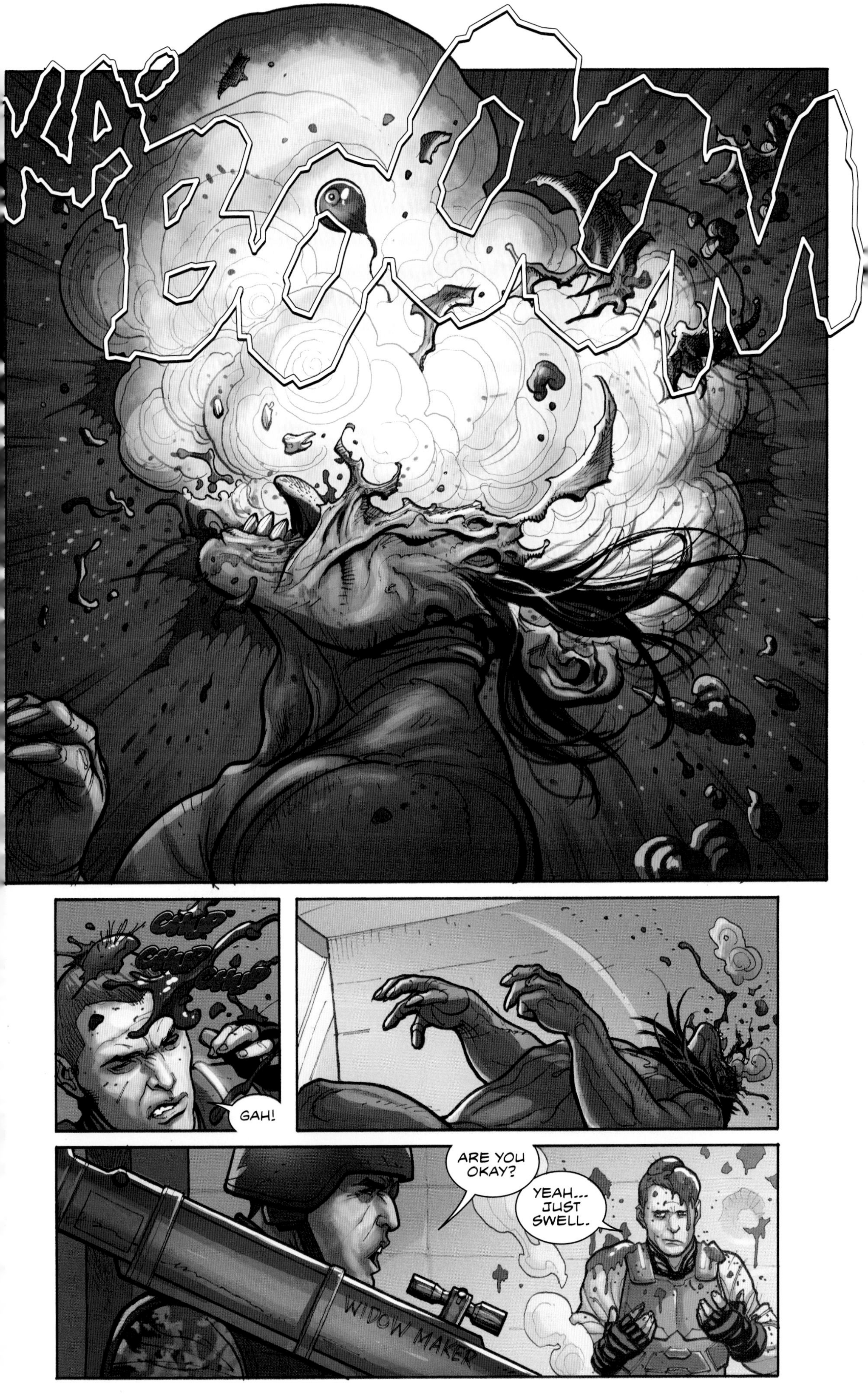
KA-BOOOOM
GAH!
ARE YOU OKAY?
YEAH... JUST SWELL.
WIDOW MAKER

LEVEL 18.

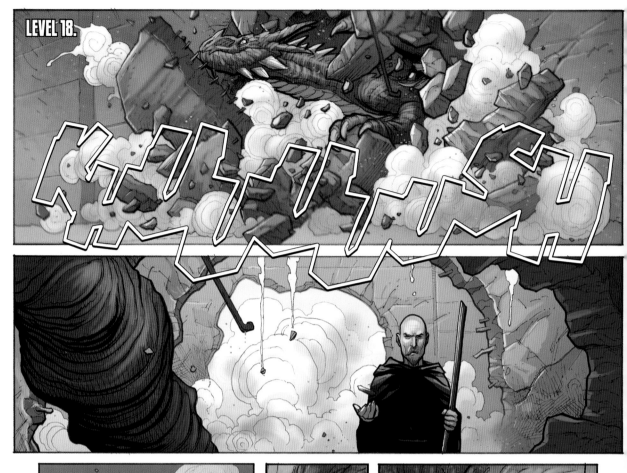

KHHHHHH

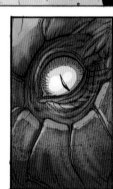

THAT WAY.

THUUM KRAK

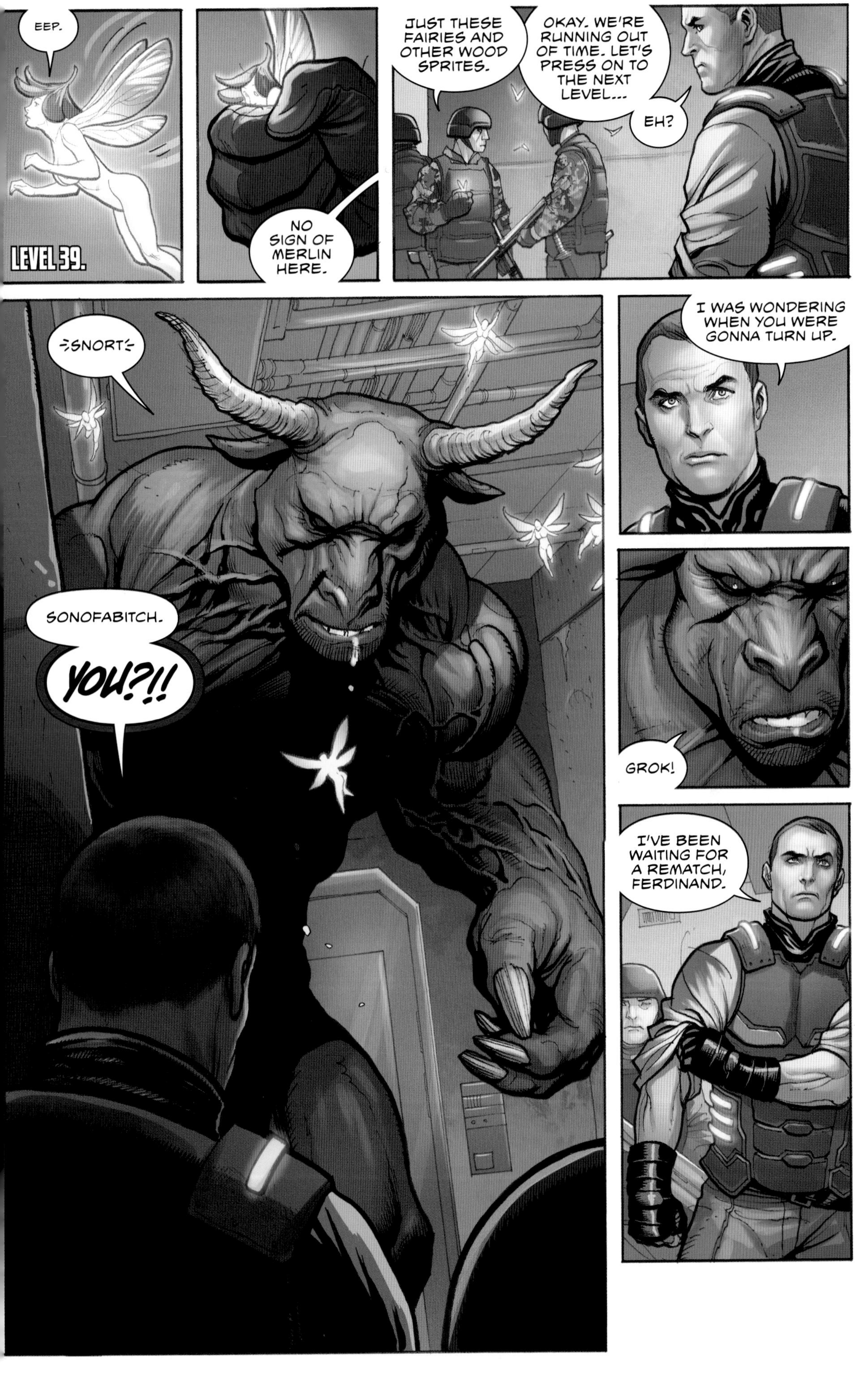
EEP.
LEVEL 39.
NO SIGN OF MERLIN HERE.
JUST THESE FAIRIES AND OTHER WOOD SPRITES.
OKAY. WE'RE RUNNING OUT OF TIME. LET'S PRESS ON TO THE NEXT LEVEL...
EH?
SNORT
SONOFABITCH.
YOU?!!
I WAS WONDERING WHEN YOU WERE GONNA TURN UP.
GROK!
I'VE BEEN WAITING FOR A REMATCH, FERDINAND.

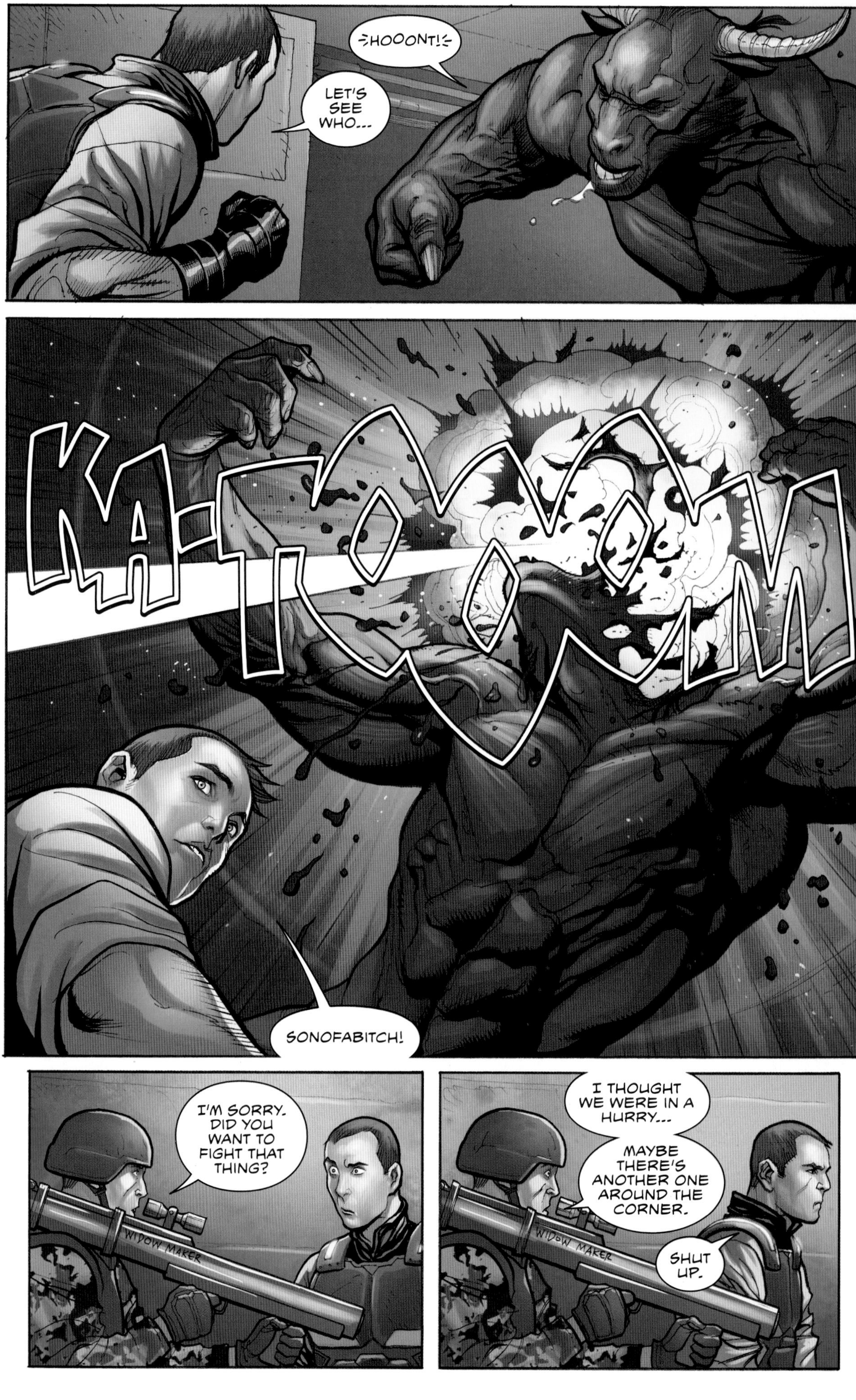

HOOONT!
LET'S SEE WHO...
KA-TROOOM
SONOFABITCH!
I'M SORRY. DID YOU WANT TO FIGHT THAT THING?
WIDOW MAKER
I THOUGHT WE WERE IN A HURRY...
MAYBE THERE'S ANOTHER ONE AROUND THE CORNER.
SHUT UP.

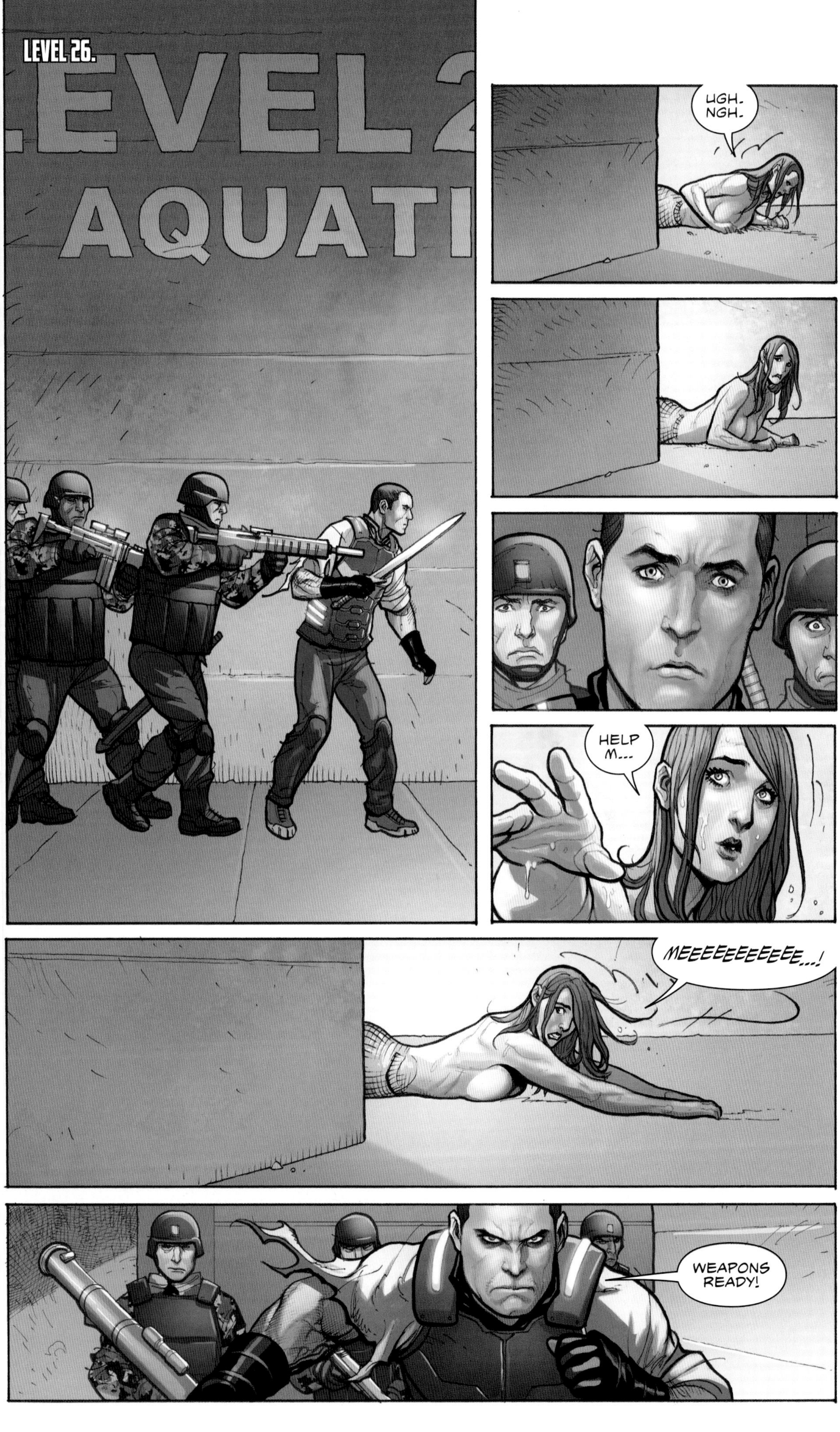
LEVEL 26.
LEVEL 2
AQUATI
UGH. NGH.
HELP M...
MEEEEEEEEEEE...!
WEAPONS READY!

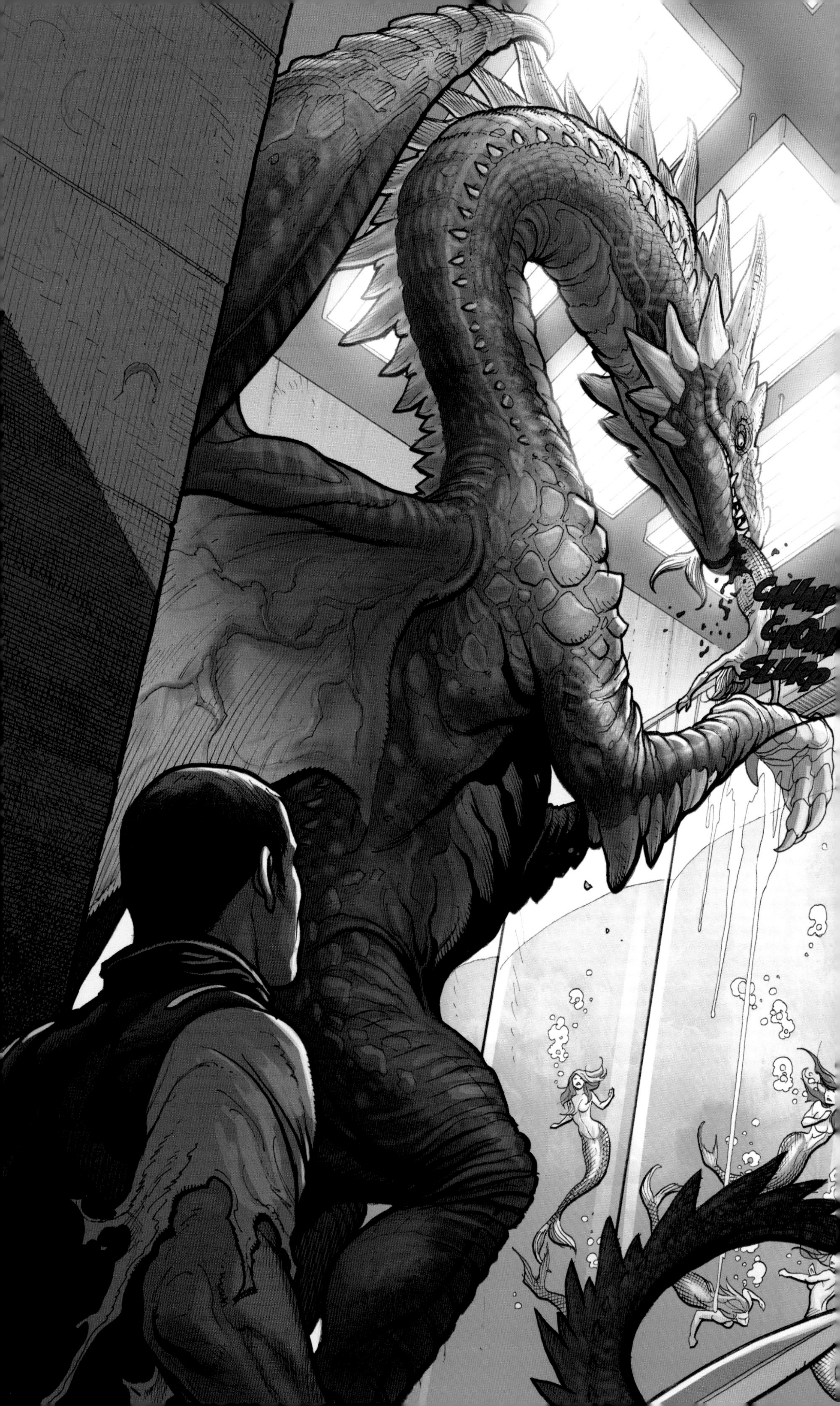
SLURP

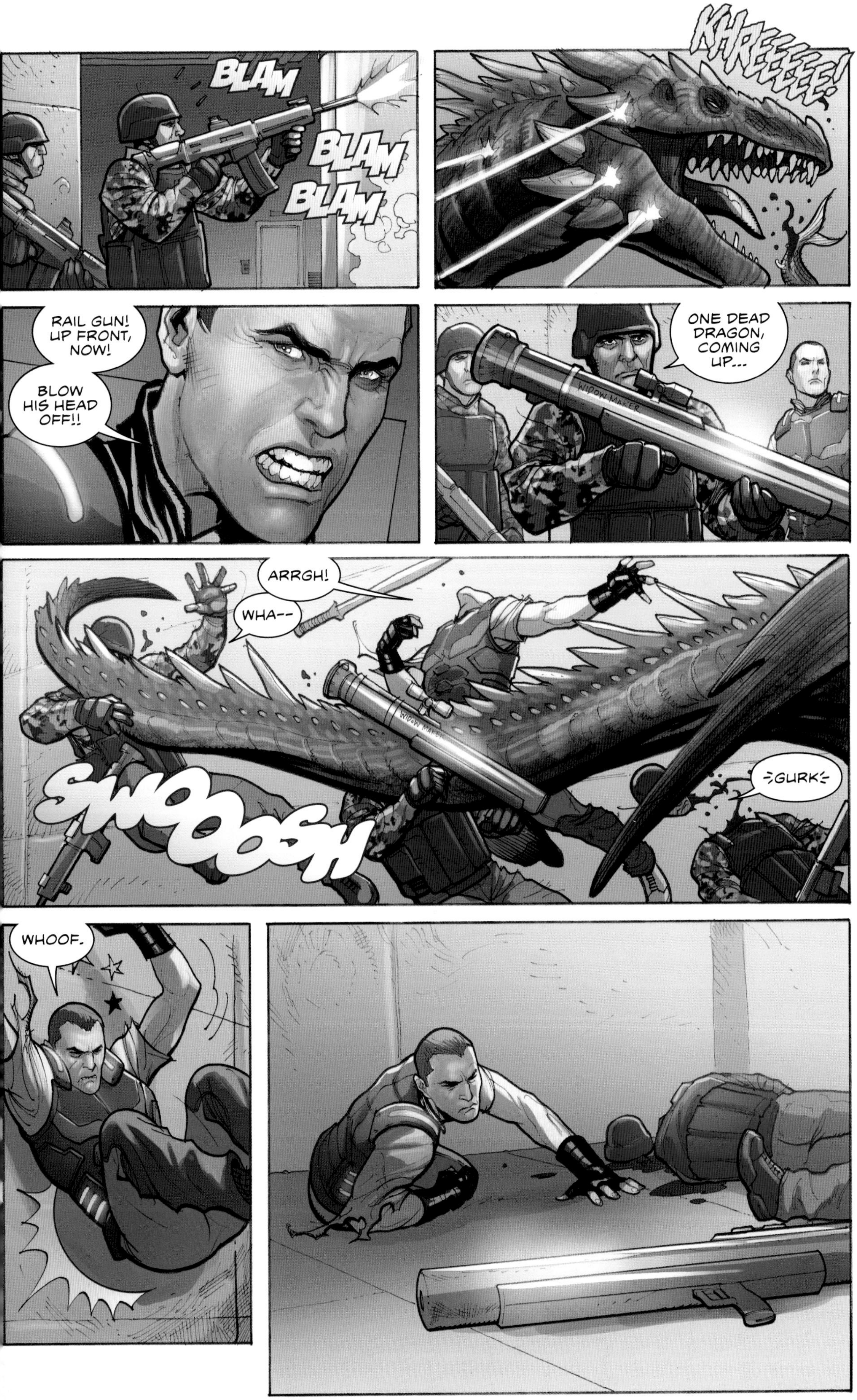
BLAM
BLAM
BLAM
KHREEEEEE!
RAIL GUN! UP FRONT, NOW!
BLOW HIS HEAD OFF!!
ONE DEAD DRAGON, COMING UP...
WIDOW MAKER
ARRGH!
WHA--
SWOOOSH
GURK
WHOOF.

KHUNN

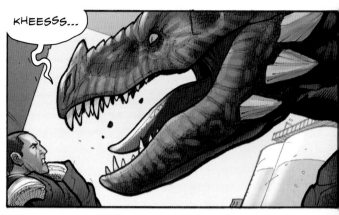

KHEESSS...

BOOOOOOOM

WHO...?

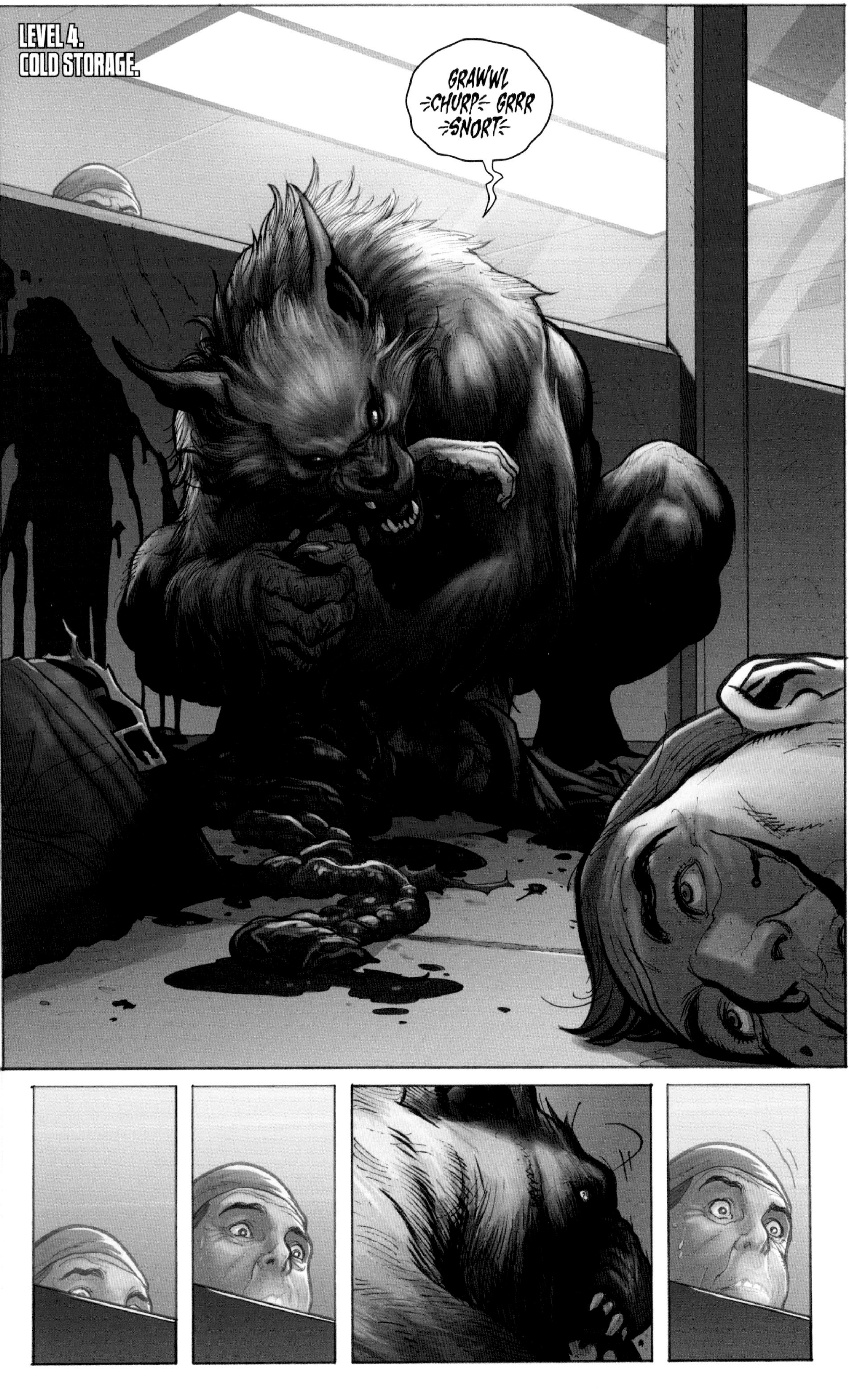
LEVEL 4.
COLD STORAGE.
GRAWWL CHURP GRRR SNORT

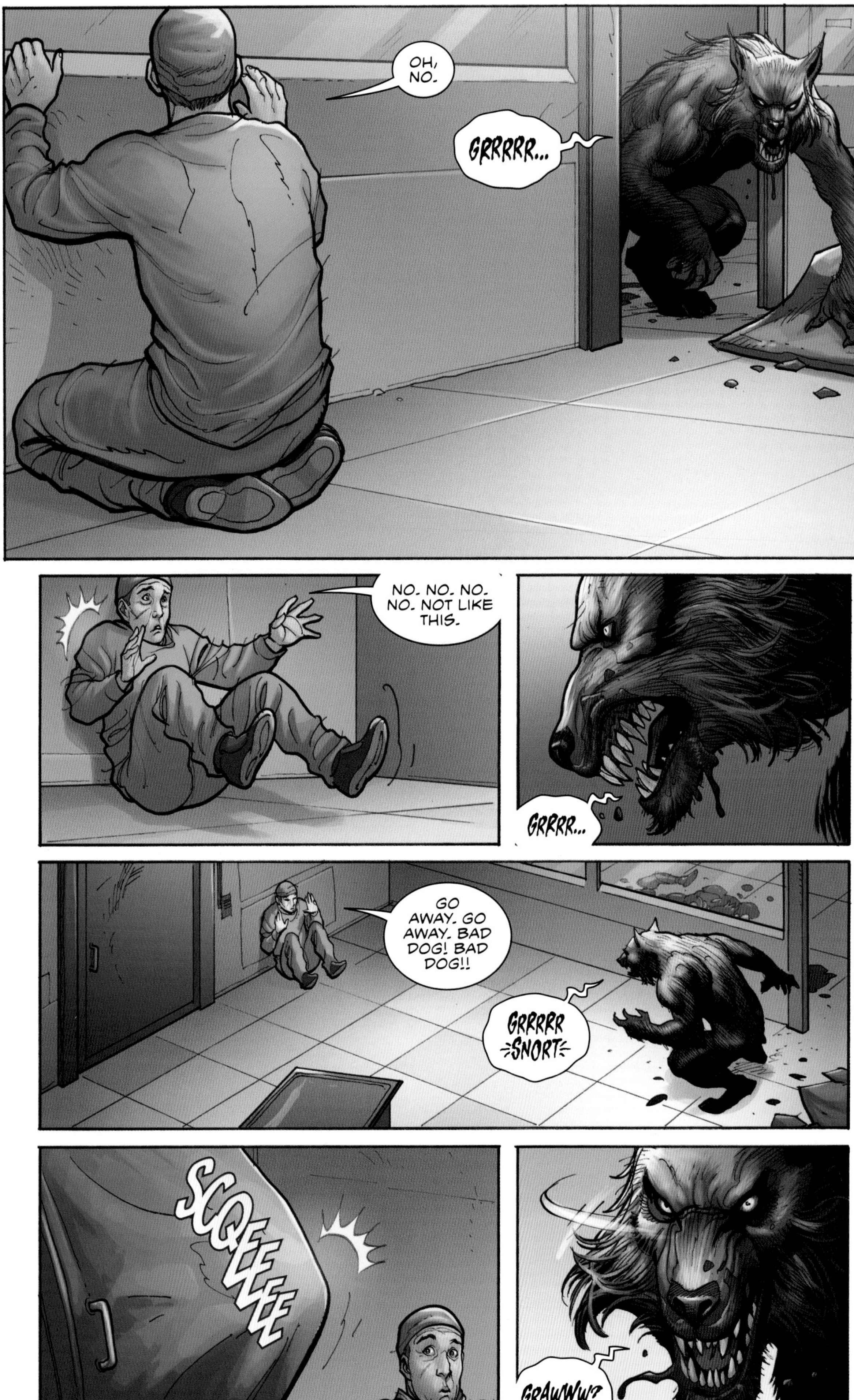
OH, NO.
GRRRRR...
NO. NO. NO. NO. NOT LIKE THIS.
GRRRR...
GO AWAY. GO AWAY. BAD DOG! BAD DOG!!
GRRRRR SNORT
SCQEEEEE
GRAWWW?

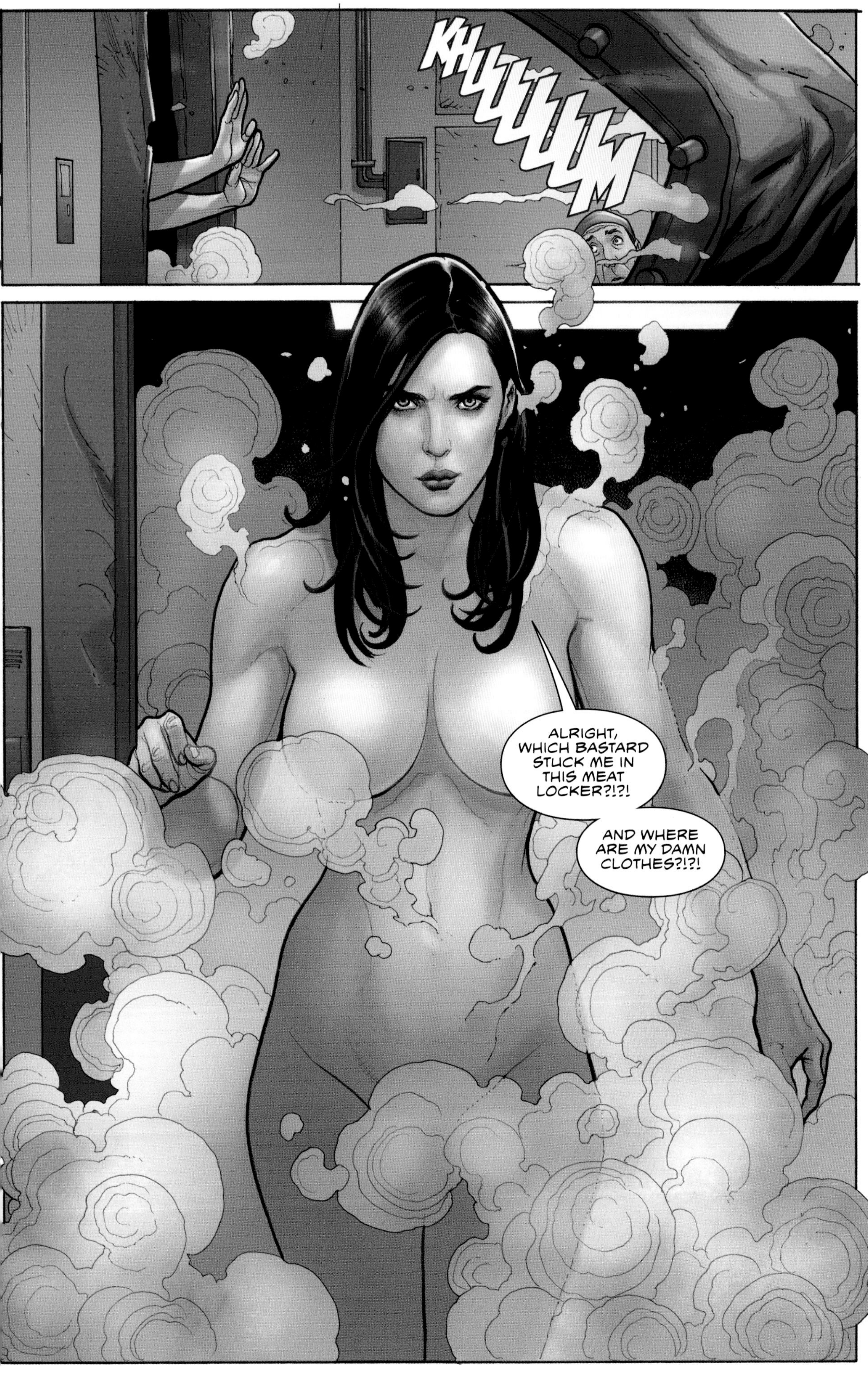

KHUUUUUM
ALRIGHT, WHICH BASTARD STUCK ME IN THIS MEAT LOCKER?!?!
AND WHERE ARE MY DAMN CLOTHES?!?!

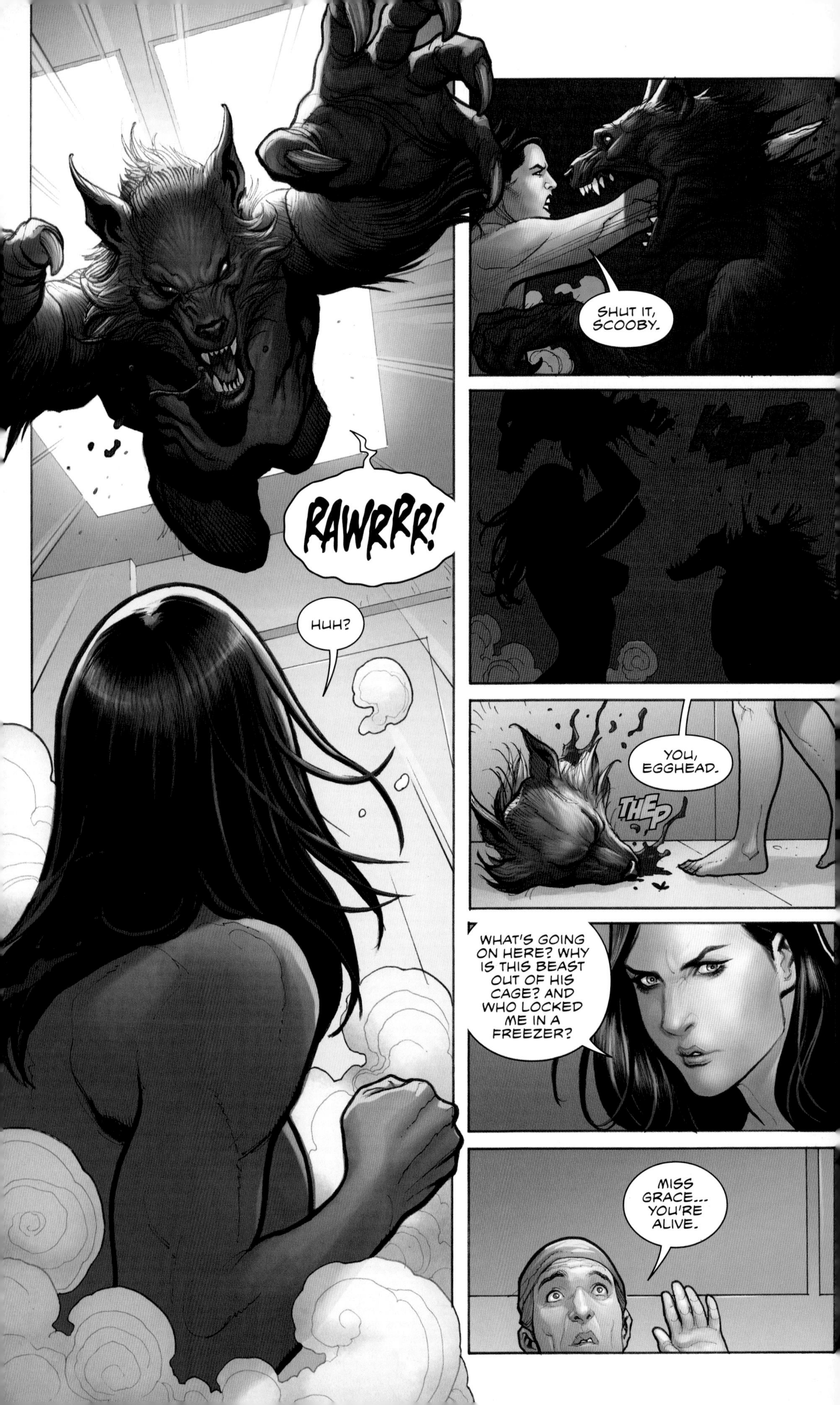
RAWRRR!
HUH?
SHUT IT, SCOOBY.
YOU, EGGHEAD.
THEP
WHAT'S GOING ON HERE? WHY IS THIS BEAST OUT OF HIS CAGE? AND WHO LOCKED ME IN A FREEZER?
MISS GRACE... YOU'RE ALIVE.

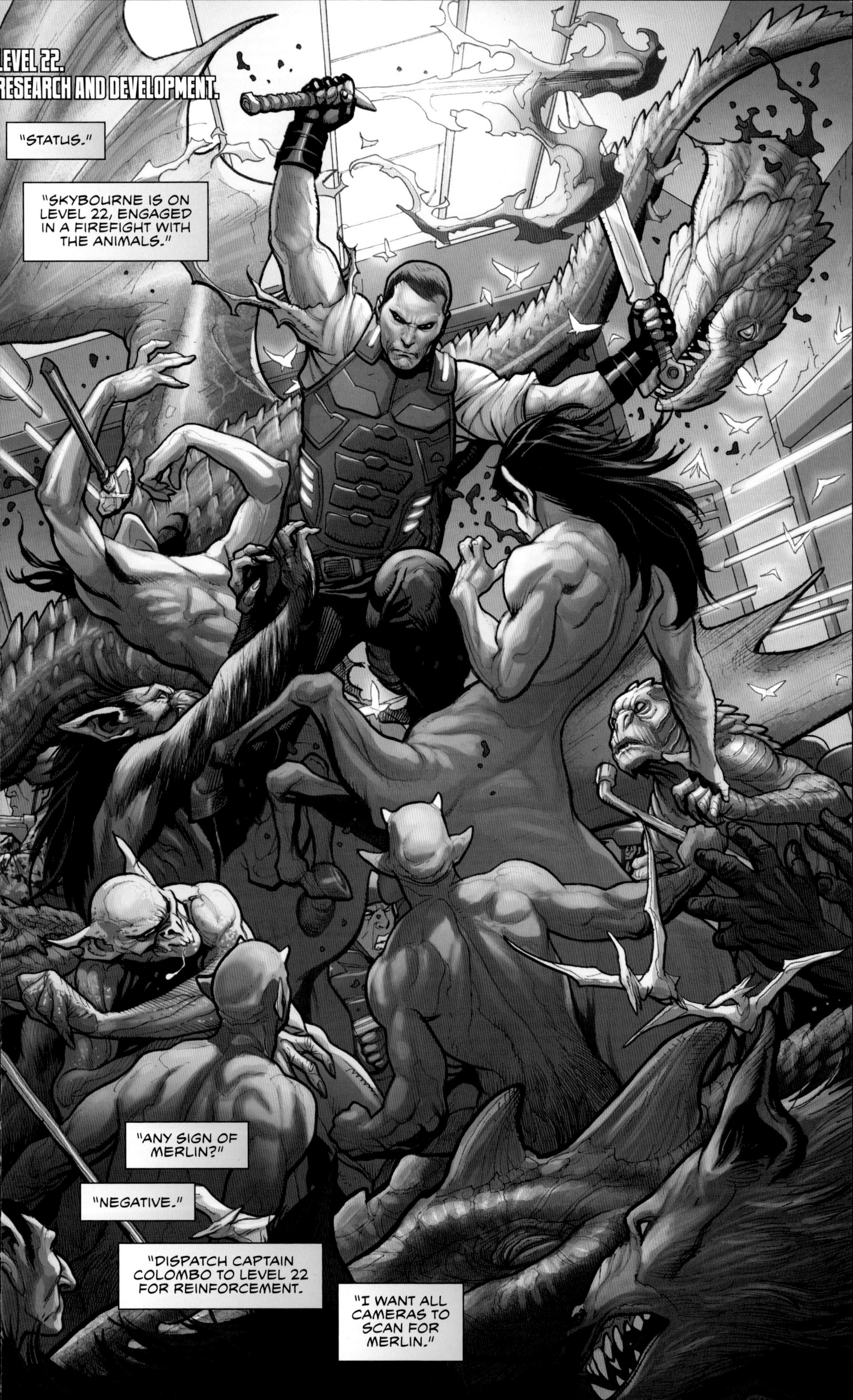
LEVEL 22.
RESEARCH AND DEVELOPMENT.
"STATUS."
"SKYBOURNE IS ON LEVEL 22, ENGAGED IN A FIREFIGHT WITH THE ANIMALS."
"ANY SIGN OF MERLIN?"
"NEGATIVE."
"DISPATCH CAPTAIN COLOMBO TO LEVEL 22 FOR REINFORCEMENT.
"I WANT ALL CAMERAS TO SCAN FOR MERLIN."

WHAT HAPPENED TO POWER?

CIRCUIT OVERLOAD. REROUTING THE GRID.

WE NEED EYES. GET THOSE CAMERAS BACK ONLINE.

WAR ROOM.

POWER INTEGRITY HOLDING.

ARCHIVE, YOU HAVE THE GREEN TO MOVE THE ARTIFACTS OFF-BASE.

HANGARS 1 AND 2 ON STANDBY FOR POSSIBLE EVAC.

CAMERAS BACK ONLINE IN 3, 2, 1...

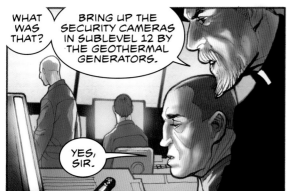

WHAT WAS THAT?

BRING UP THE SECURITY CAMERAS IN SUBLEVEL 12 BY THE GEOTHERMAL GENERATORS.

YES, SIR.

OH, $#!&.

SKYBOURNE! GET YOUR ASS TO SUBLEVEL 12!!

RIGHT NOW!!!

MERLIN HAS UNEARTHED PANDORA'S GATE!!!

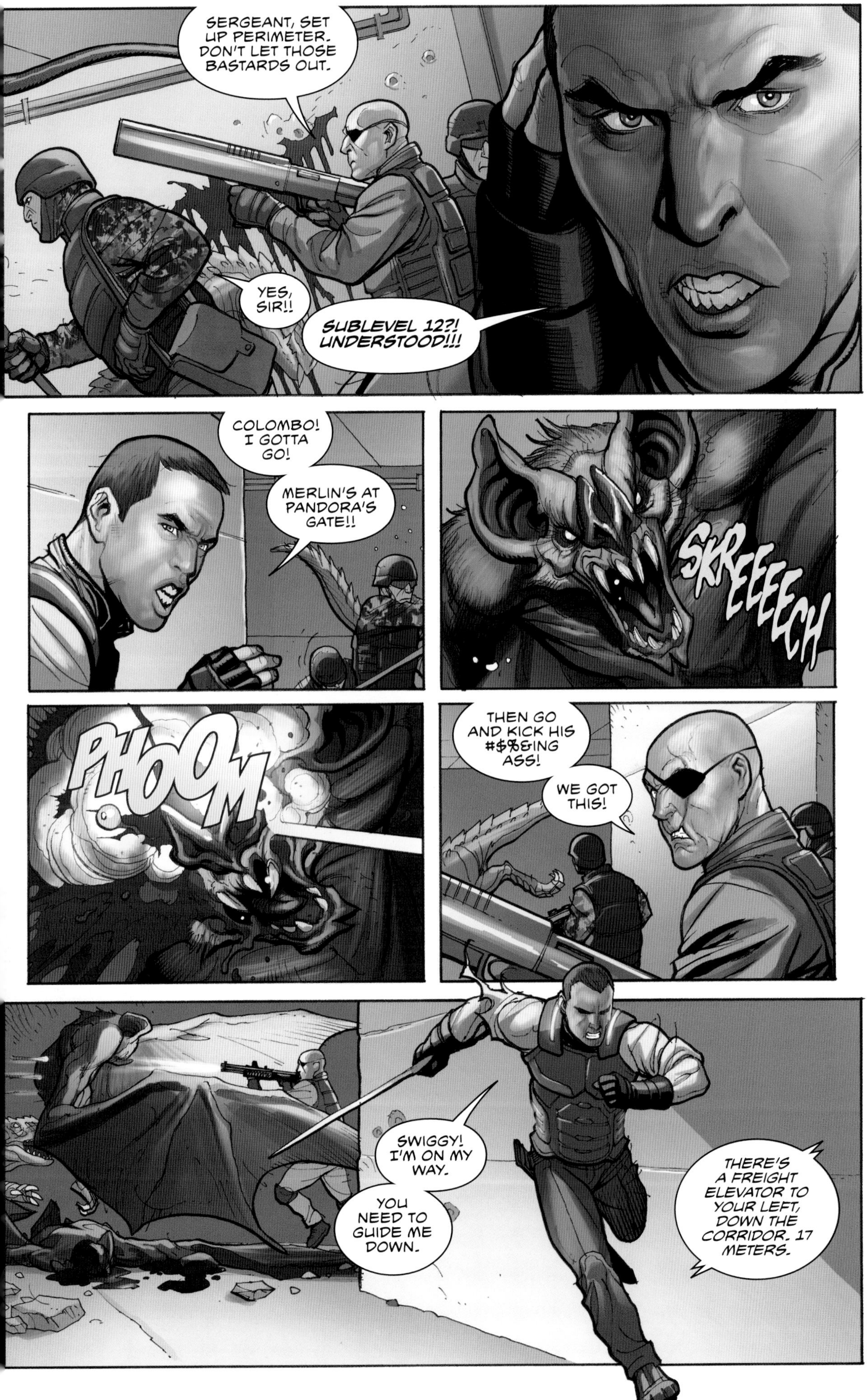
SERGEANT, SET UP PERIMETER. DON'T LET THOSE BASTARDS OUT.
YES, SIR!!
SUBLEVEL 12?! UNDERSTOOD!!!
COLOMBO! I GOTTA GO!
MERLIN'S AT PANDORA'S GATE!!
SKREEEEECH
PHOOM
THEN GO AND KICK HIS #$%&ING ASS!
WE GOT THIS!
SWIGGY! I'M ON MY WAY.
YOU NEED TO GUIDE ME DOWN.
THERE'S A FREIGHT ELEVATOR TO YOUR LEFT, DOWN THE CORRIDOR. 17 METERS.

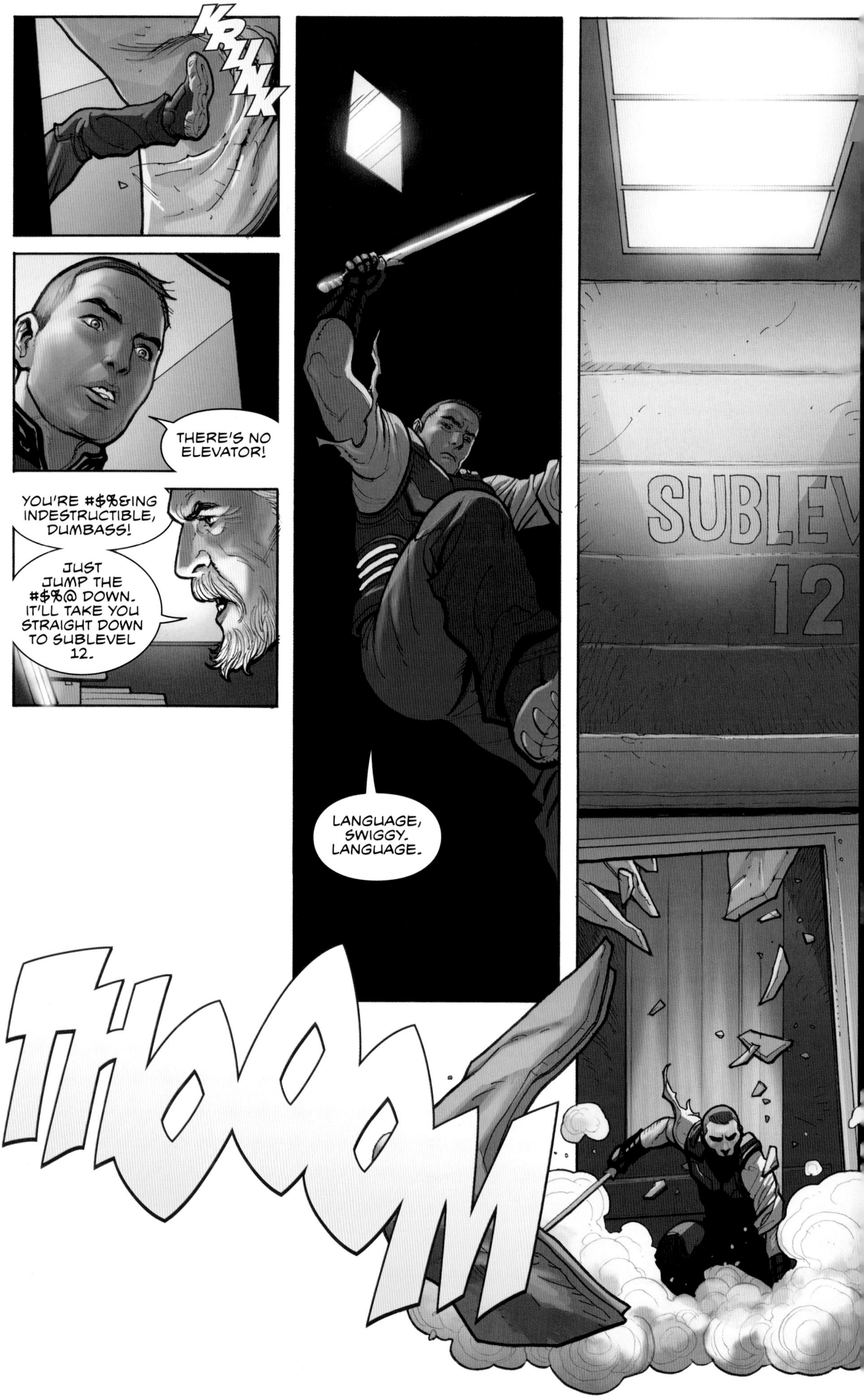
KRUNK
THERE'S NO ELEVATOR!
YOU'RE #$%&ING INDESTRUCTIBLE, DUMBASS!
JUST JUMP THE #$%@ DOWN. IT'LL TAKE YOU STRAIGHT DOWN TO SUBLEVEL 12.
LANGUAGE, SWIGGY. LANGUAGE.
SUBLEV
12
THOOM

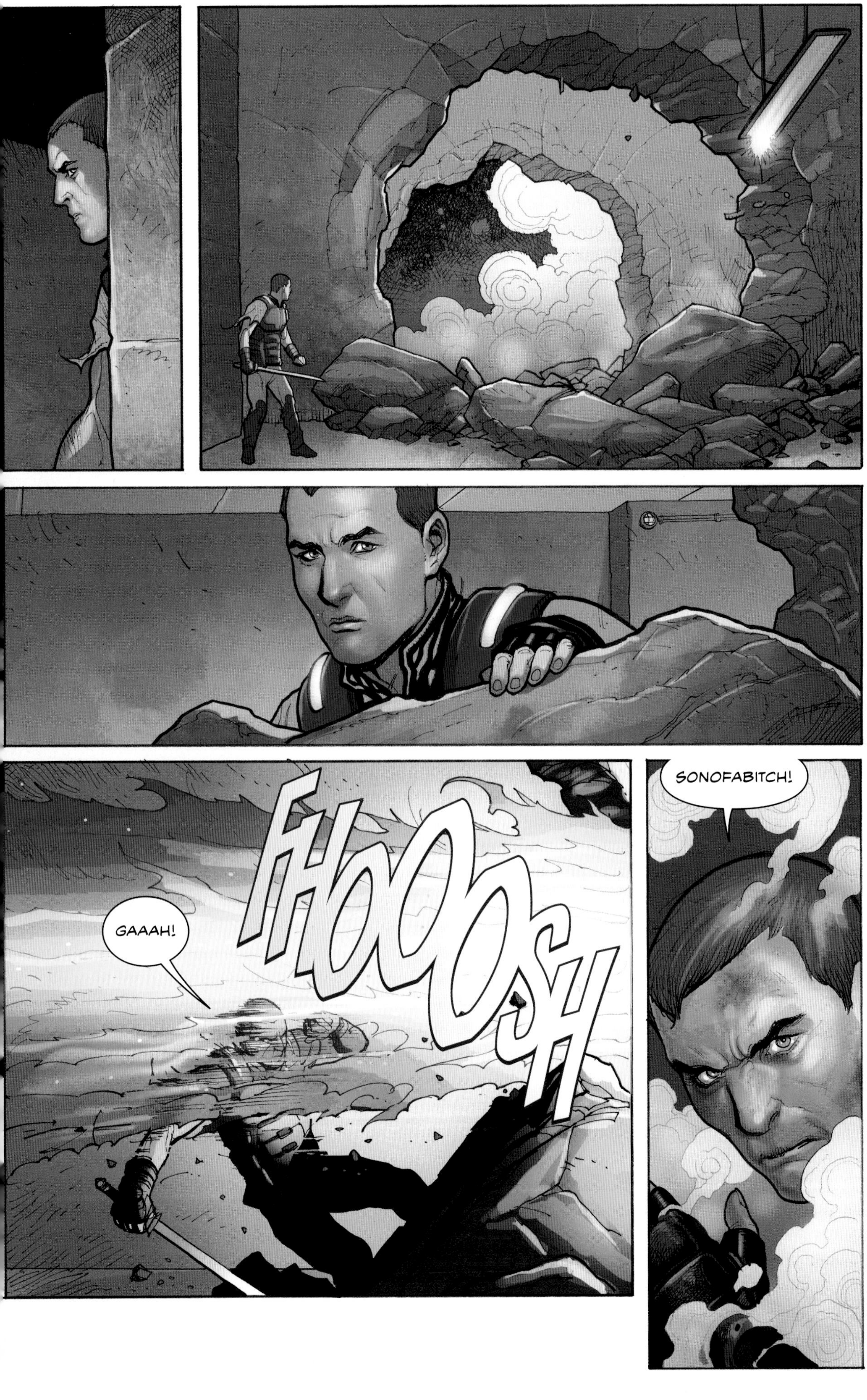
FHOOOSH
GAAAH!
SONOFABITCH!

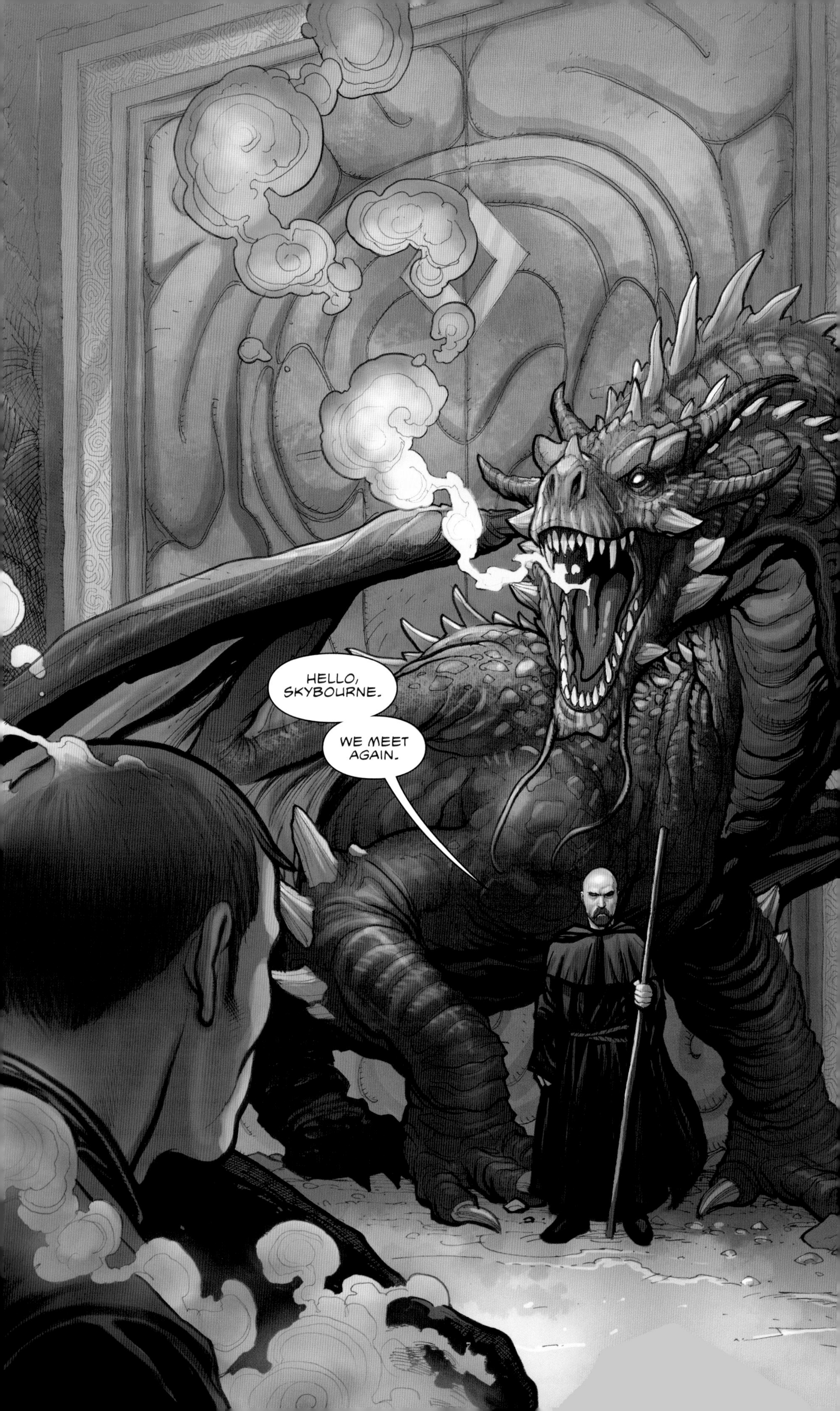
HELLO, SKYBOURNE.
WE MEET AGAIN.

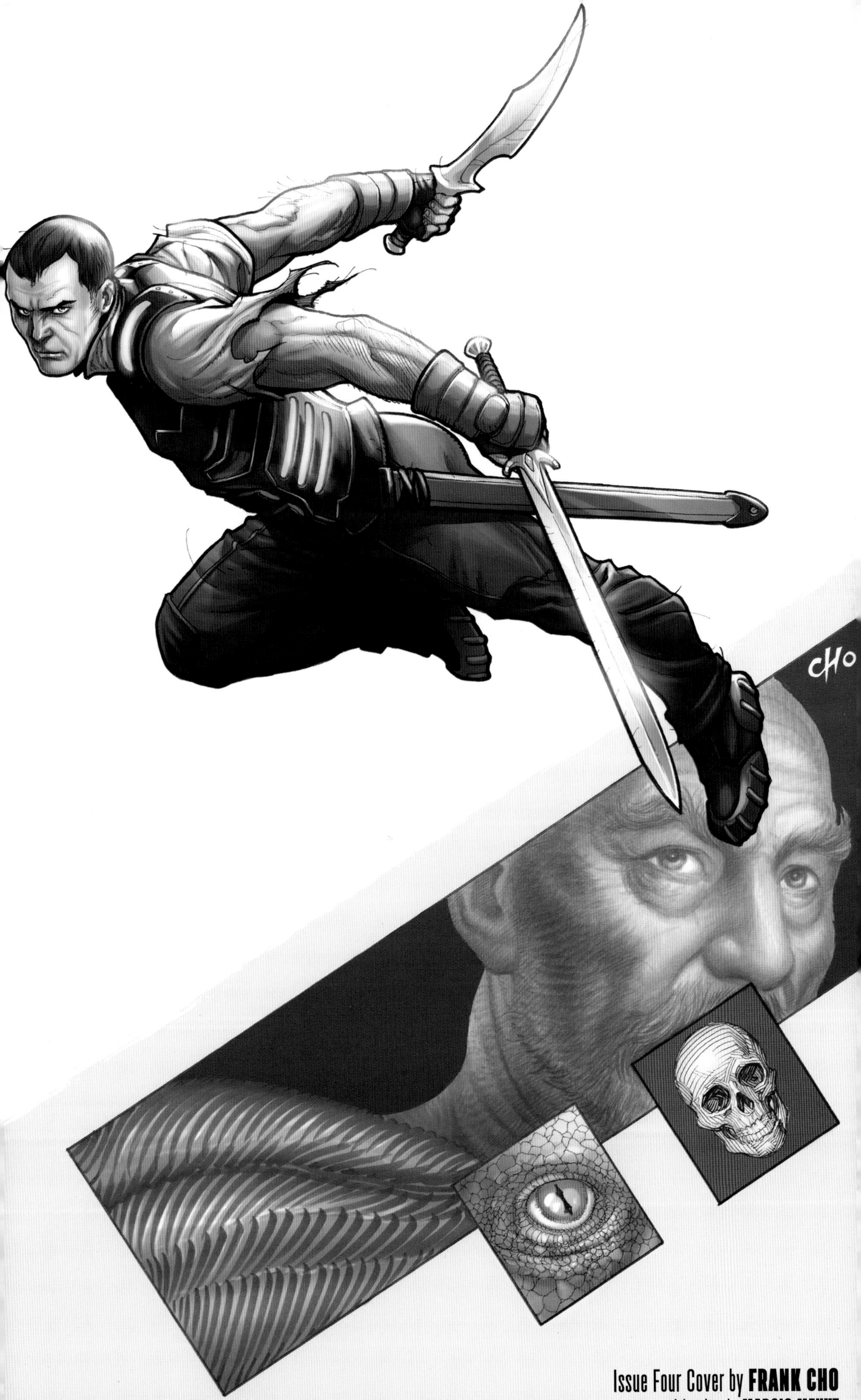
CHO

Issue Four Cover by **FRANK CHO**
with colors by **MARCIO MENYZ**

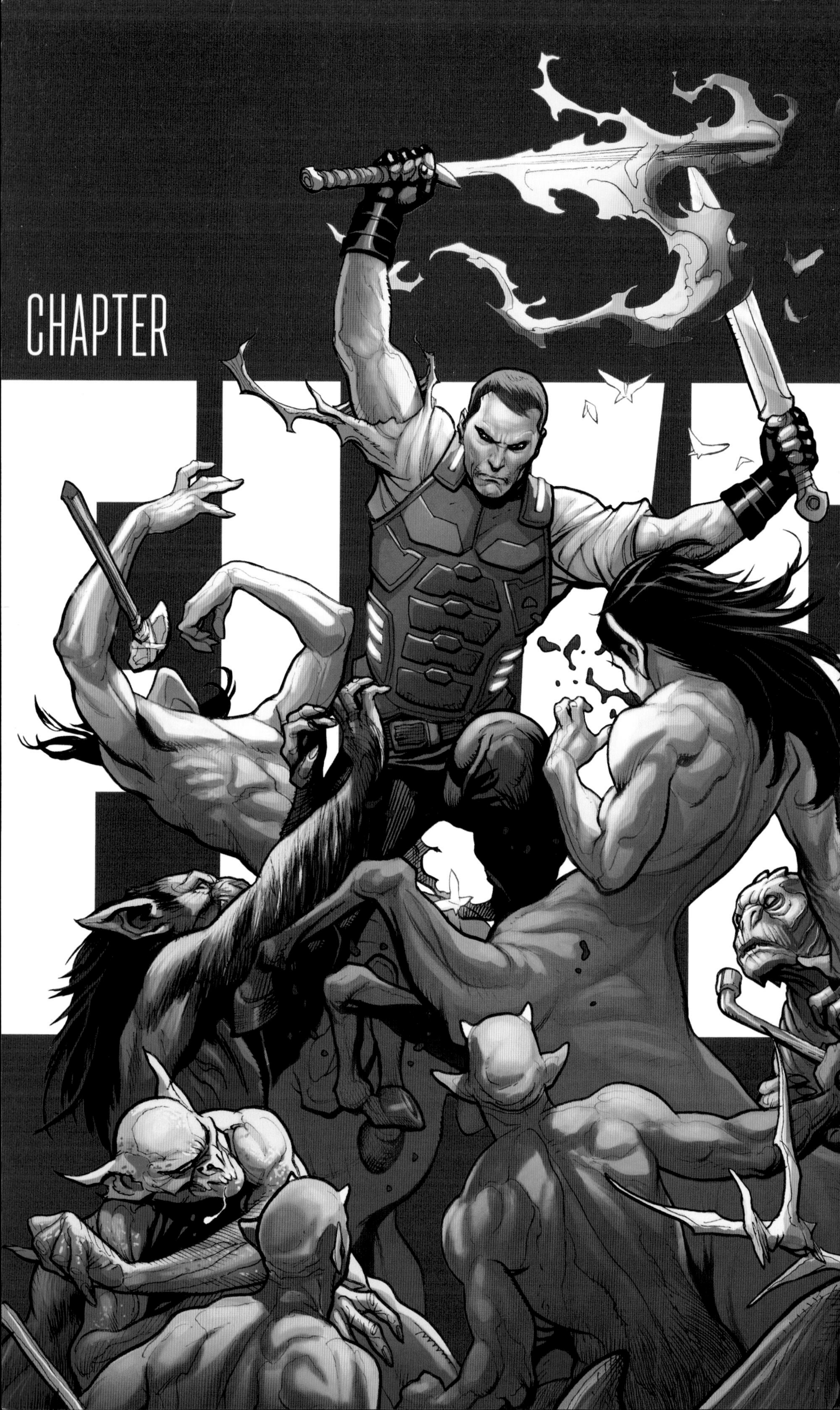
CHAPTER

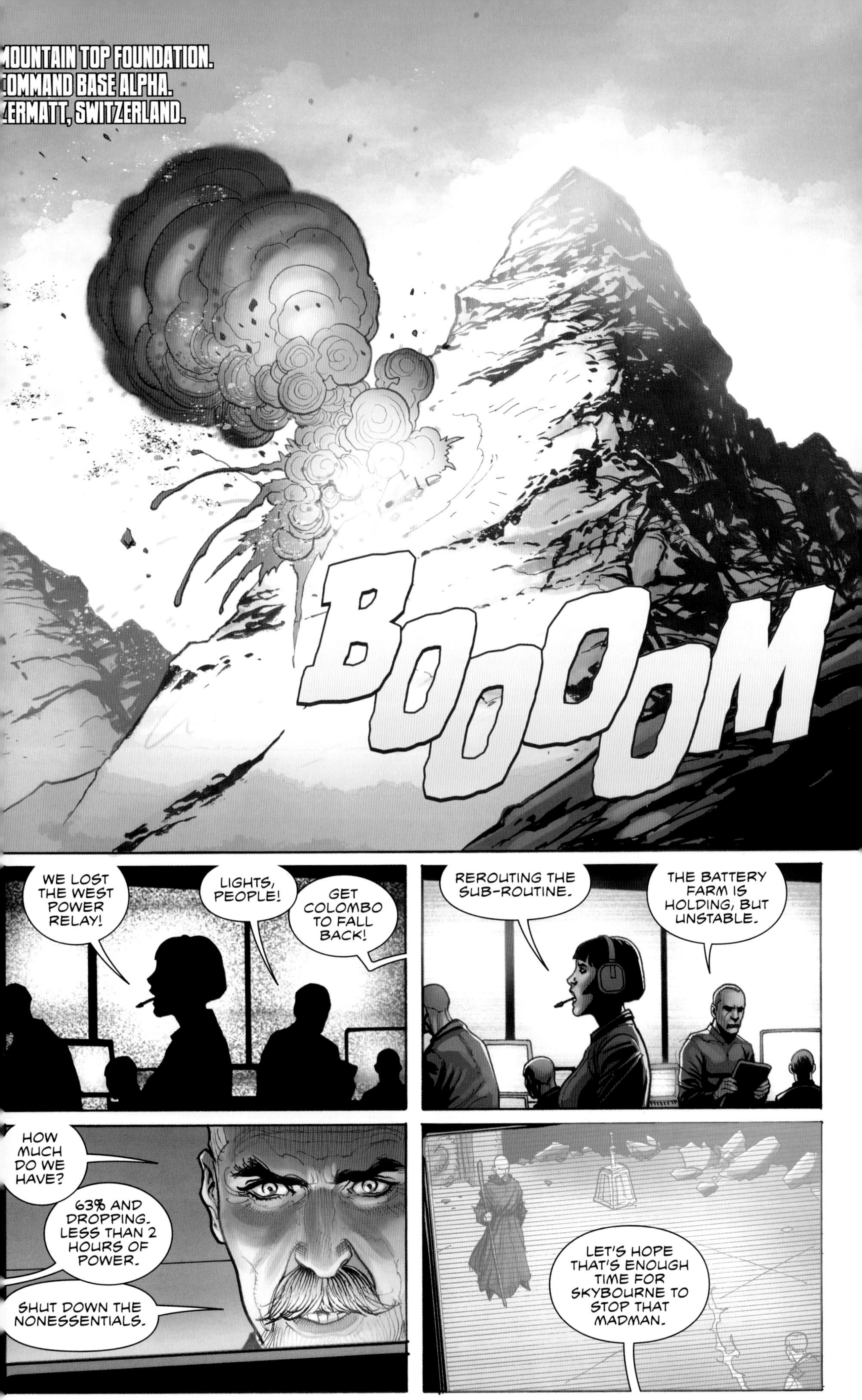
MOUNTAIN TOP FOUNDATION.
COMMAND BASE ALPHA.
ZERMATT, SWITZERLAND.
BOOOOOM
WE LOST THE WEST POWER RELAY!
LIGHTS, PEOPLE!
GET COLOMBO TO FALL BACK!
REROUTING THE SUB-ROUTINE.
THE BATTERY FARM IS HOLDING, BUT UNSTABLE.
HOW MUCH DO WE HAVE?
63% AND DROPPING. LESS THAN 2 HOURS OF POWER.
SHUT DOWN THE NONESSENTIALS.
LET'S HOPE THAT'S ENOUGH TIME FOR SKYBOURNE TO STOP THAT MADMAN.

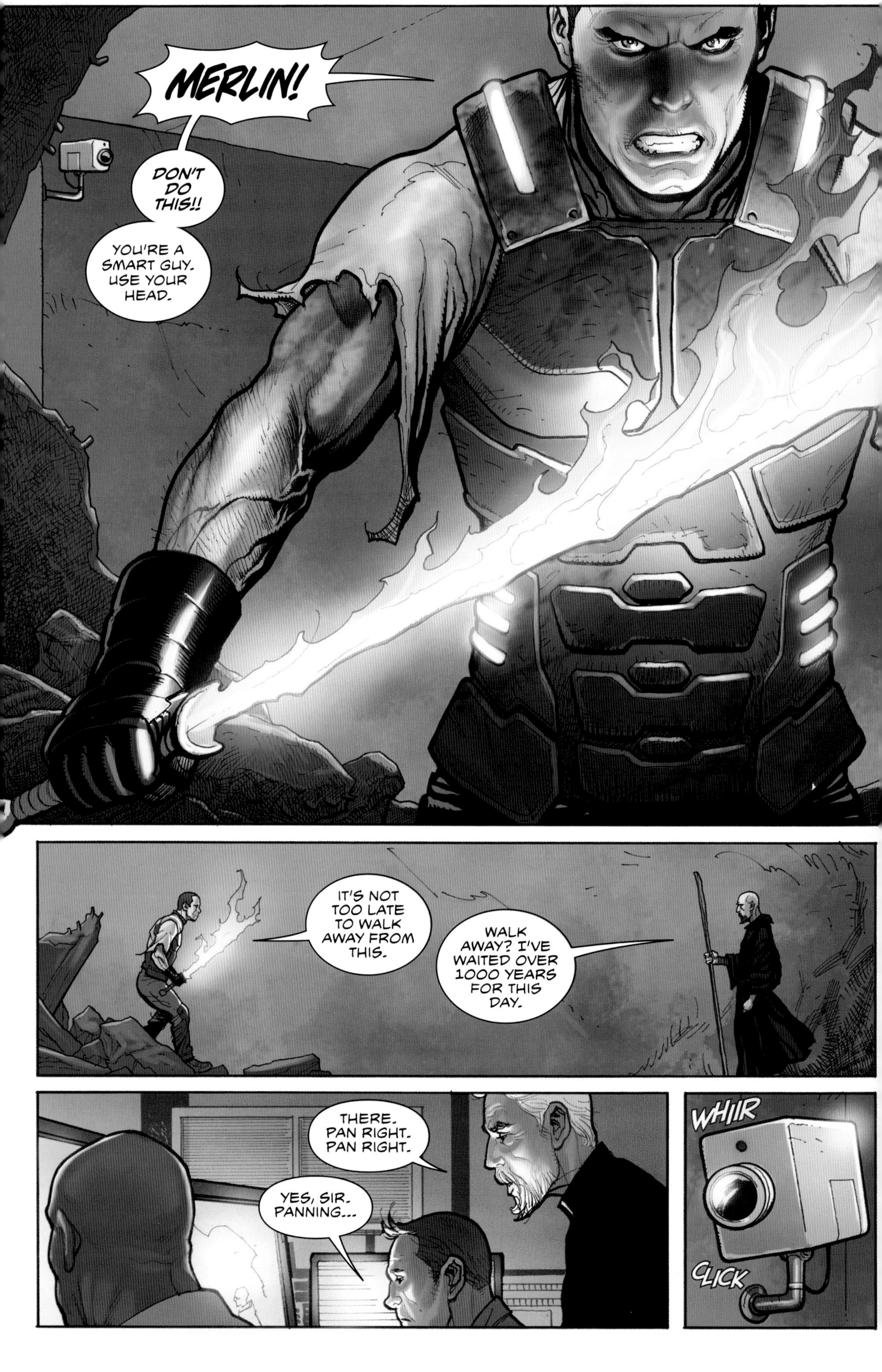
MERLIN!
DON'T DO THIS!!
YOU'RE A SMART GUY. USE YOUR HEAD.
IT'S NOT TOO LATE TO WALK AWAY FROM THIS.
WALK AWAY? I'VE WAITED OVER 1000 YEARS FOR THIS DAY.
THERE. PAN RIGHT. PAN RIGHT.
YES, SIR. PANNING...
WHIIR
CLICK

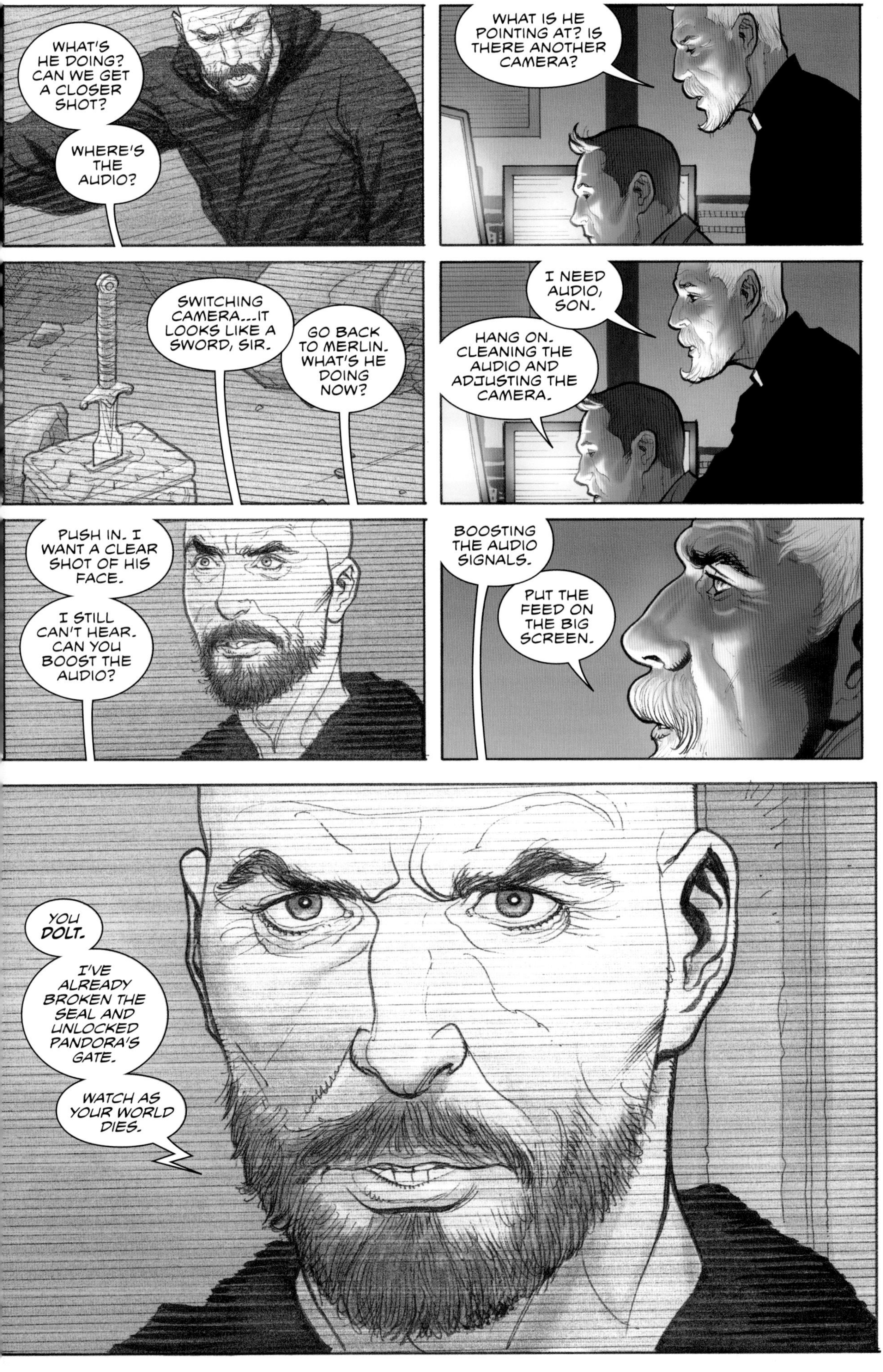

WHAT'S HE DOING? CAN WE GET A CLOSER SHOT?
WHERE'S THE AUDIO?
WHAT IS HE POINTING AT? IS THERE ANOTHER CAMERA?
SWITCHING CAMERA...IT LOOKS LIKE A SWORD, SIR.
GO BACK TO MERLIN. WHAT'S HE DOING NOW?
I NEED AUDIO, SON.
HANG ON. CLEANING THE AUDIO AND ADJUSTING THE CAMERA.
PUSH IN. I WANT A CLEAR SHOT OF HIS FACE.
I STILL CAN'T HEAR. CAN YOU BOOST THE AUDIO?
BOOSTING THE AUDIO SIGNALS.
PUT THE FEED ON THE BIG SCREEN.
YOU DOLT.
I'VE ALREADY BROKEN THE SEAL AND UNLOCKED PANDORA'S GATE.
WATCH AS YOUR WORLD DIES.

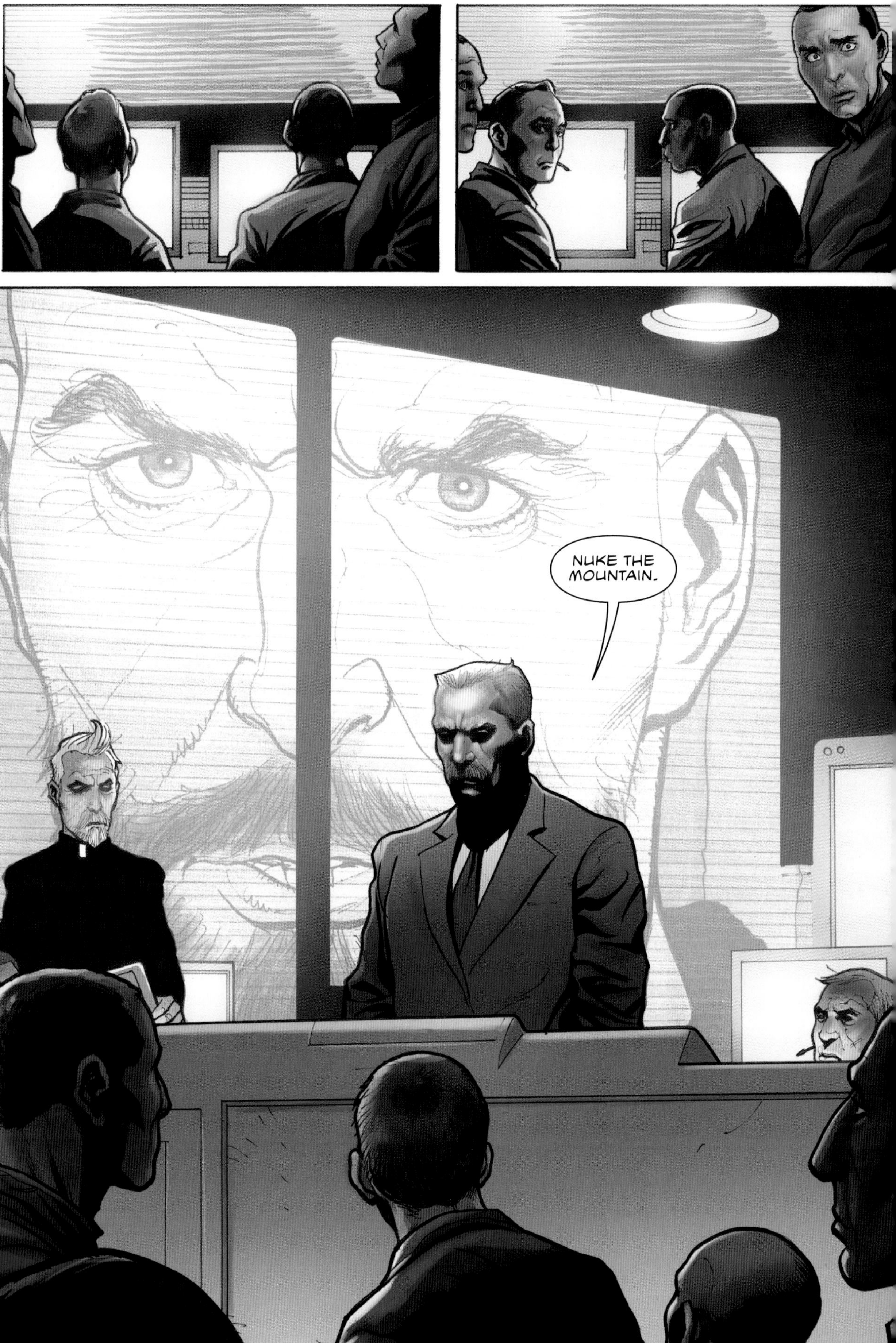
NUKE THE
MOUNTAIN.

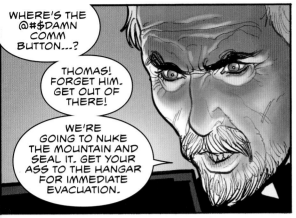

WHERE'S THE @#$DAMN COMM BUTTON...?

THOMAS! FORGET HIM. GET OUT OF THERE!

WE'RE GOING TO NUKE THE MOUNTAIN AND SEAL IT. GET YOUR ASS TO THE HANGAR FOR IMMEDIATE EVACUATION.

THIS IS THE END OF THE LINE FOR ME. REMEMBER YOUR PROMISE.

GOODBYE, SWIGGY.

WELL?

HE'S NOT COMING.

SO BE IT.

ALL RIGHT, PEOPLE! SOUND THE ALARM!

THE MOUNTAIN IS LOST! ALL PERSONNEL, FULL EVAC NOW!

CAPTAIN COLOMBO! PREP THE NUKE. WE'RE COLLAPSING THE MOUNTAIN AND SEALING THE GATE.

COUNTDOWN, 30 MINUTES.

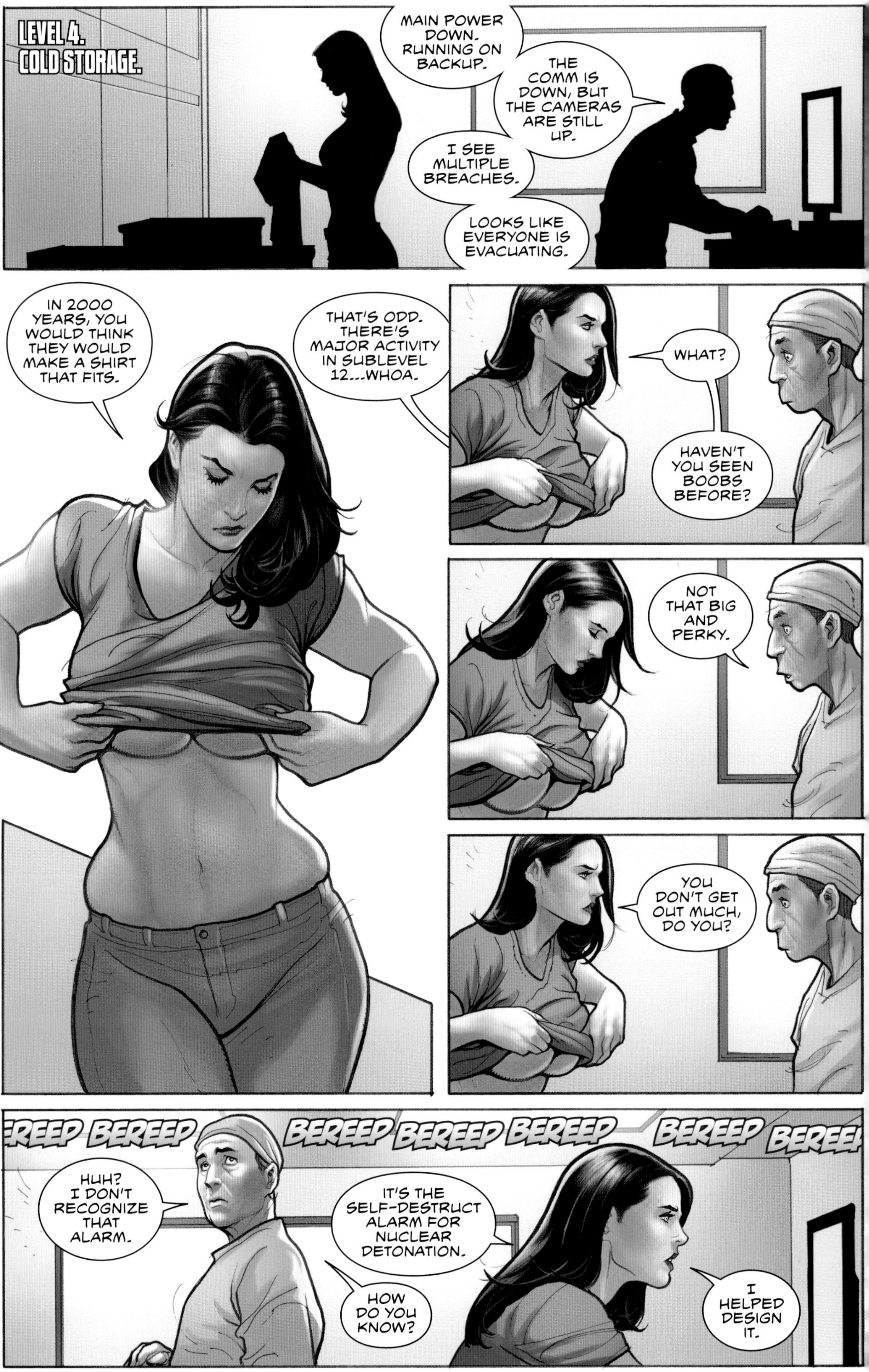

LEVEL 4. COLD STORAGE.
MAIN POWER DOWN. RUNNING ON BACKUP.
THE COMM IS DOWN, BUT THE CAMERAS ARE STILL UP.
I SEE MULTIPLE BREACHES.
LOOKS LIKE EVERYONE IS EVACUATING.
IN 2000 YEARS, YOU WOULD THINK THEY WOULD MAKE A SHIRT THAT FITS.
THAT'S ODD. THERE'S MAJOR ACTIVITY IN SUBLEVEL 12...WHOA.
WHAT?
HAVEN'T YOU SEEN BOOBS BEFORE?
NOT THAT BIG AND PERKY.
YOU DON'T GET OUT MUCH, DO YOU?
BEREEP BEREEP BEREEP BEREEP BEREEP BEREEP BEREEP
HUH? I DON'T RECOGNIZE THAT ALARM.
IT'S THE SELF-DESTRUCT ALARM FOR NUCLEAR DETONATION.
HOW DO YOU KNOW?
I HELPED DESIGN IT.

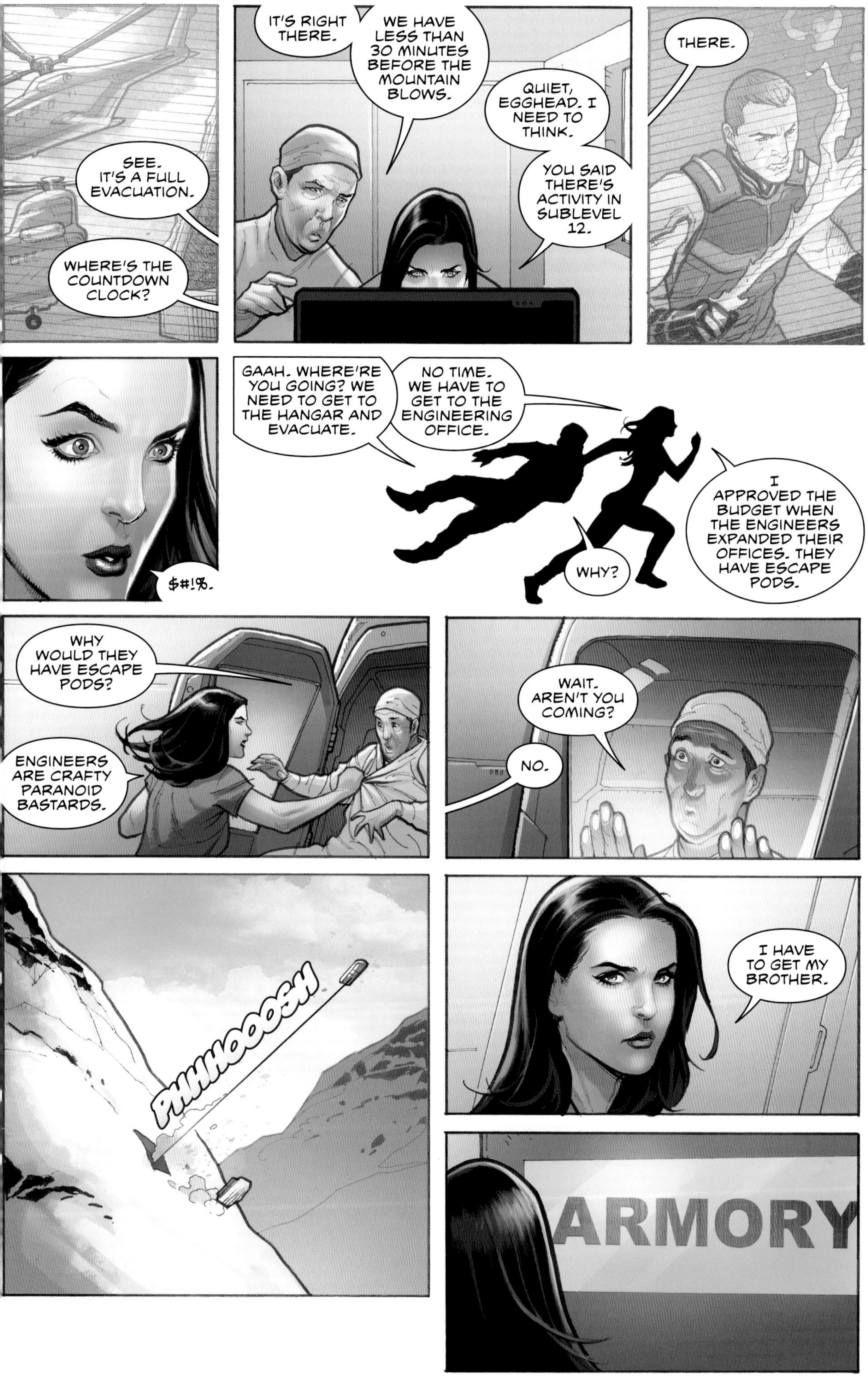
SEE. IT'S A FULL EVACUATION.
WHERE'S THE COUNTDOWN CLOCK?
IT'S RIGHT THERE.
WE HAVE LESS THAN 30 MINUTES BEFORE THE MOUNTAIN BLOWS.
QUIET, EGGHEAD. I NEED TO THINK.
YOU SAID THERE'S ACTIVITY IN SUBLEVEL 12.
THERE.
$#!%.
GAAH. WHERE'RE YOU GOING? WE NEED TO GET TO THE HANGAR AND EVACUATE.
NO TIME. WE HAVE TO GET TO THE ENGINEERING OFFICE.
WHY?
I APPROVED THE BUDGET WHEN THE ENGINEERS EXPANDED THEIR OFFICES. THEY HAVE ESCAPE PODS.
WHY WOULD THEY HAVE ESCAPE PODS?
ENGINEERS ARE CRAFTY PARANOID BASTARDS.
WAIT. AREN'T YOU COMING?
NO.
PHHHOOOSH
I HAVE TO GET MY BROTHER.
ARMORY

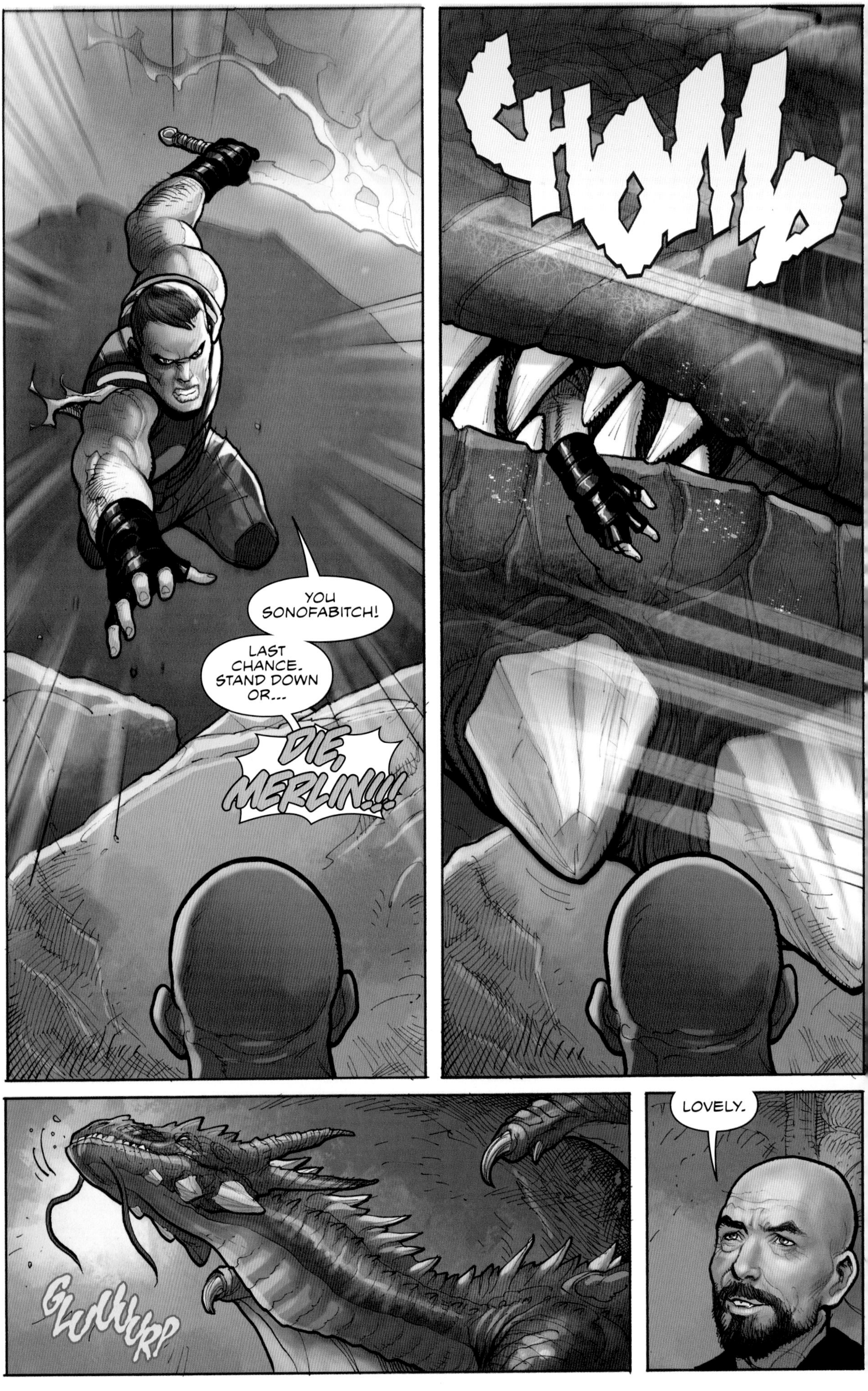
YOU SONOFABITCH!
LAST CHANCE. STAND DOWN OR...
DIE, MERLIN!!!
CHOMP
GLUUURP
LOVELY.

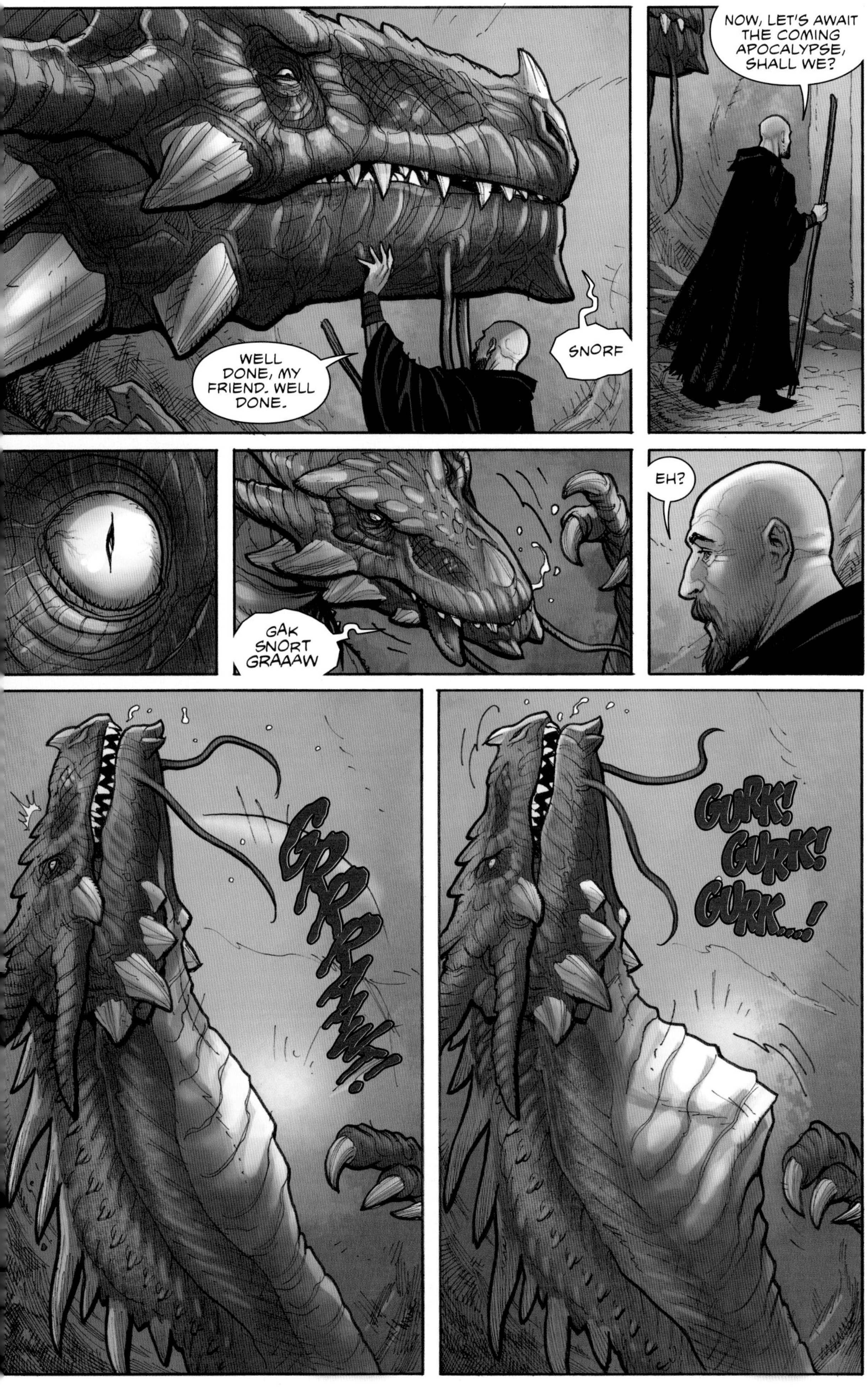
WELL DONE, MY FRIEND. WELL DONE.
SNORF
NOW, LET'S AWAIT THE COMING APOCALYPSE, SHALL WE?
GAK SNORT GRAAAW
EH?
GRRAAWK!!
GURK! GURK! GURK...!

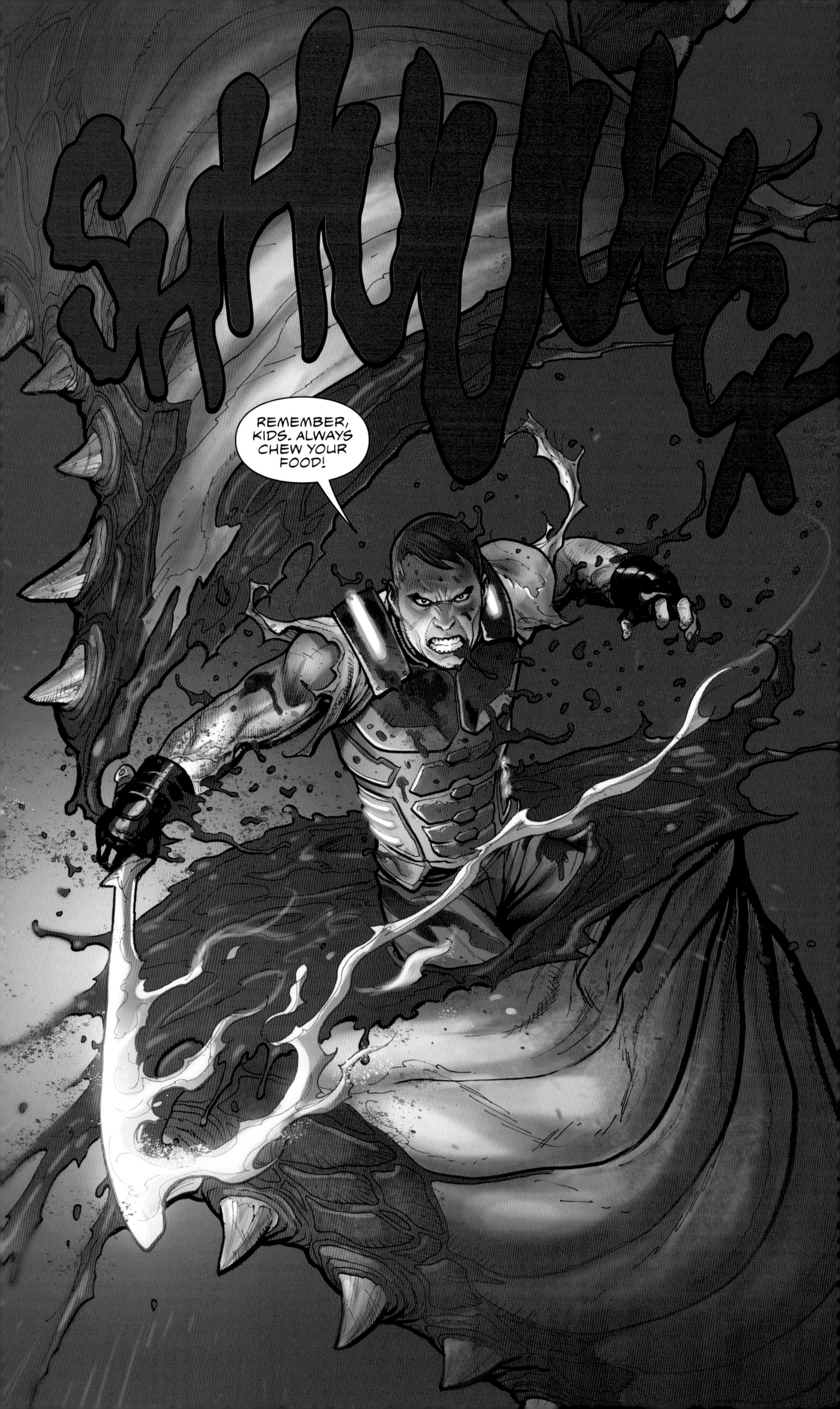

SHHUNNKK
REMEMBER, KIDS. ALWAYS CHEW YOUR FOOD!

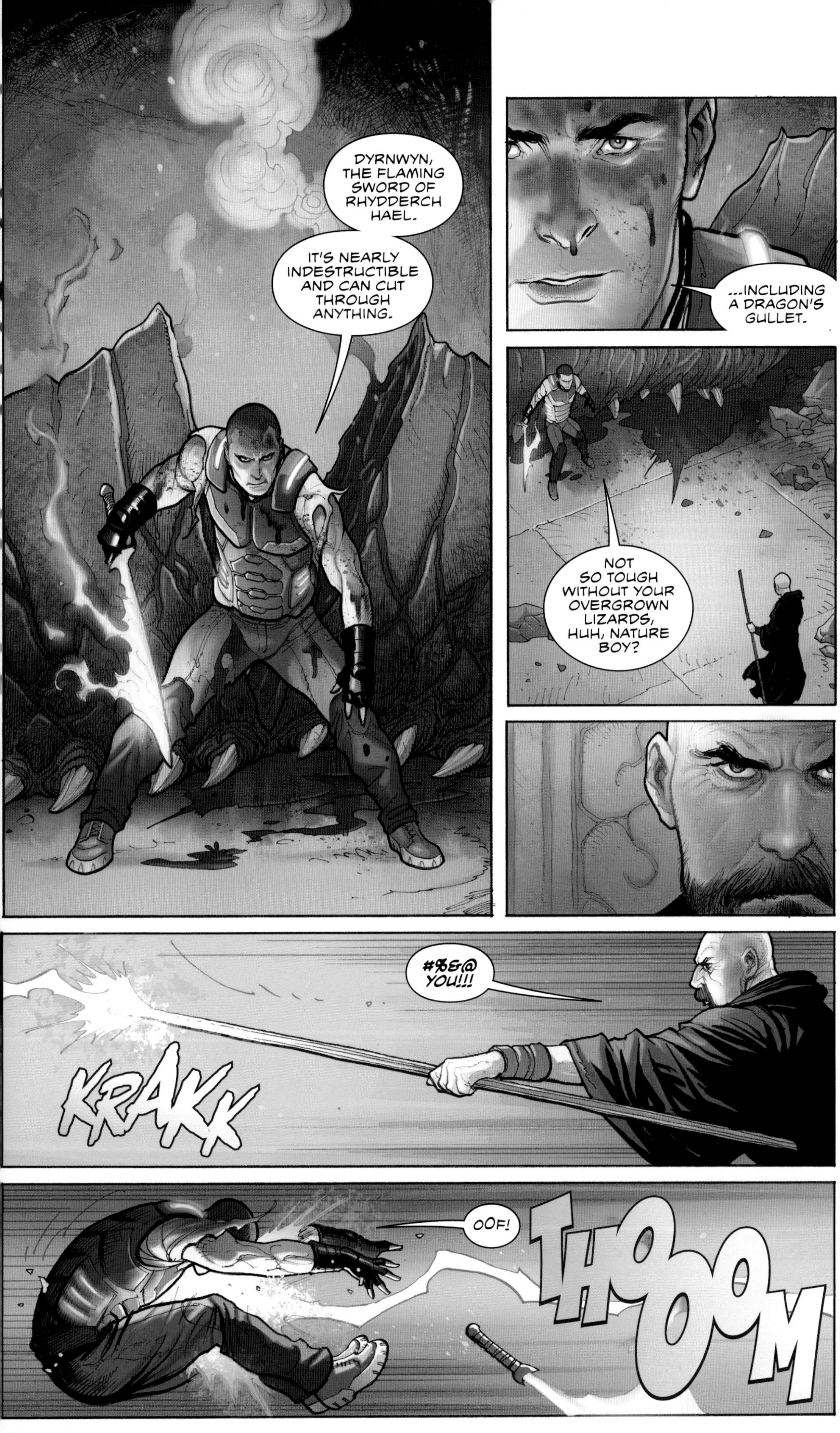
DYRNWYN, THE FLAMING SWORD OF RHYDDERCH HAEL.
IT'S NEARLY INDESTRUCTIBLE AND CAN CUT THROUGH ANYTHING.
...INCLUDING A DRAGON'S GULLET.
NOT SO TOUGH WITHOUT YOUR OVERGROWN LIZARDS, HUH, NATURE BOY?
#%&@ YOU!!!
KRAKK
OOF!
THOOOM

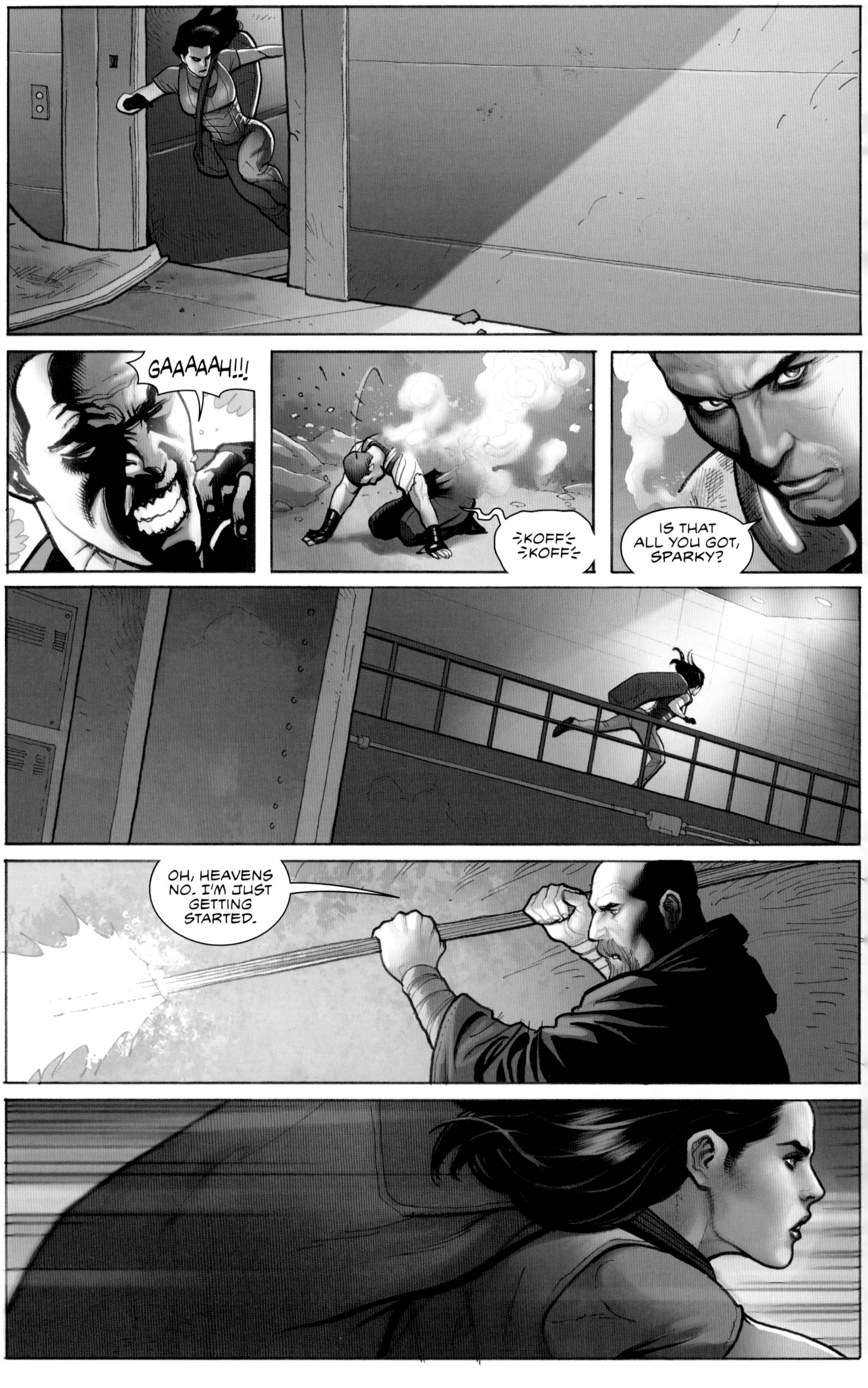
GAAAAAH!!!
KOFF KOFF
IS THAT ALL YOU GOT, SPARKY?
OH, HEAVENS NO. I'M JUST GETTING STARTED.

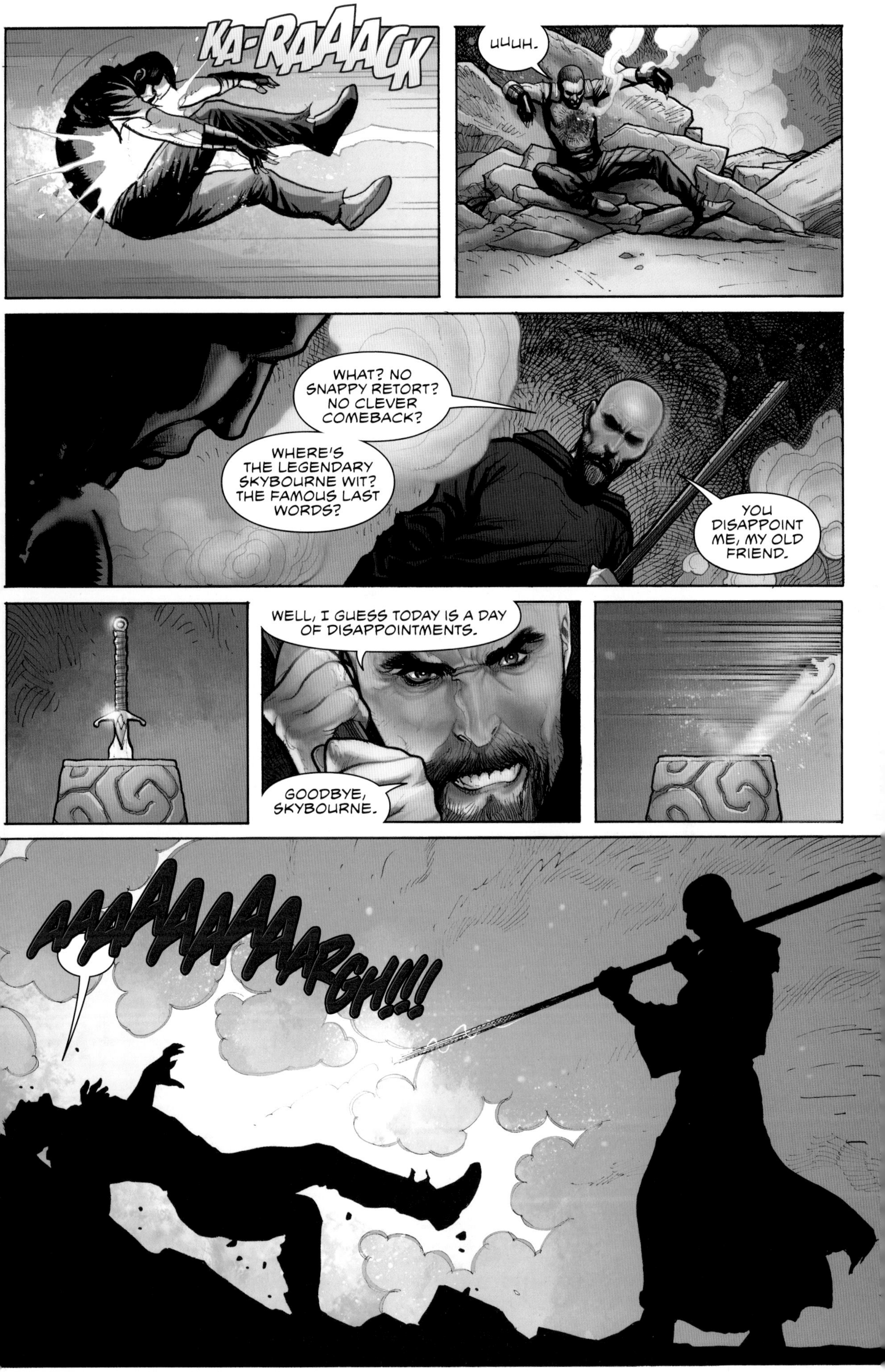
KA-RAAACK
UUUH.
WHAT? NO SNAPPY RETORT? NO CLEVER COMEBACK?
WHERE'S THE LEGENDARY SKYBOURNE WIT? THE FAMOUS LAST WORDS?
YOU DISAPPOINT ME, MY OLD FRIEND.
WELL, I GUESS TODAY IS A DAY OF DISAPPOINTMENTS.
GOODBYE, SKYBOURNE.
AAAAAAAAAARGH!!!

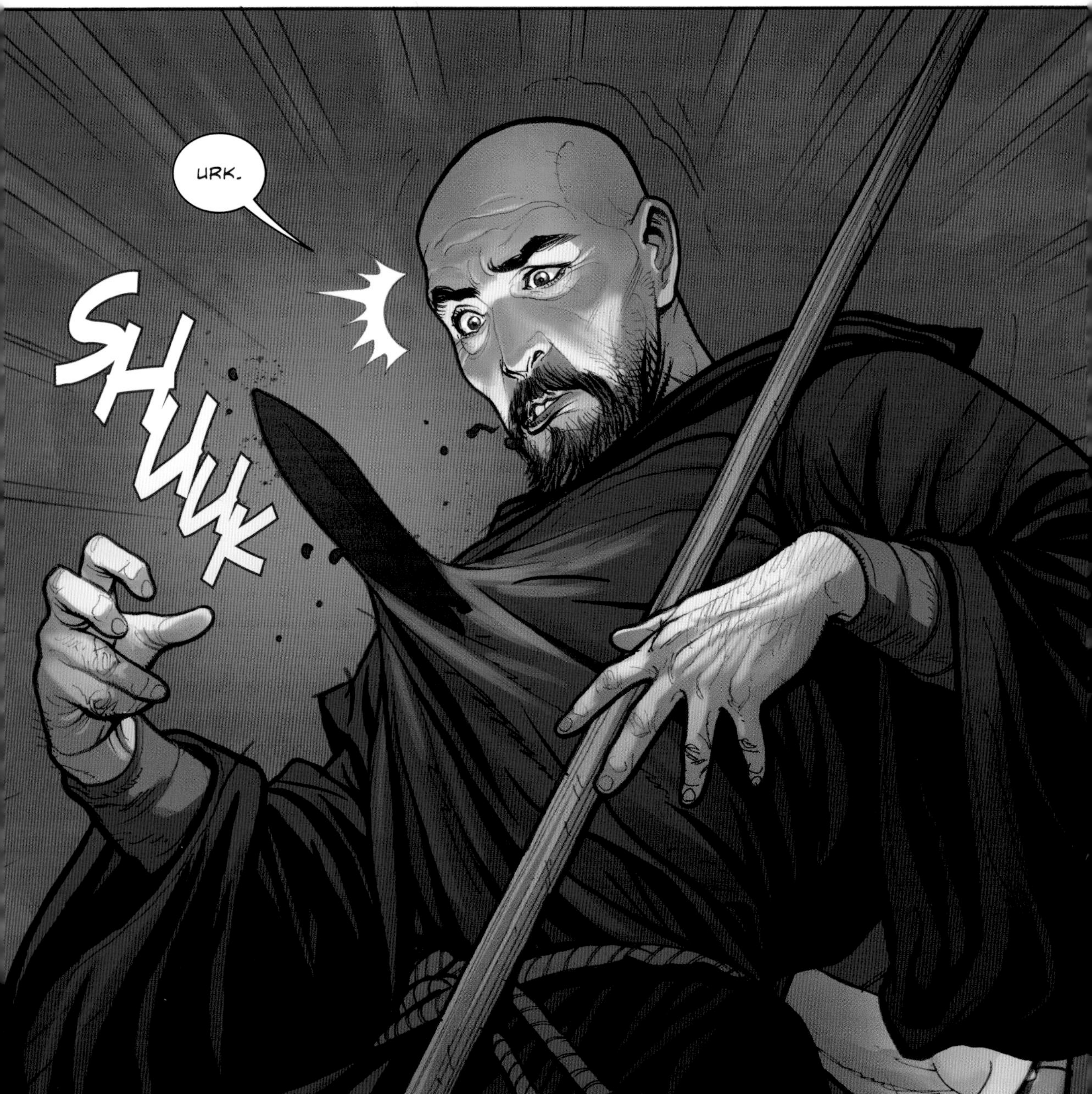
URK.
SHUNK

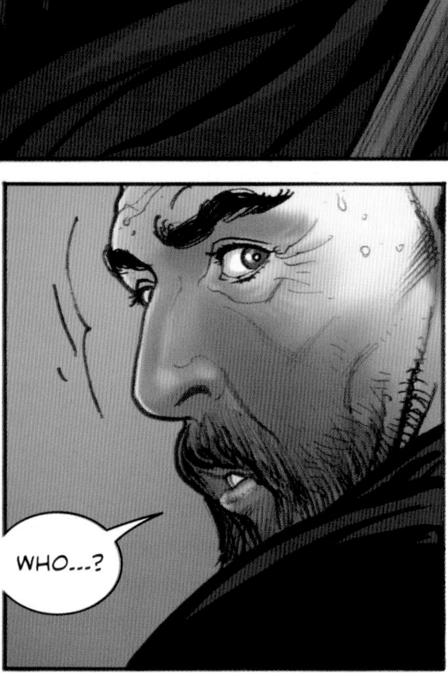
WHO...?

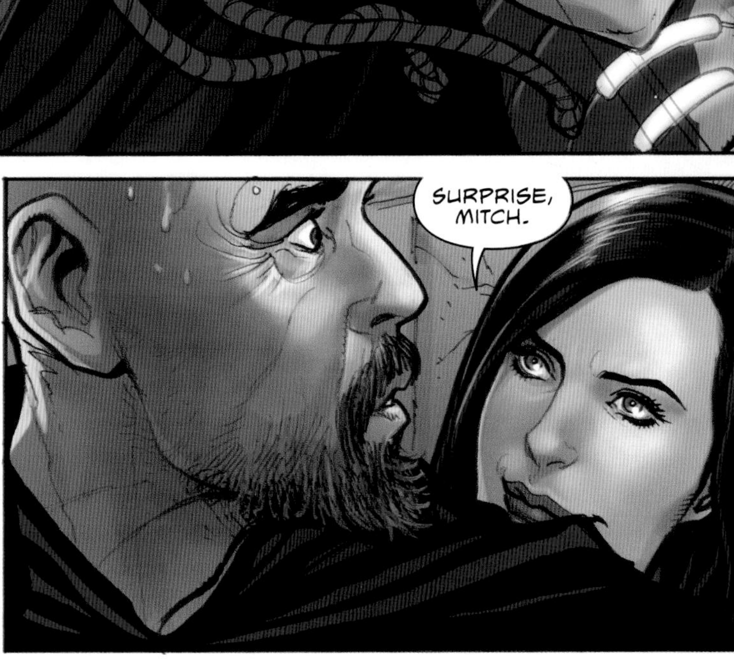
SURPRISE, MITCH.

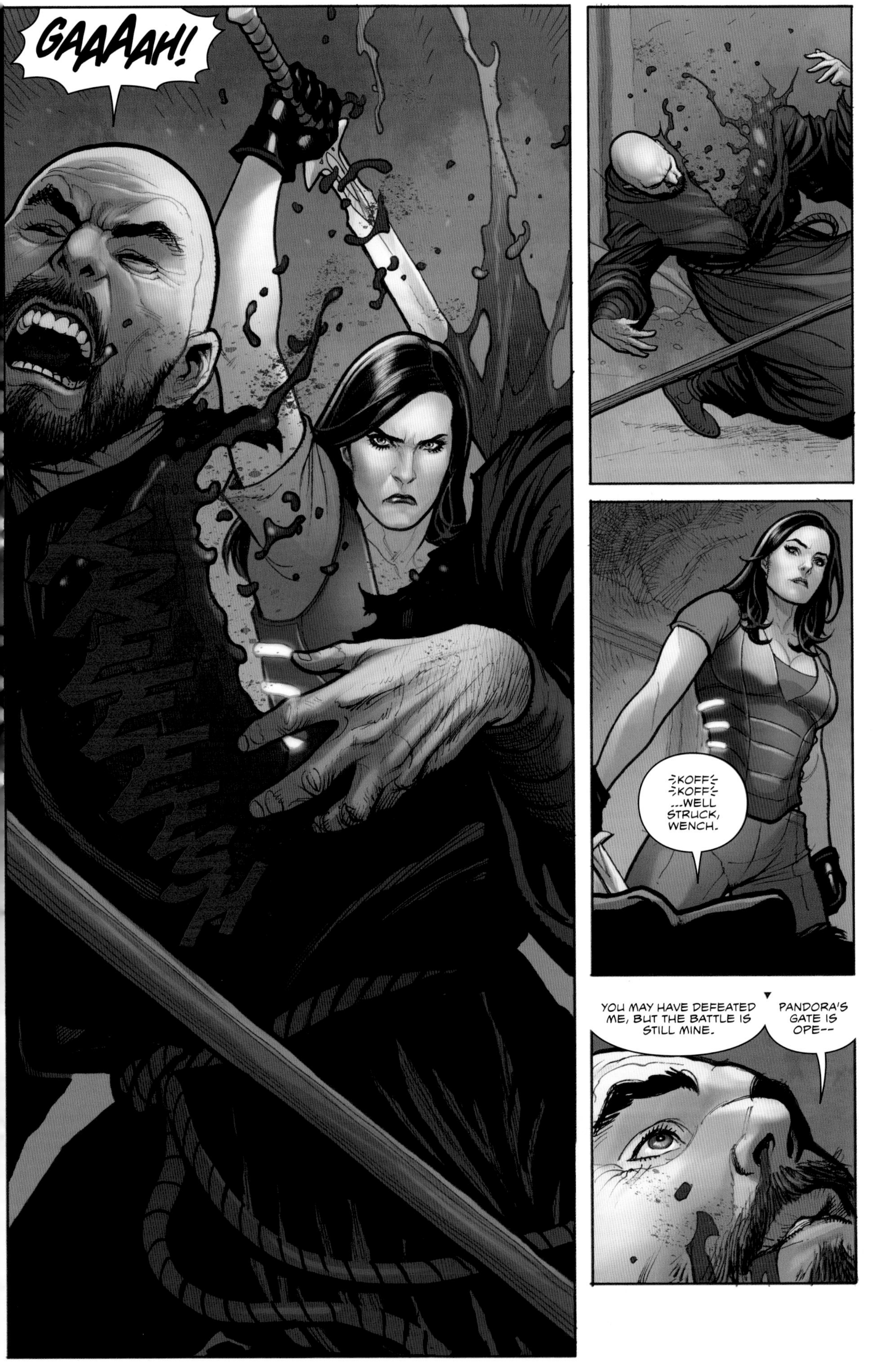
GAAAAAH!
KOFF KOFF ...WELL STRUCK, WENCH.
YOU MAY HAVE DEFEATED ME, BUT THE BATTLE IS STILL MINE.
PANDORA'S GATE IS OPE--

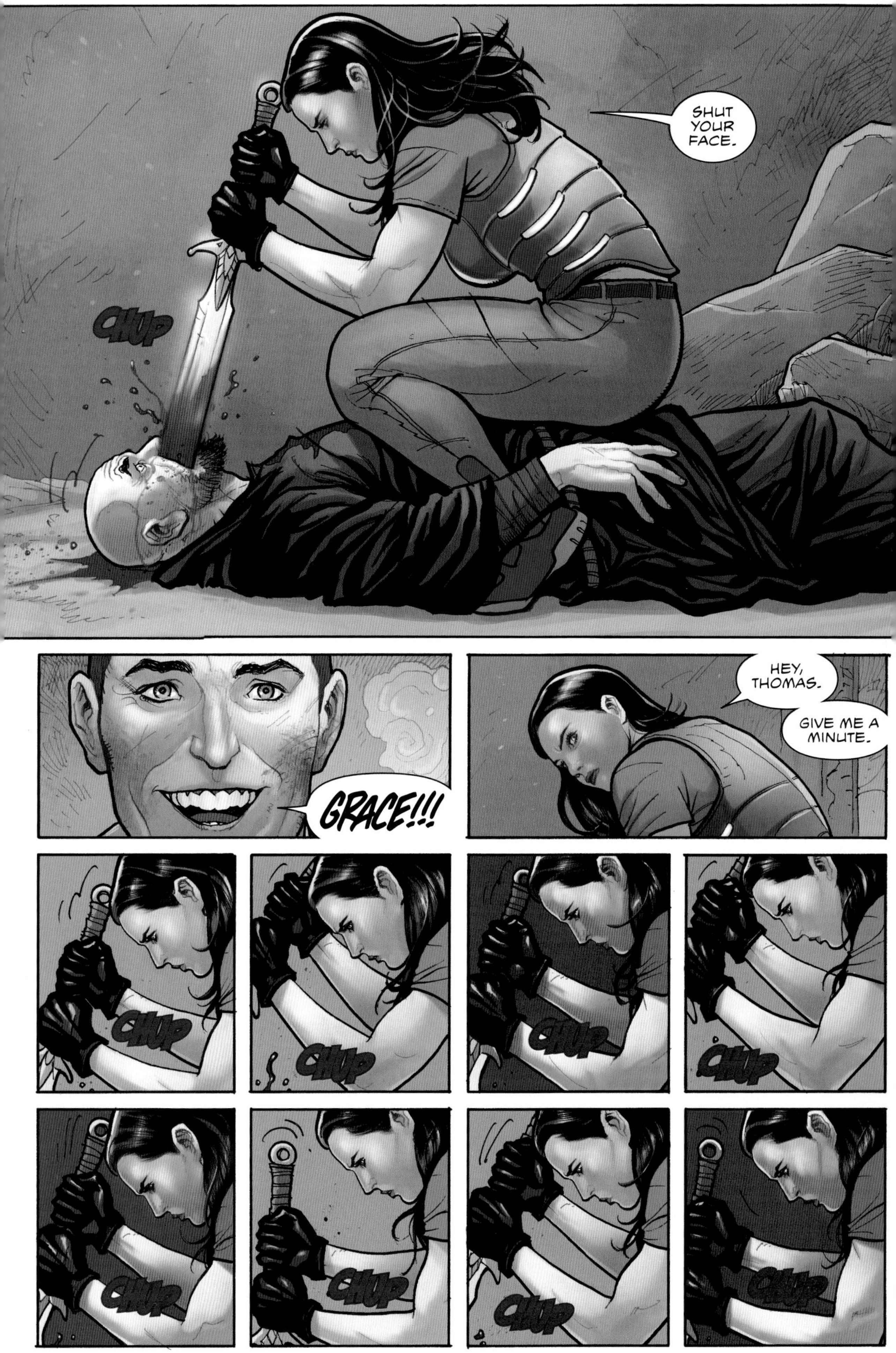

SHUT YOUR FACE.
CHUP
GRACE!!!
HEY, THOMAS.
GIVE ME A MINUTE.
CHUP
CHUP
CHUP
CHUP
CHUP
CHUP
CHUP
CHUP

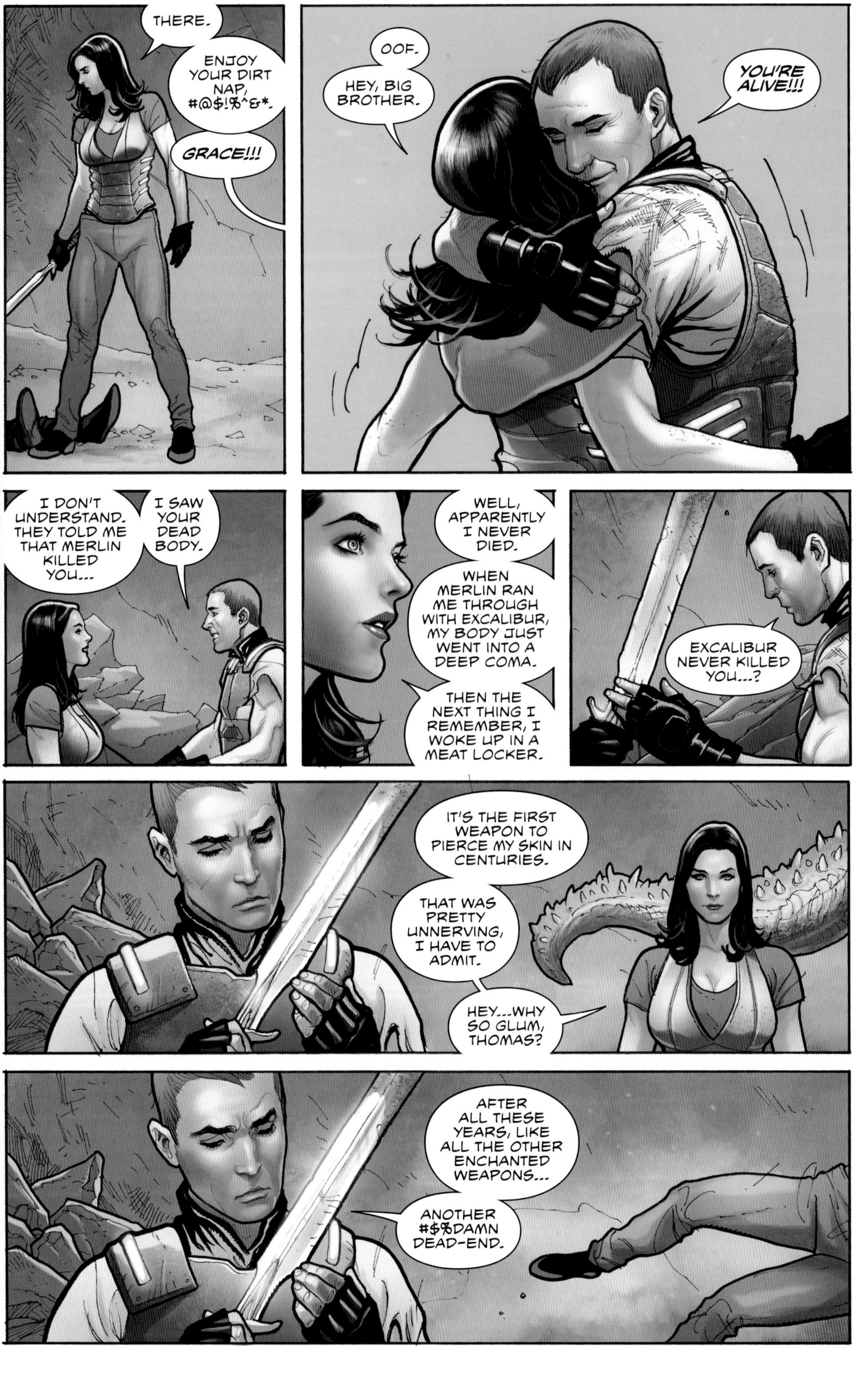

THERE.
ENJOY YOUR DIRT NAP, #@$!%^&*.
GRACE!!!
OOF.
HEY, BIG BROTHER.
YOU'RE ALIVE!!!
I DON'T UNDERSTAND. THEY TOLD ME THAT MERLIN KILLED YOU...
I SAW YOUR DEAD BODY.
WELL, APPARENTLY I NEVER DIED.
WHEN MERLIN RAN ME THROUGH WITH EXCALIBUR, MY BODY JUST WENT INTO A DEEP COMA.
THEN THE NEXT THING I REMEMBER, I WOKE UP IN A MEAT LOCKER.
EXCALIBUR NEVER KILLED YOU...?
IT'S THE FIRST WEAPON TO PIERCE MY SKIN IN CENTURIES.
THAT WAS PRETTY UNNERVING, I HAVE TO ADMIT.
HEY...WHY SO GLUM, THOMAS?
AFTER ALL THESE YEARS, LIKE ALL THE OTHER ENCHANTED WEAPONS...
ANOTHER #$%DAMN DEAD-END.

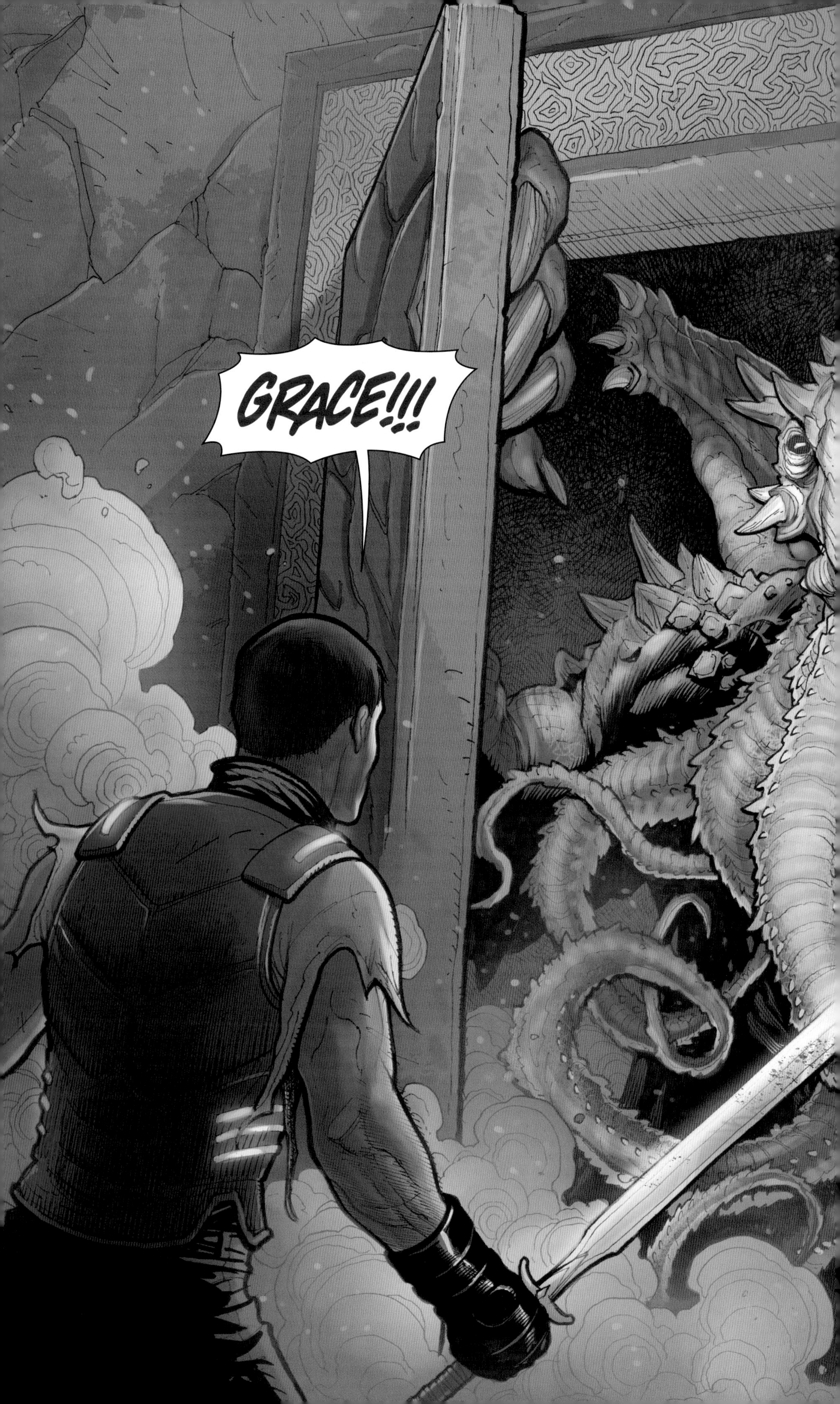
GRACE!!!

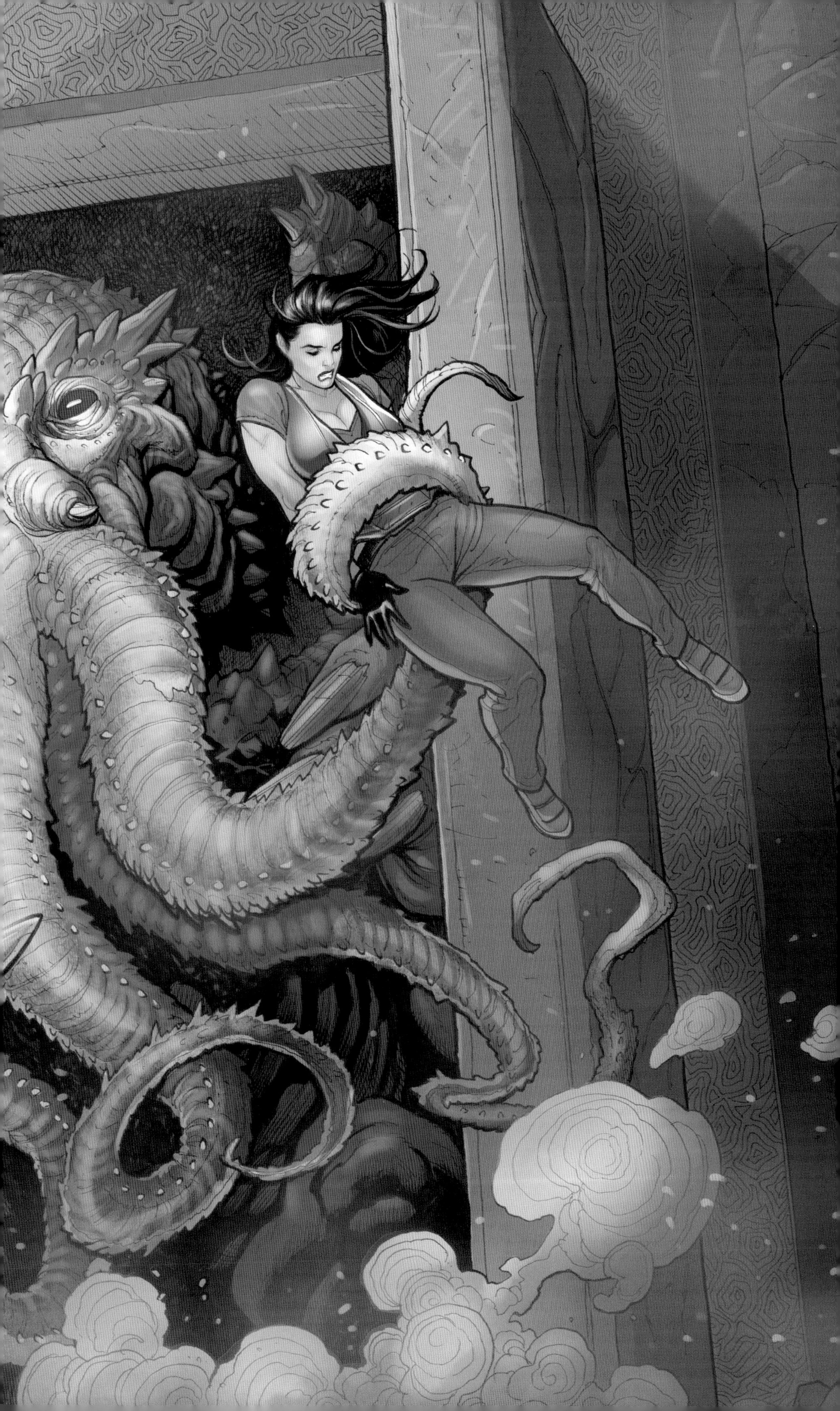

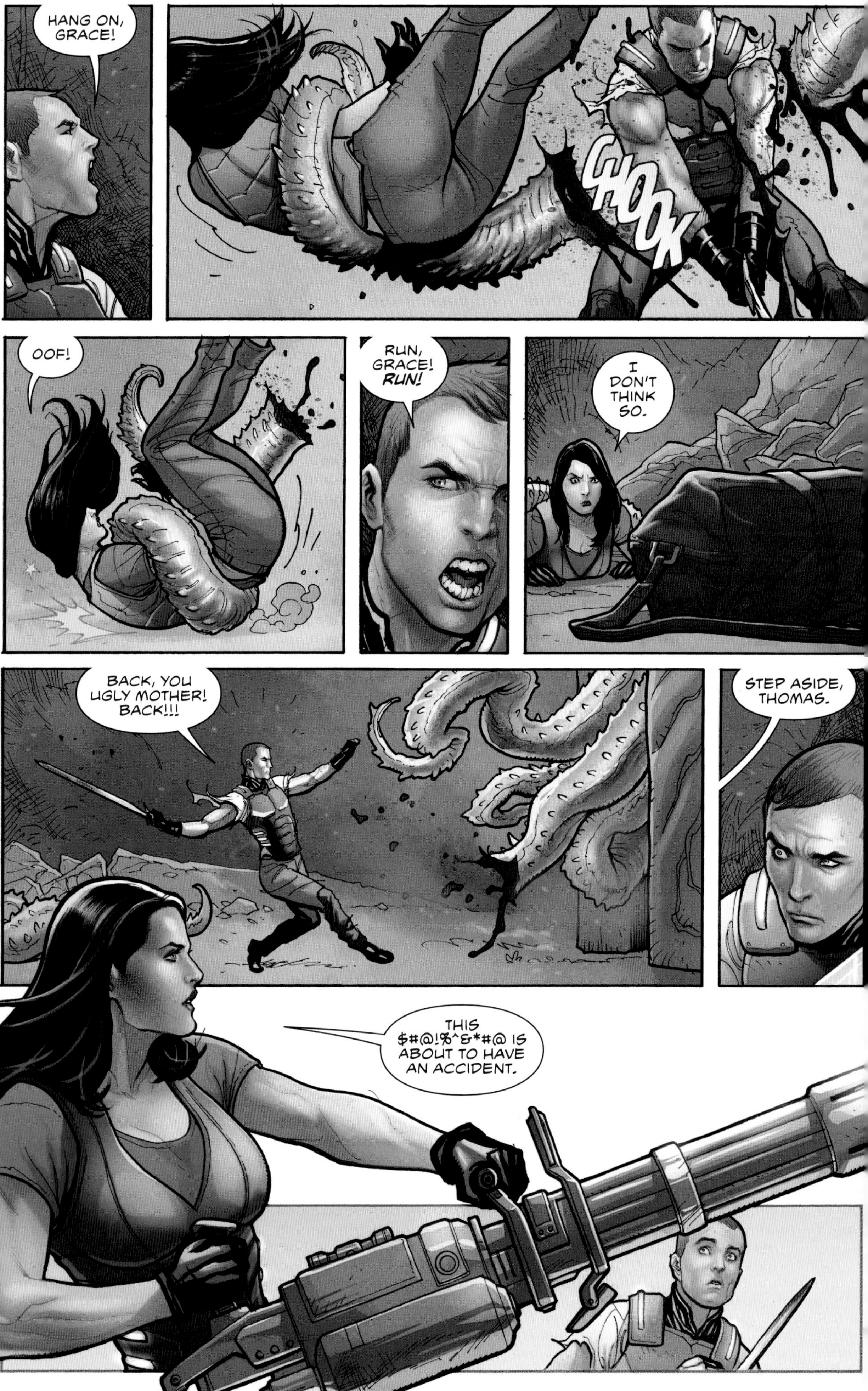
HANG ON, GRACE!
CHOOK
OOF!
RUN, GRACE! RUN!
I DON'T THINK SO.
BACK, YOU UGLY MOTHER! BACK!!!
STEP ASIDE, THOMAS.
THIS $#@!%^&*#@ IS ABOUT TO HAVE AN ACCIDENT.

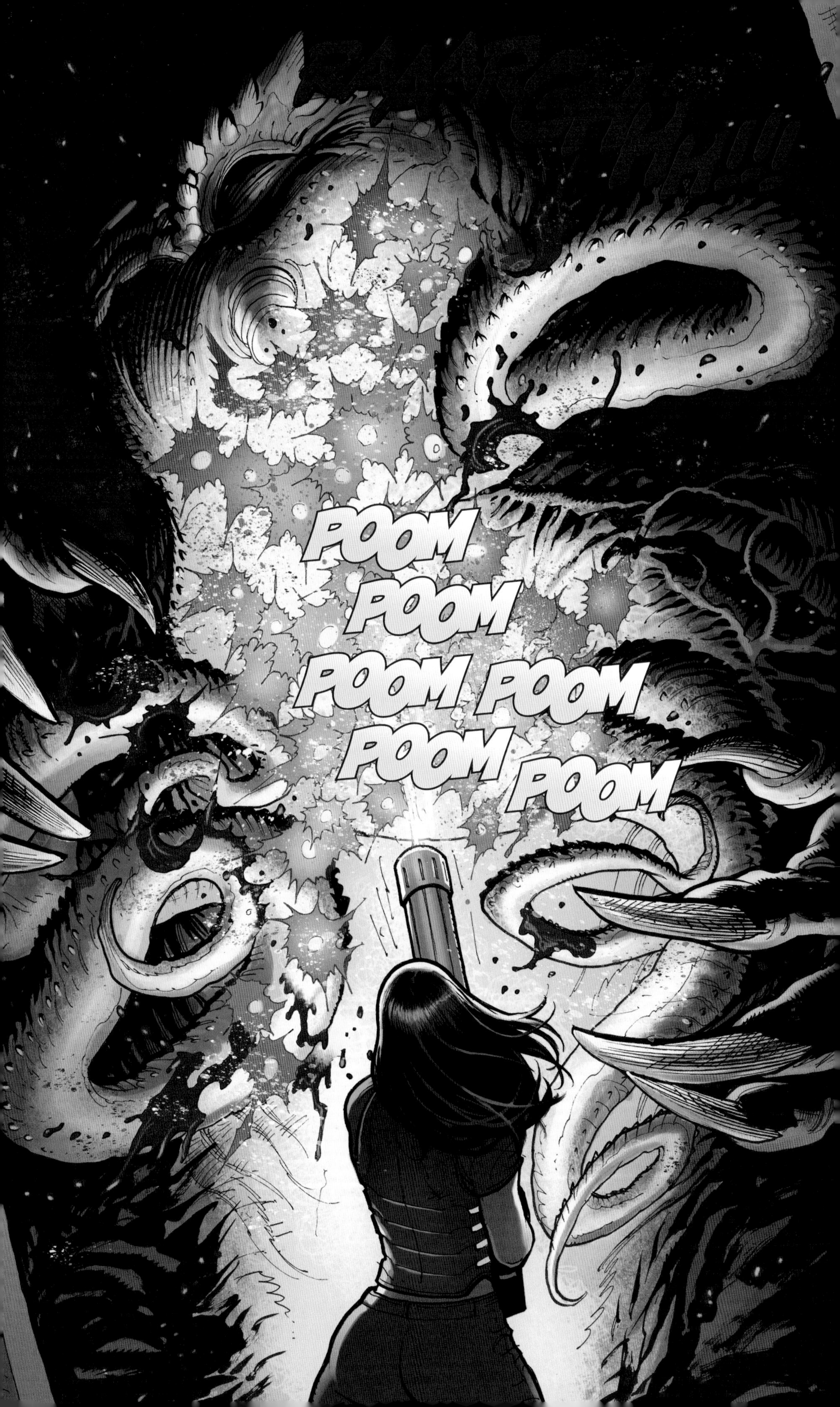
POOM
POOM
POOM POOM
POOM
POOM

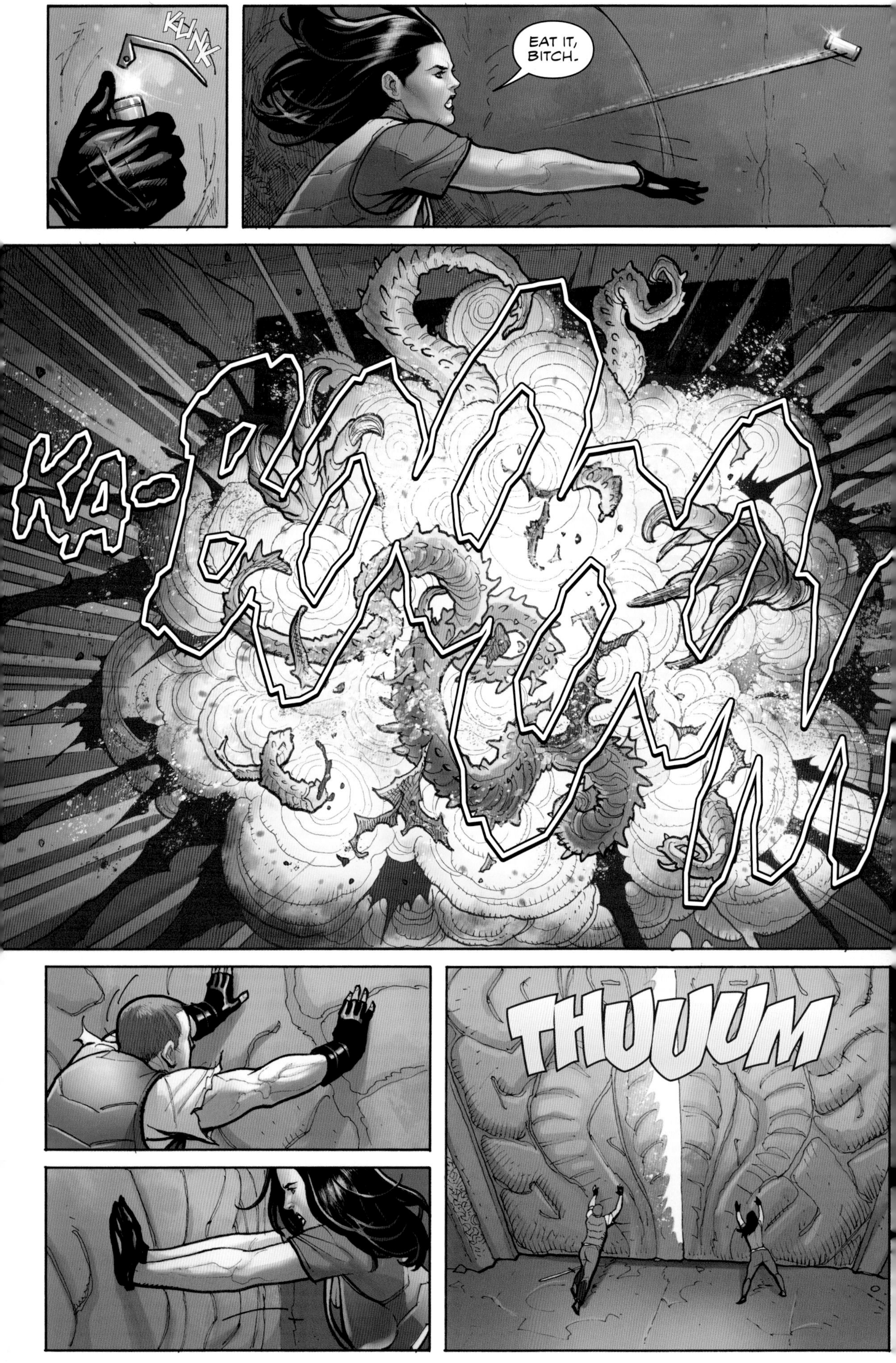
KLUNK
EAT IT, BITCH.
KA-BOOOOOM
THUUUM

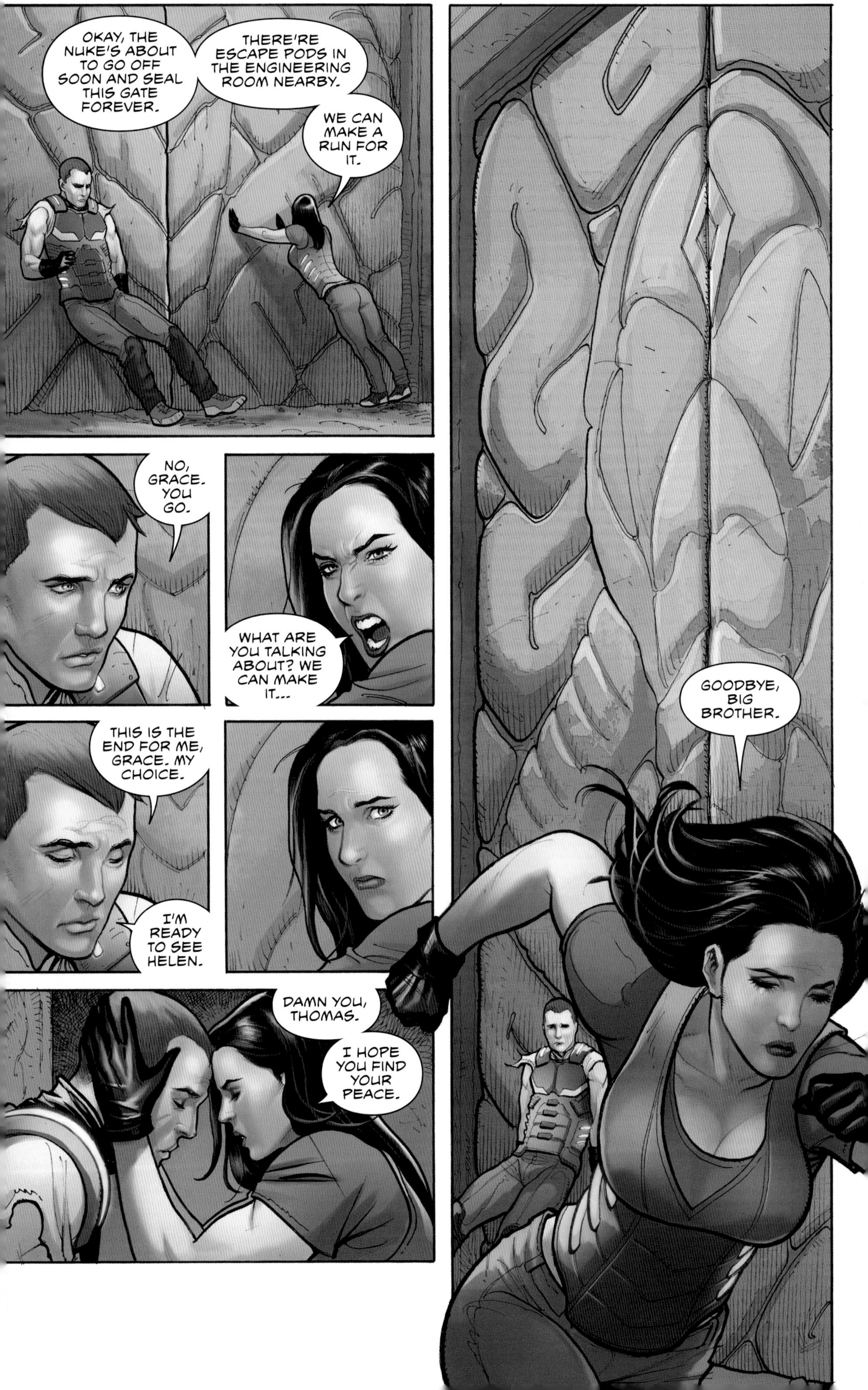
OKAY, THE NUKE'S ABOUT TO GO OFF SOON AND SEAL THIS GATE FOREVER.
THERE'RE ESCAPE PODS IN THE ENGINEERING ROOM NEARBY.
WE CAN MAKE A RUN FOR IT.
NO, GRACE. YOU GO.
WHAT ARE YOU TALKING ABOUT? WE CAN MAKE IT...
THIS IS THE END FOR ME, GRACE. MY CHOICE.
I'M READY TO SEE HELEN.
DAMN YOU, THOMAS.
I HOPE YOU FIND YOUR PEACE.
GOODBYE, BIG BROTHER.

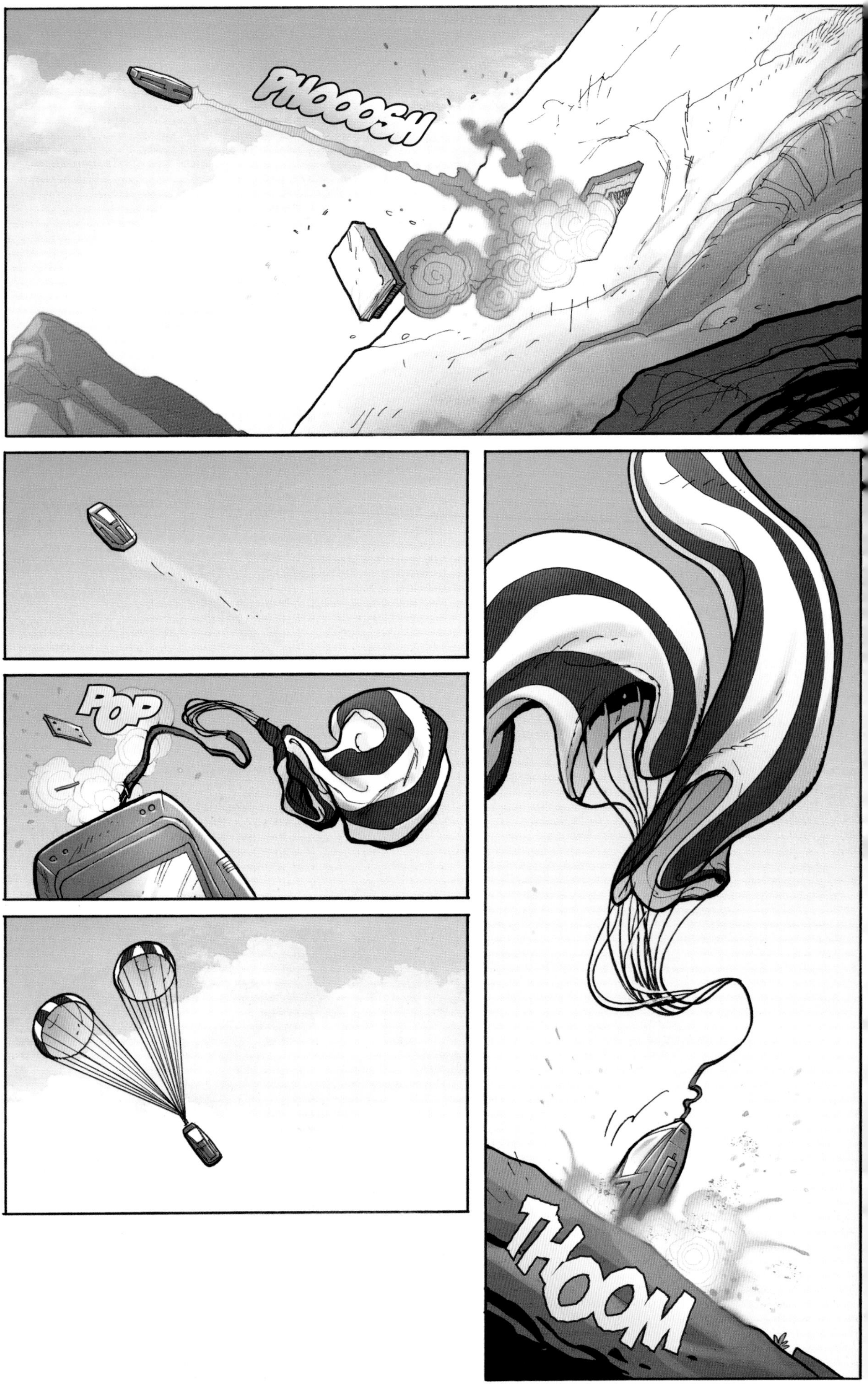
PHOOOSH
POP
THOOM

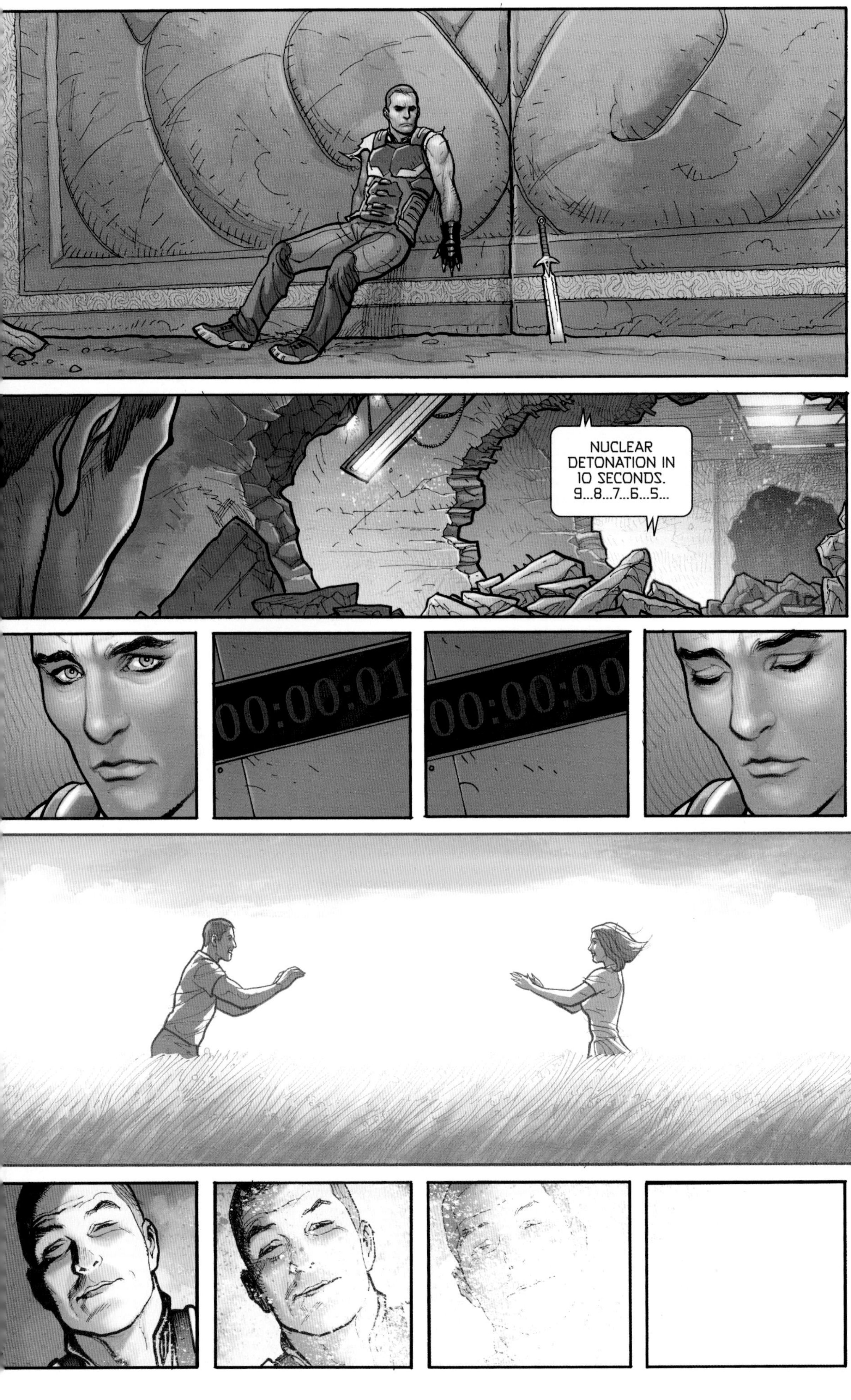
NUCLEAR DETONATION IN 10 SECONDS. 9...8...7...6...5...
00:00:01
00:00:00

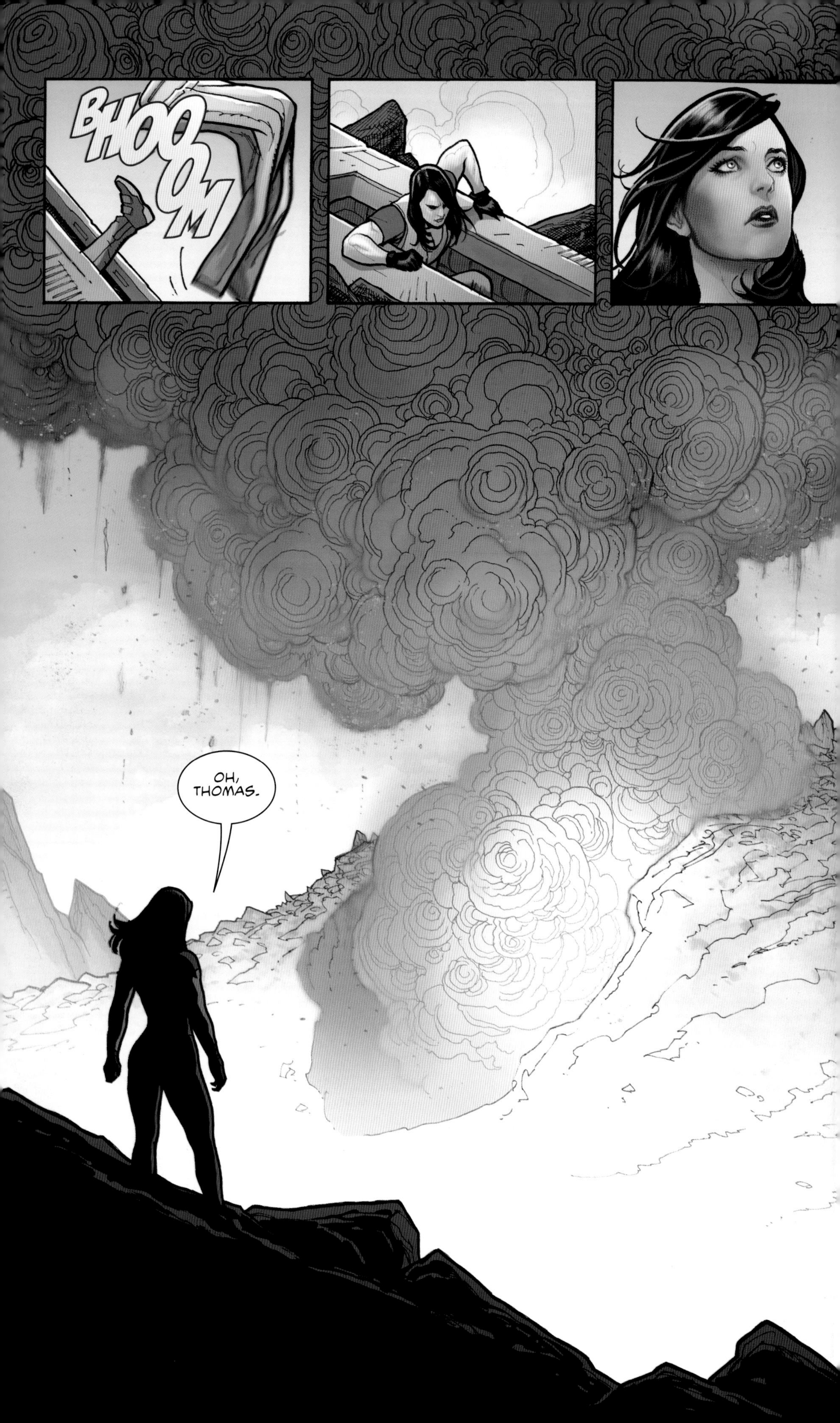
BHOOOOM
OH, THOMAS.

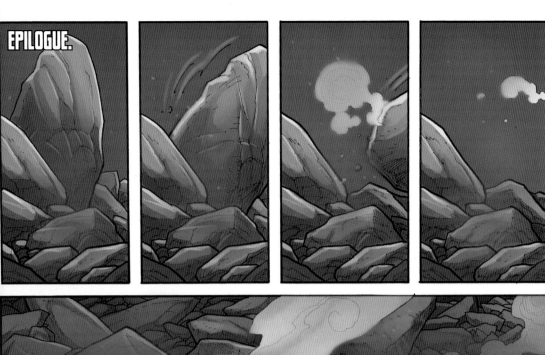

EPILOGUE.

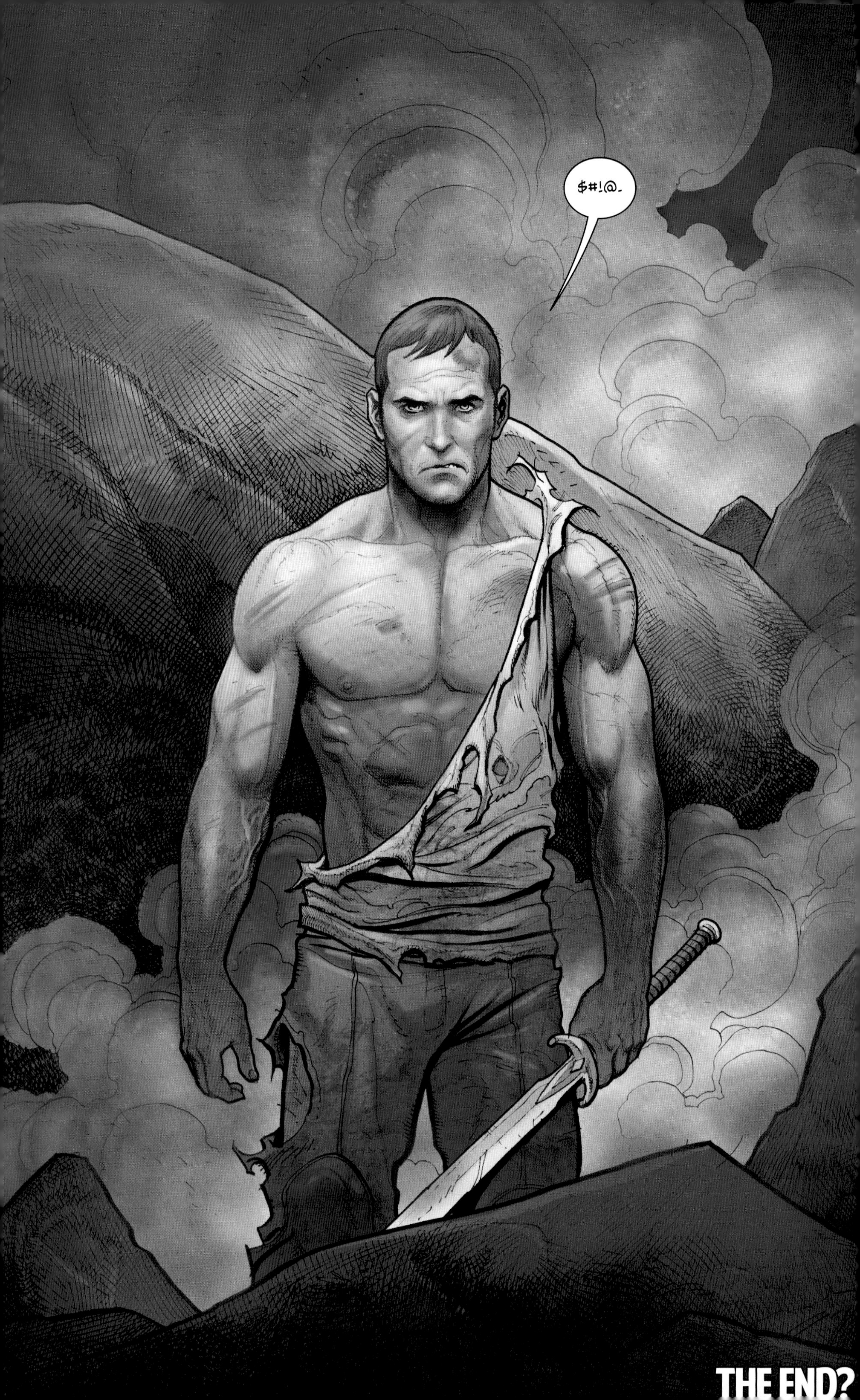
$#!@-
THE END?

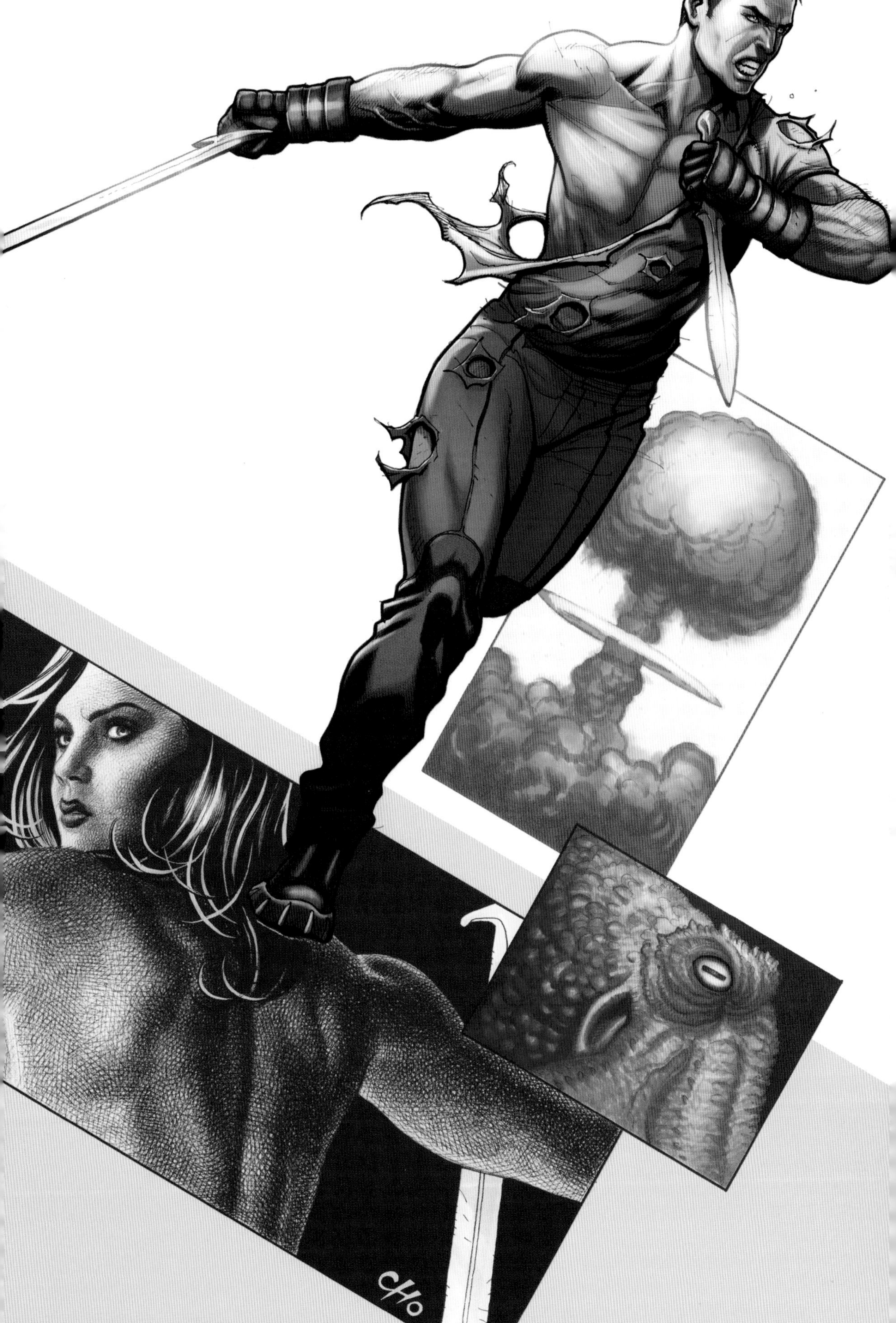
CHO

Issue Five Cover by **FRANK CHO**
with colors by **MARCIO MENYZ**

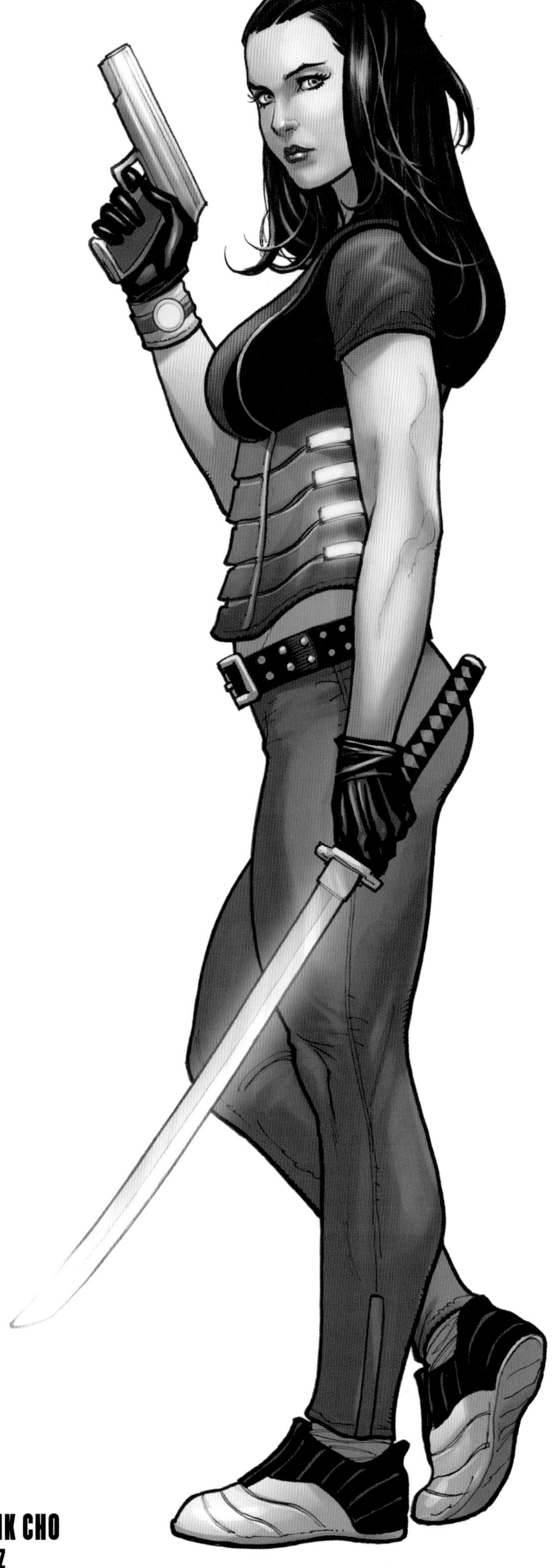

Issue One Cover by **FRANK CHO**
with colors by **MARCIO MENYZ**

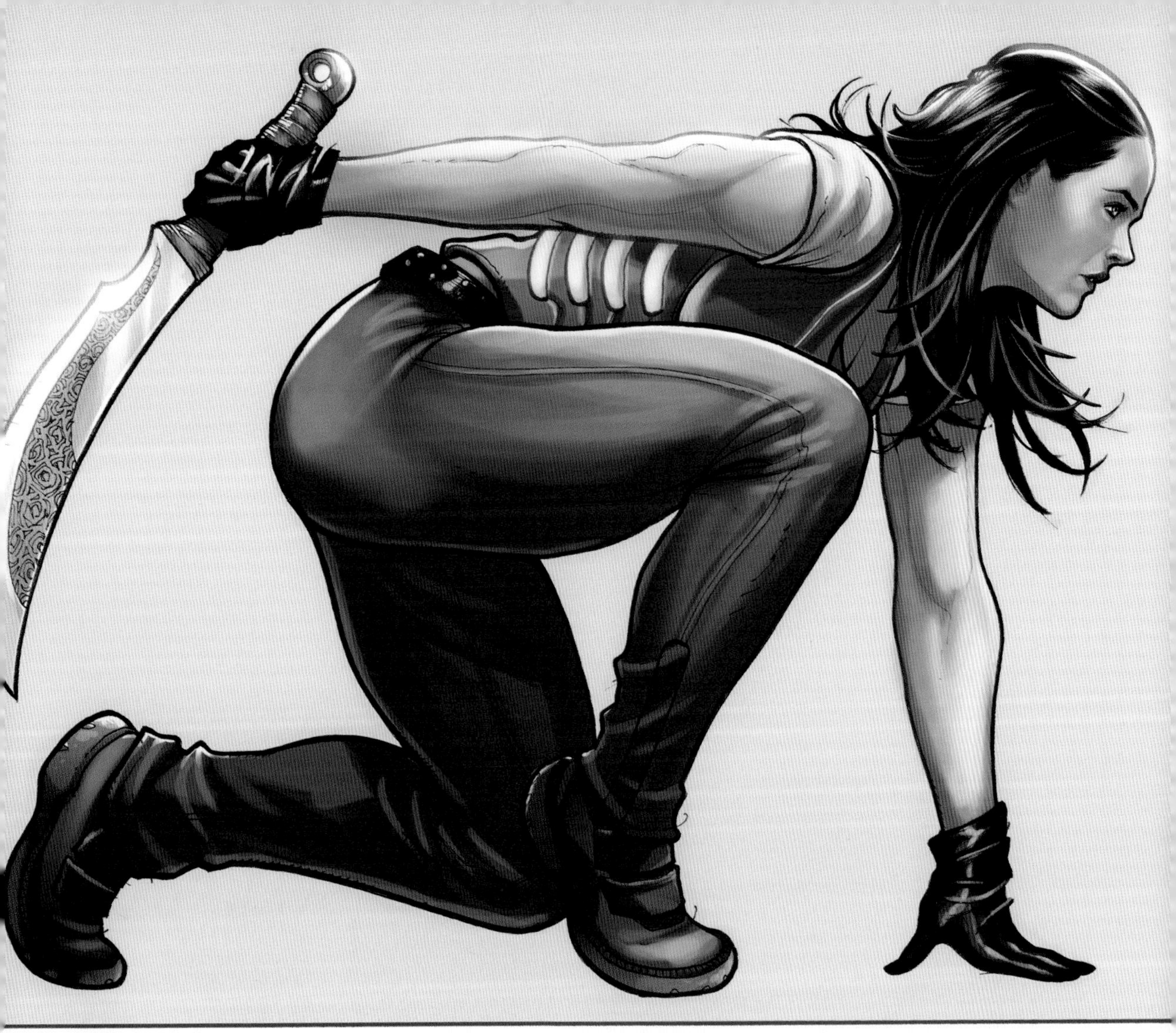

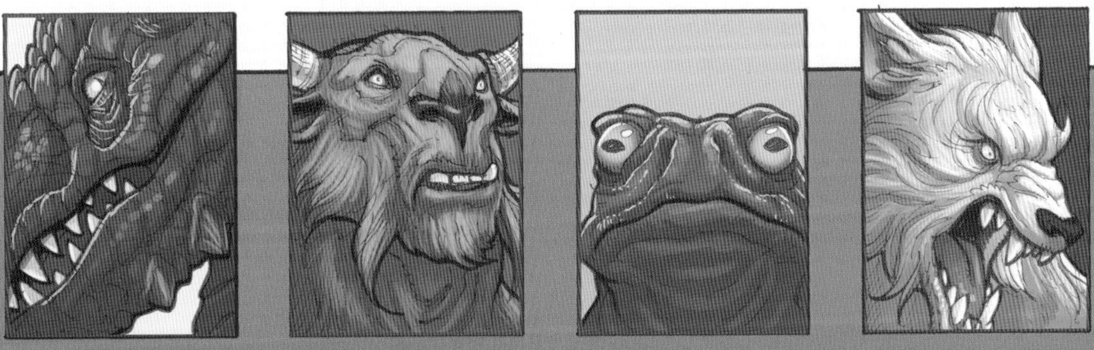

Issue One Baltimore Comic-Con Exclusive Cover by **FRANK CHO**
with colors by **MARCIO MENYZ**

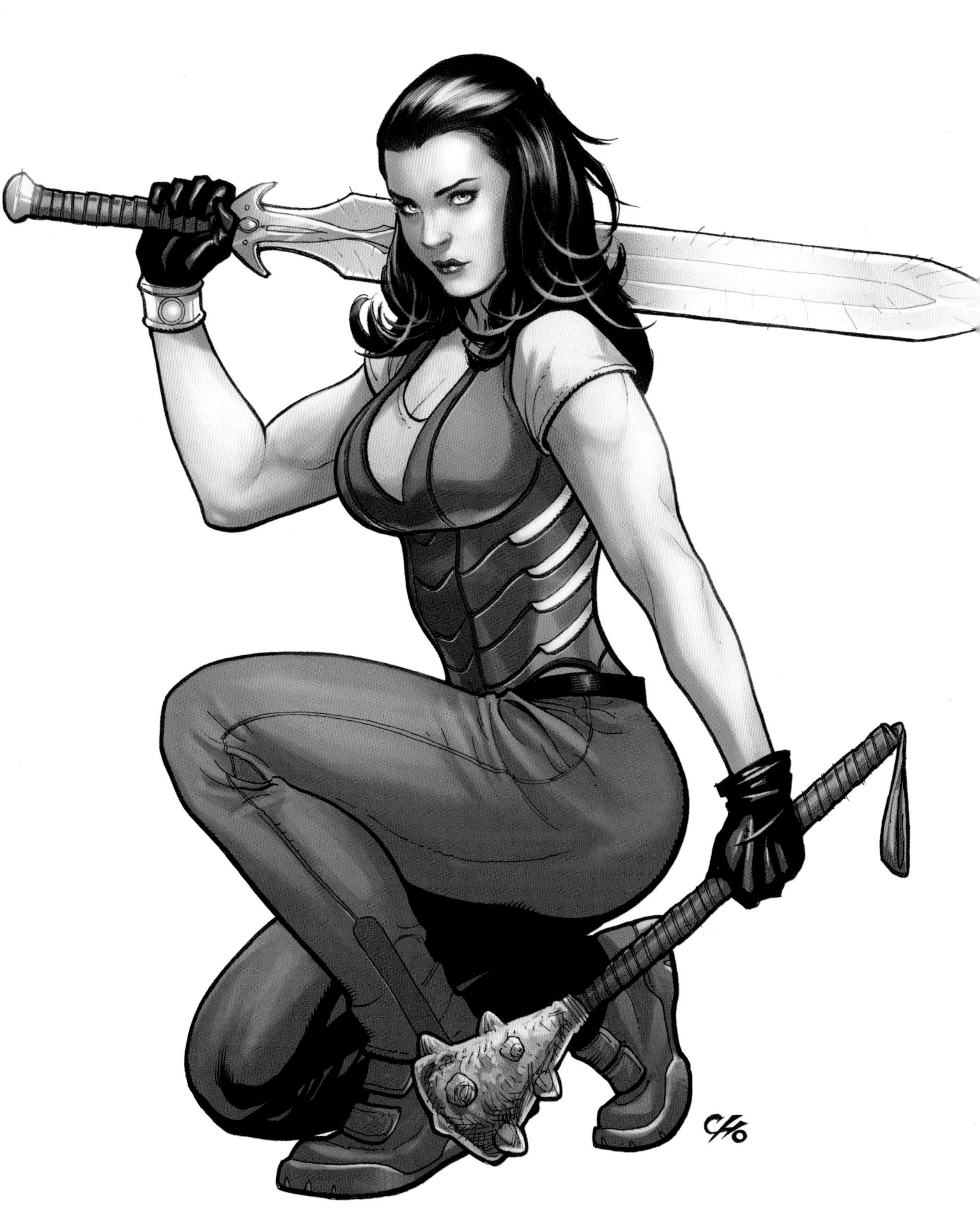
CHO

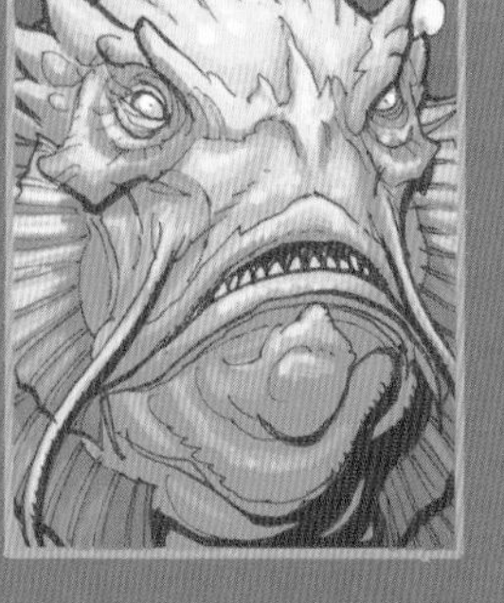

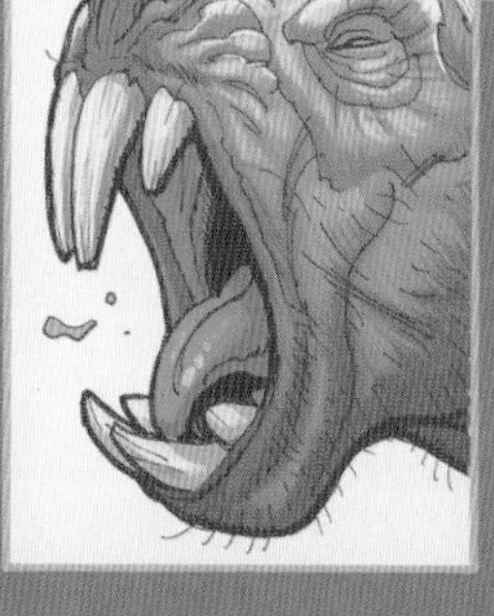

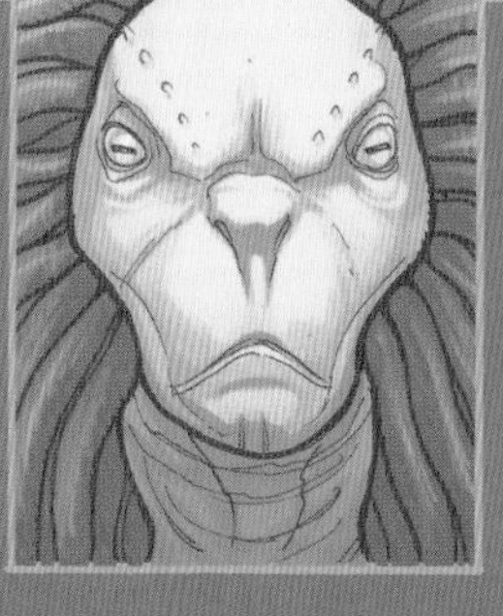

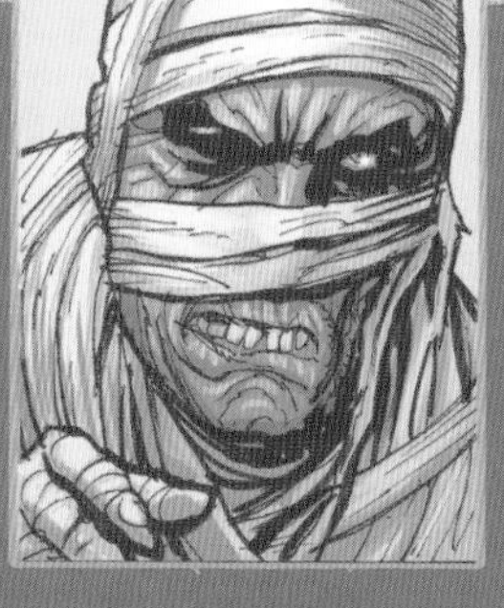

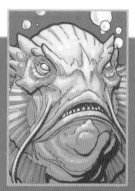

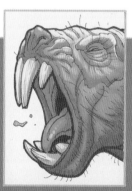

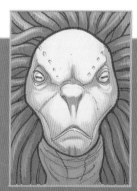

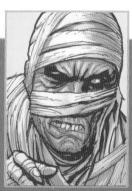

Issue One Midtown Comics Exclusive Cover by **FRANK CHO**
with colors by **MARCIO MENYZ**

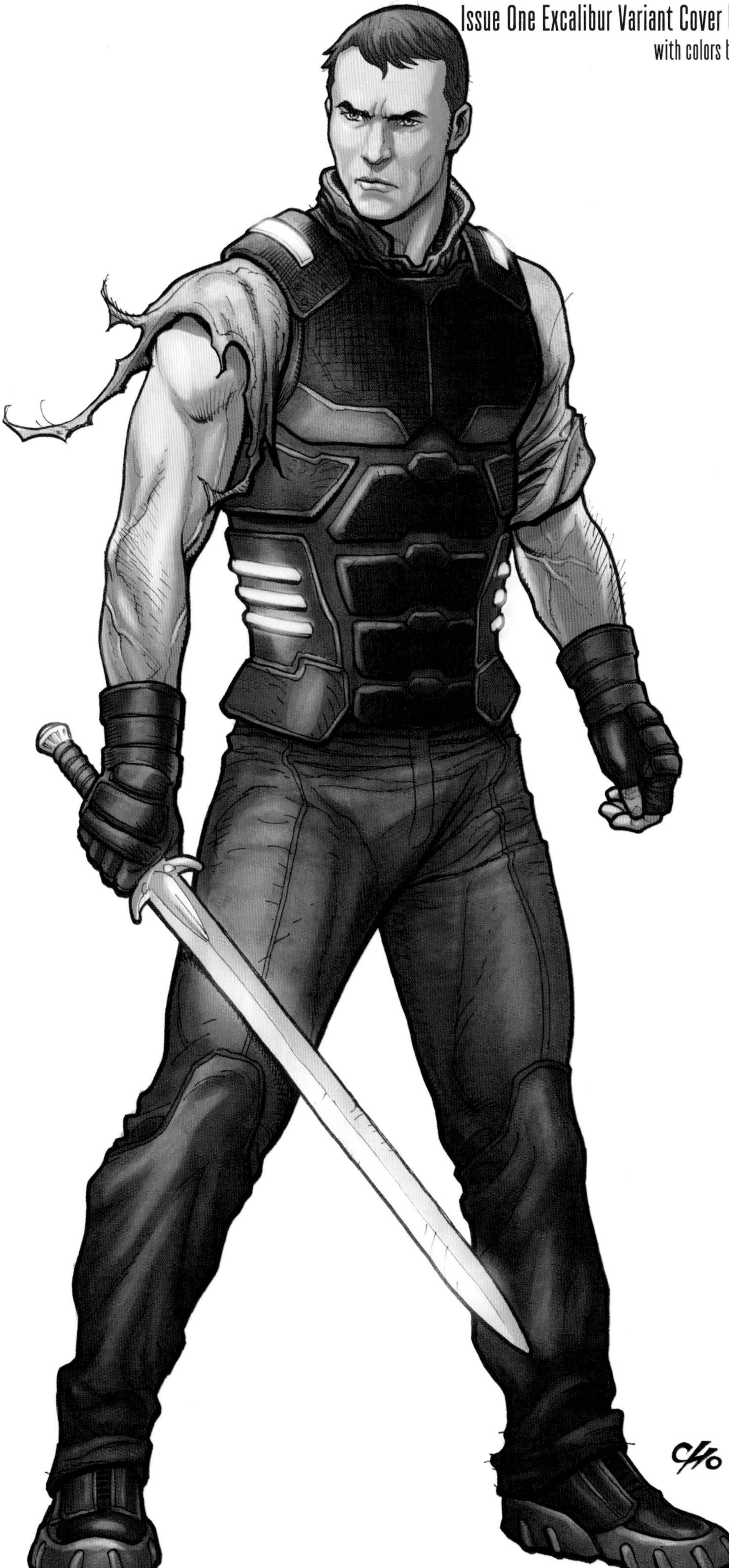
CHO

Issue One Excalibur Variant Cover by **FRANK CHO**
with colors by **MARCIO MENYZ**

Issue One Artifact Variant Cover by **FRANK CHO**

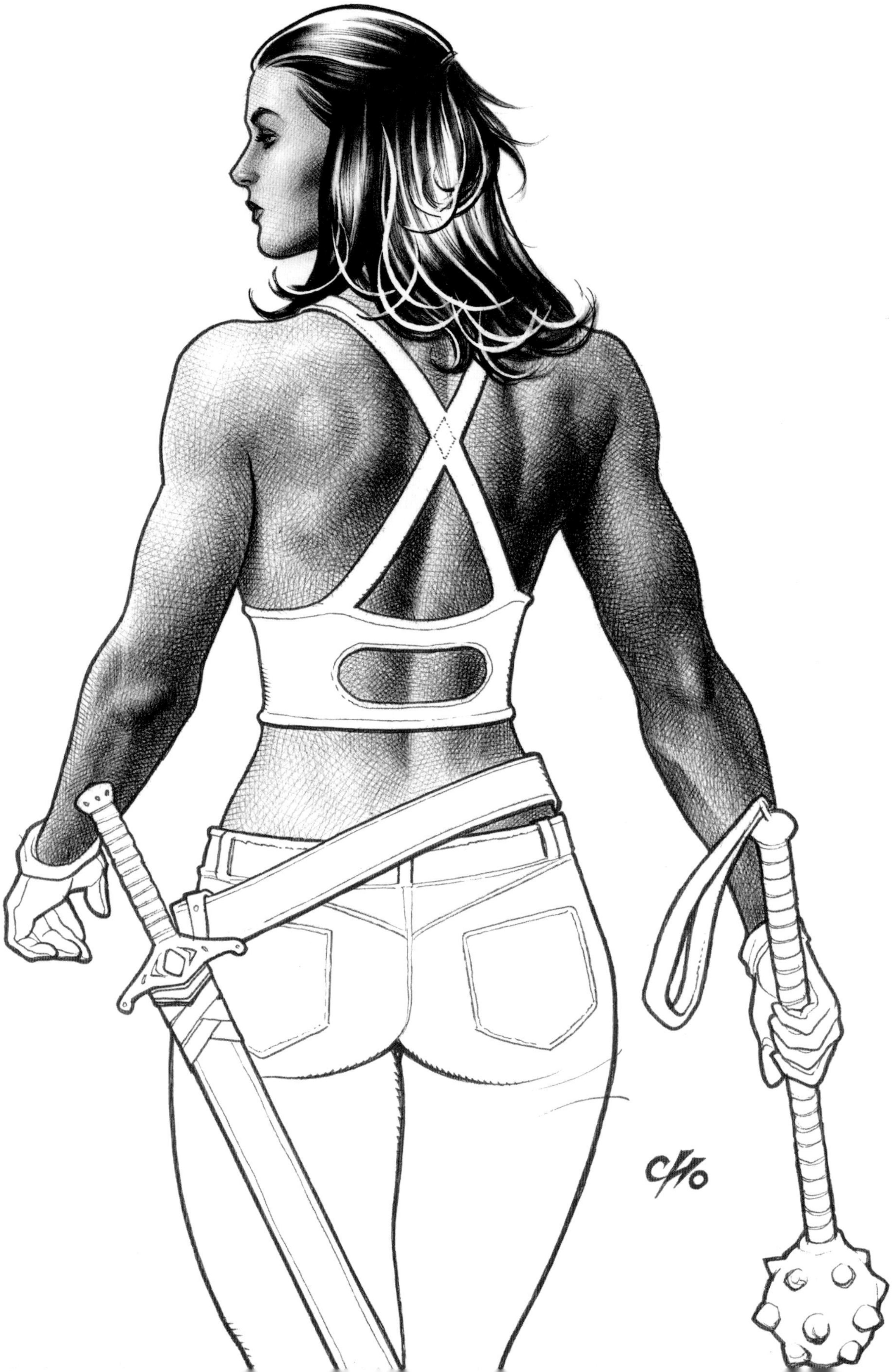
CHO

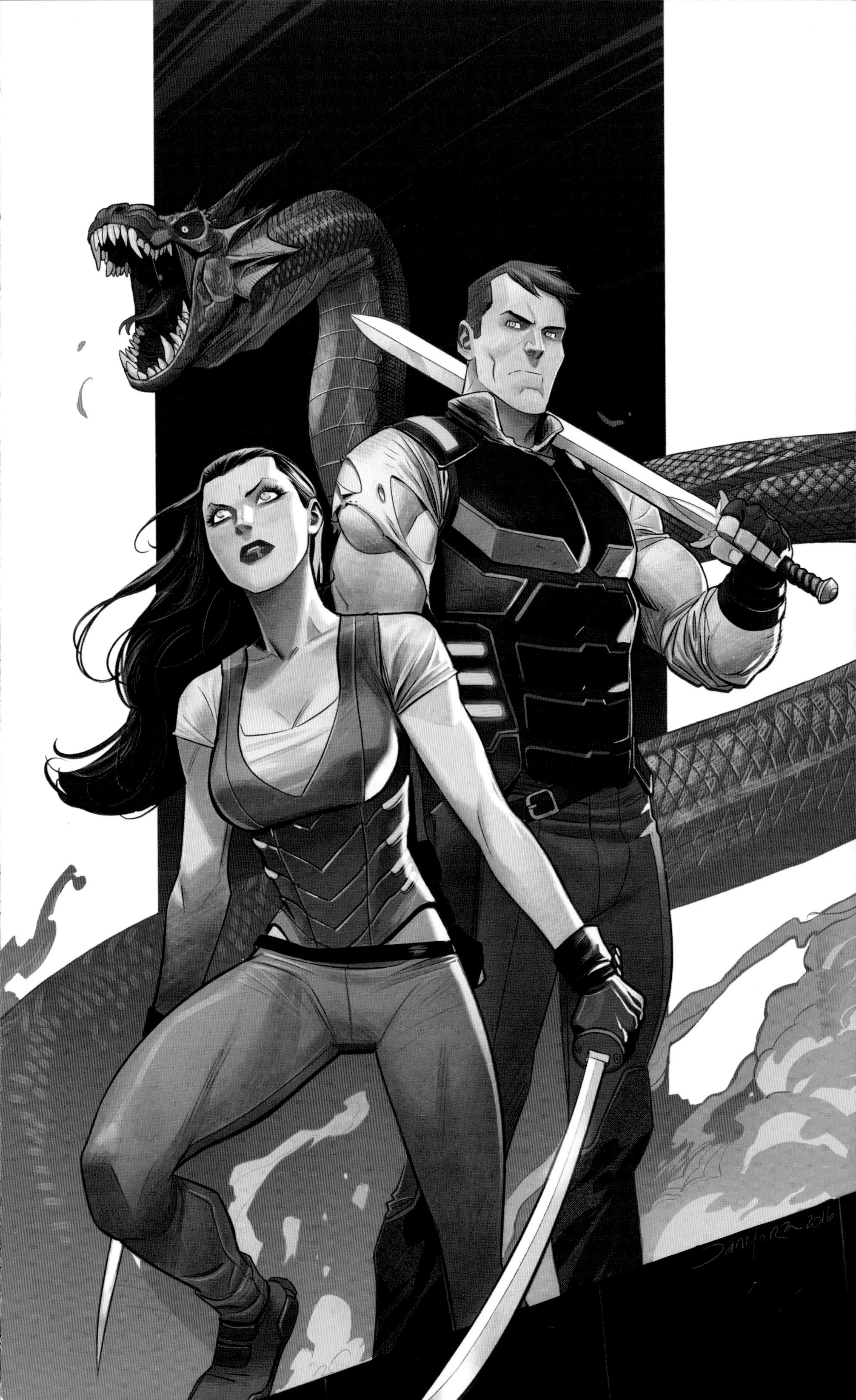

Issue One Mountain Top Variant Cover by **DAN MORA**

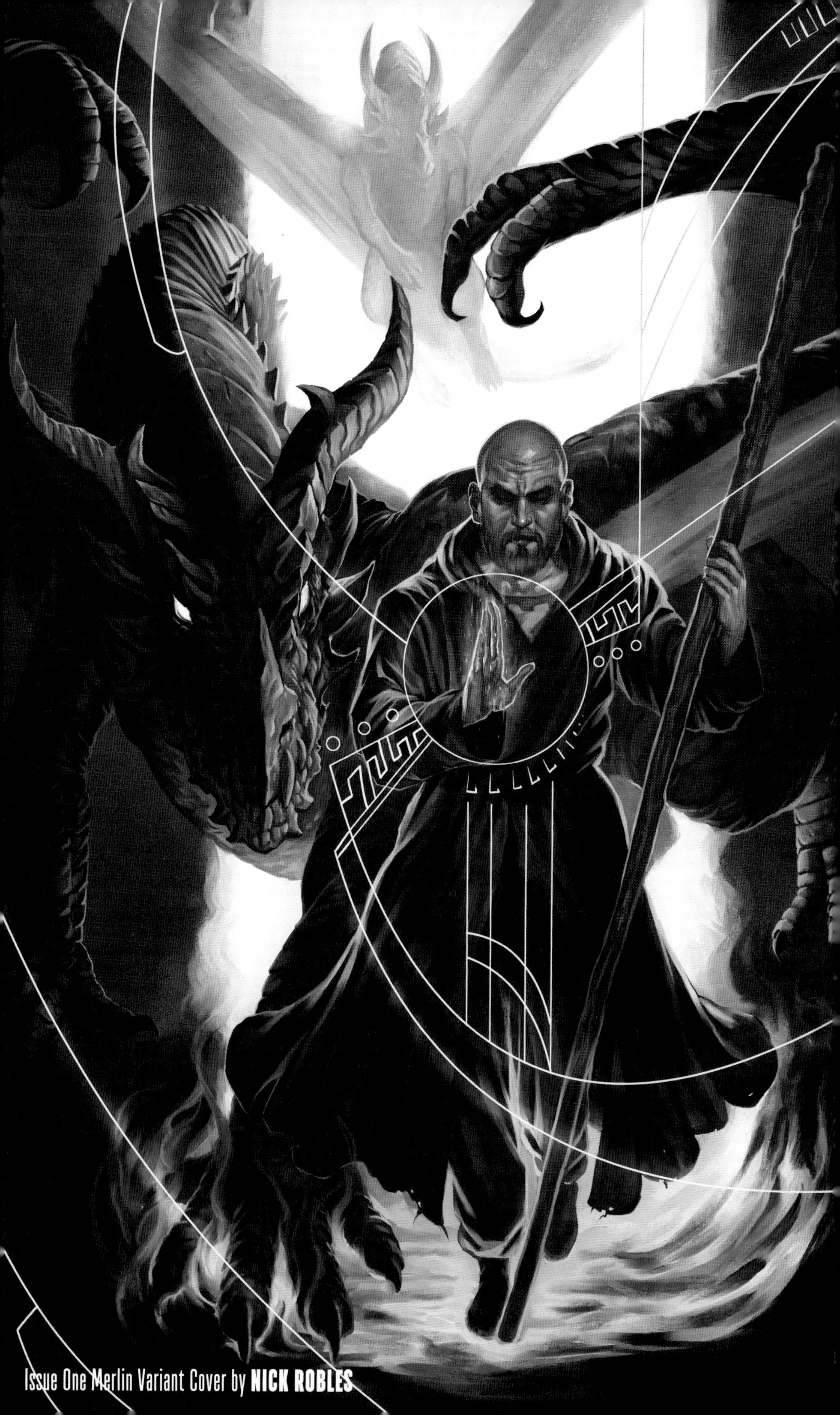

Issue One Merlin Variant Cover by **NICK ROBLES**

Issue One Lazarus Variant Cover by **CARLOS MAGNO**
with colors by **CHRIS BLYTHE**

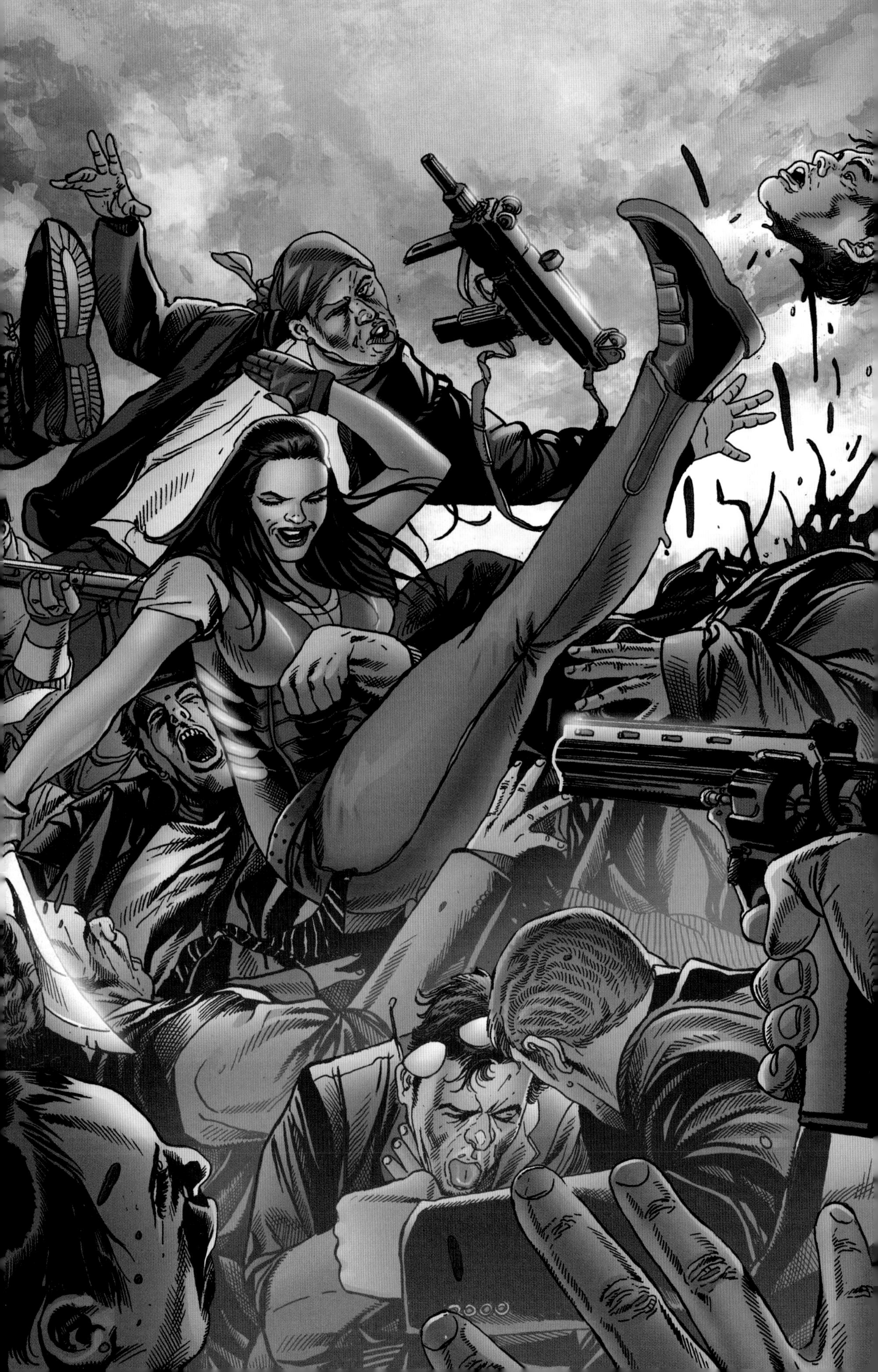

Issue One Variant Cover by **BRANDON PETERSON**

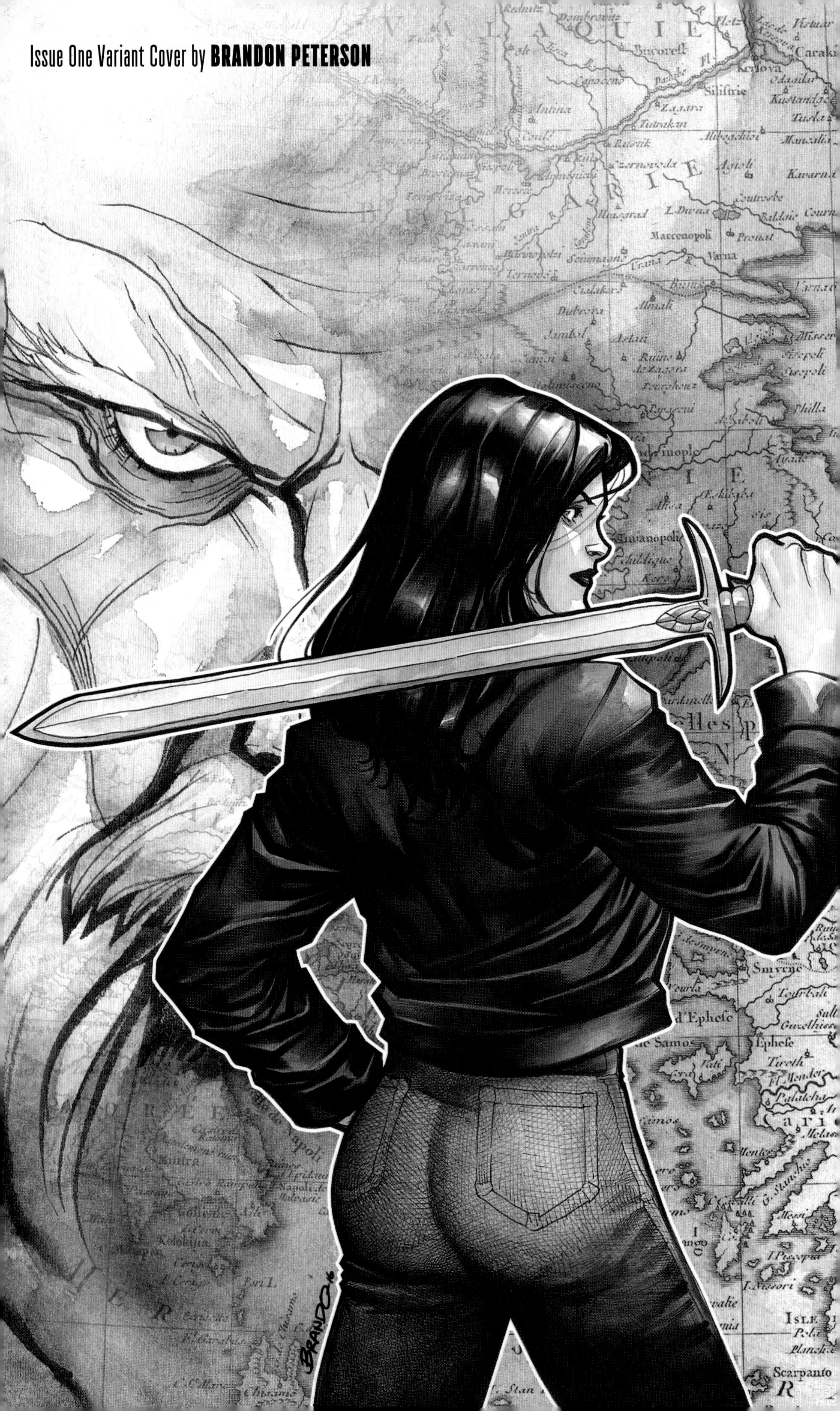
VALAQUIE
Bucoreſt
Silistrie
Tutrakan
Caraki
Kavarna
Marcenopoli
Varna
Dubrova
Jambol
Trajanopoli
Smyrne
d'Ephese
Ephese
Samos
Napoli
Scarpanto
BRANDO '16

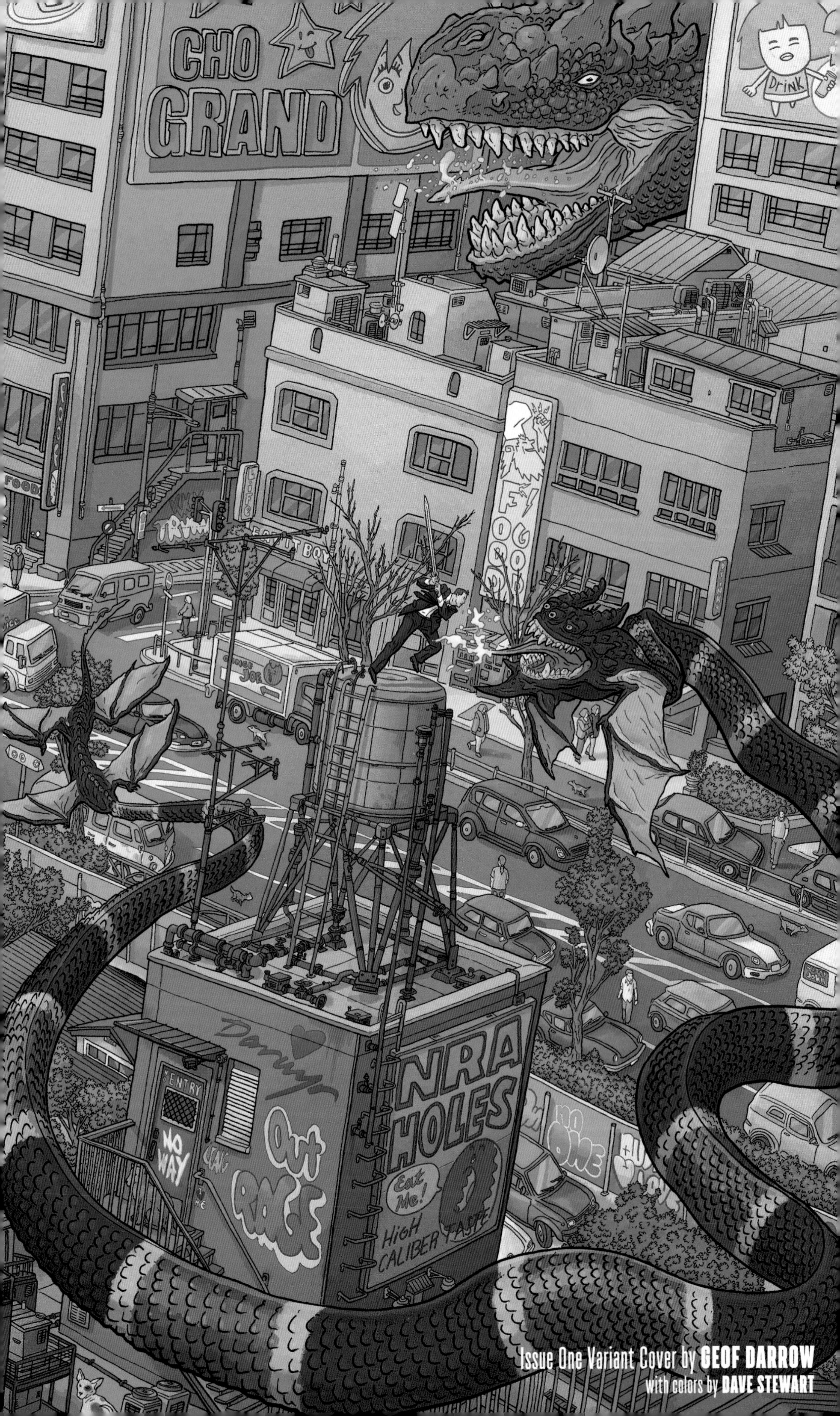
CHO
GRAND
Drink
FOOD
ENTRY
NO WAY
Out RAGE
NRA
HOLES
Eat Me!
HIGH
CALIBER
TASTE

Issue One Variant Cover by **GEOF DARROW**
with colors by **DAVE STEWART**

DISCOVER
VISIONARY CREATORS

THE
WOODS
JAMES TYNION IV • MICHAEL DIALYNAS
"The Woods is creepy, funny, charming, and mysterious. My favorite kind of comic, a deep mythology mixed with equally deep character work. Get in on the ground floor of something great!" –Jeff Lemire
VOL. 1
THE ARROW

"The Spire is fantastic! My kind of genre free-for-all." —BRIAN K. VAUGHAN (Saga)
THE
SPIRE
SIMON SPURRIER
JEFF STOKELY
ANDRÉ MAY

MARK WAID · PETER KRAUSE
IRREDEEMABLE
AFTERWORD BY GRANT MORRISON

J.G.
JONES
MARK
WAID
STRANGE
FRUIT
Foreword by
ELVIS MITCHELL

MICHAEL ALAN NELSON
DAN MORA
GABRIEL CASSATA
HEXED
THE HARLOT & THE THIEF VOLUME ONE

ABNETT & CULBARD
WILD'S
END
FIRST LIGHT
"IT'S REALLY, GREAT!" JEFF LEMIRE

BOOM! STUDIOS

AVAILABLE AT YOUR LOCAL COMICS SHOP AND BOOKSTORE
WWW.**BOOM-STUDIOS**.COM

James Tynion IV
The Woods
Volume 1
ISBN: 978-1-60886-454-6 | $9.99 US
Volume 2
ISBN: 978-1-60886-495-9 | $14.99 US
Volume 3
ISBN: 978-1-60886-773-8 | $14.99 US

The Backstagers
Volume 1
ISBN: 978-1-60886-993-0 | $14.99 US

Simon Spurrier
Six-Gun Gorilla
ISBN: 978-1-60886-390-7 | $19.99 US

The Spire
ISBN: 978-1-60886-913-8 | $29.99 US

Weavers
ISBN: 978-1-60886-963-3 | $19.99 US

Mark Waid
Irredeemable
Volume 1
ISBN: 978-1-93450-690-5 | $16.99 US
Volume 2
ISBN: 978-1-60886-000-5 | $16.99 US

Incorruptible
Volume 1
ISBN: 978-1-60886-015-9 | $16.99 US
Volume 2
ISBN: 978-1-60886-028-9 | $16.99 US

Strange Fruit
ISBN: 978-1-60886-872-8 | $24.99 US

Michael Alan Nelson
Hexed The Harlot & The Thief
Volume 1
ISBN: 978-1-60886-718-9 | $14.99 US
Volume 2
ISBN: 978-1-60886-816-2 | $14.99 US

Day Men
Volume 1
ISBN: 978-1-60886-393-8 | $9.99 US
Volume 2
ISBN: 978-1-60886-852-0 | $9.99 US

Dan Abnett
Wild's End
Volume 1: First Light
ISBN: 978-1-60886-735-6 | $19.99 US
Volume 2: The Enemy Within
ISBN: 978-1-60886-877-3 | $19.99 US

Hypernaturals
Volume 1
ISBN: 978-1-60886-298-6 | $16.99 US
Volume 2
ISBN: 978-1-60886-319-8 | $19.99 US

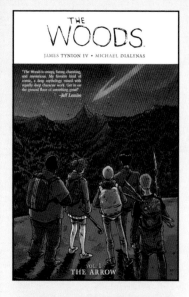

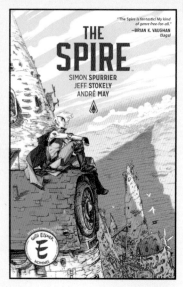

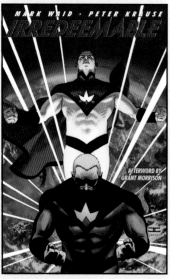

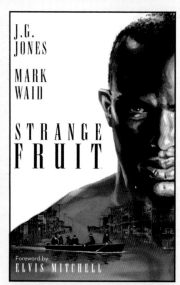

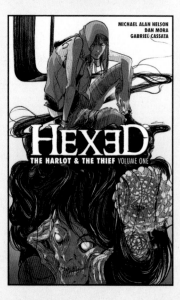

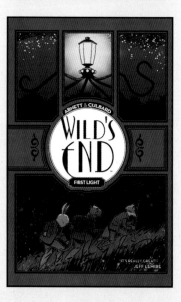

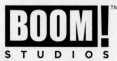